VALUING WALL STREET

VALUING WALL STREET

Protecting Wealth in Turbulent Markets

ANDREW SMITHERS
STEPHEN WRIGHT

McGraw-Hill

New York   San Francisco   Washington, D.C.   Auckland   Bogotá
Caracas   Lisbon   London   Madrid   Mexico City   Milan
Montreal   New Delhi   Singapore
Sydney   Tokyo   Toronto

Library of Congress Cataloging-in-Publication Data

Smithers, Andrew.
  Valuing Wall Street / by Andrew Smithers and Stephen Wright.
    p. cm.
  ISBN 0-07-135461-1
    1. Investment analysis. I. Wright, Stephen. II. Title.

HG4529.S554   2000
332.6—dc21
                                    99-057874

McGraw-Hill

A Division of The McGraw·Hill Companies

2 3 4 5 6 7 8 9 0   DOC/DOC 0 9 8 7 6 5 4 3 2 1 0

ISBN 0-07-135461-1

This book was typeset in 11/13 New Century Schoolbook by Lisa Hernandez of Editorial and Production Services.

Printed and bound by R. R. Donnelley & Sons Company.

This publication is designed to provide accurate and authoritative information in regard to the subject matter covered. It is sold with the understanding that the author nor the publisher is engaged in rendering legal, accounting, futures/securities trading, or other professional service. If legal advice or other expert assistance is required, the services of a competent professional person should be sought.

> *—From a Declaration of Principles jointly adopted by a Committee of the American Bar Association and a Committee of Publishers.*

McGraw-Hill books are available at special quantity discounts to use as premiums and sales promotions, or for use in corporate training programs. For more information, please write to the Director of Special Sales, McGraw-Hill, Professional Publishing, Two Penn Plaza, New York, NY 10121-2298. Or contact your local bookstore.

 This book is printed on recycled, acid-free paper containing a minimum of 50% recycled de-inked fiber.

CONTENTS

ACKNOWLEDGMENTS ix

PART ONE

THE CASE FOR q

Chapter 1

The Good News and the Bad News About q 3

Chapter 2

On q 9

Chapter 3

q and the Long-Term Investor 19

Chapter 4

q Versus the Competition 29

PART TWO

STOCK MARKET RISK AND RETURN

Chapter 5

The Power of Compound Interest (or How to Oversell Stocks) 39

Chapter 6

The True Impact of Stock Returns 47

Chapter 7

Stock Market Risks: Some History 55

Chapter 8

Stock Market Risks: The Impact on Investors 65

PART THREE

q AND THE VALUE OF WALL STREET

Chapter 9

The Meaning of Stock Market Value   77

Chapter 10

Stock Picking or Aggregate Value?   87

Chapter 11

What Hindsight Tells Us About Stock Market Value   95

Chapter 12

A Closer Look at *q*   107

Chapter 13

What *q* Could Have Told Investors About Value
in the Past   111

Chapter 14

q as an Investor Tool   117

PART FOUR

q AND THE FUTURE OF WALL STREET

Chapter 15

The Bad News About Stocks as Investments for
the Long Run   129

Chapter 16

Why *q* Has Risen, and Why q Will Fall   143

Chapter 17

The Good News About Stocks as Investments for the
Long Run   155

PART FIVE

SURVIVING THE BEAR MARKET

Chapter 18

What to Do with Your Money   169

Chapter 19

What Not to Do with Your Money   185

PART SIX

HOW TO VALUE THE STOCK MARKET

Chapter 20

How to Value the Stock Market: Four Key Tests for Any Indicator of Value   201

Chapter 21

The Dividend Yield   213

Chapter 22

The Price-Earnings Multiple   223

Chapter 23

The Adjusted Price-Earnings Multiple   233

Chapter 24

Yield Ratios and Yield Differences   243

Chapter 25

Corporate Net Worth and q 253

Chapter 26

q-Equivalence   263

Chapter 27

q and the Dividend Discount Model   273

PART SEVEN

q AND THE ANTI-*q*s

Chapter 28

The *q* Debate Among Economists   287

Chapter 29

The Equity Risk Premium and Stock
Market Valuations   301

Chapter 30

The *q* Debate Among Stockbrokers   313

PART EIGHT

q AND THE U.S. ECONOMY

Chapter 31

Past Falls in *q* and Their Economic Impact   329

Chapter 32

The Economic Consequences of Alan Greenspan   339

INDEX   345

ACKNOWLEDGMENTS

In writing this book we have received a great deal of help from many people:

Our colleagues at Smithers & Co. and at the University of Cambridge have been a constant help – most notably Daniel Murray, Martin Weale, Donald Robertson and Jean Roscoe. Martin has shared in many of our discussions over the past ten years, to the extent that we sometimes find it hard to distinguish our own ideas from his. It will also become evident that in this book we have at times shamelessly borrowed from Daniel's work for Smithers & Co. Donald's contribution, as the coauthor of the academic research paper that underpins much of the statistical work we exploit here, was indispensable. Jean Roscoe's help was also indispensable, but in a rather different way—with great good humor and patience she kept Smithers & Co. going at many times when both the authors were more preoccupied than they should have been with the production of this book. Her tragic death just after Christmas 1999 was a great blow. We would also both like to thank Professor Brian Reddaway, from whom, as pupils, at intervals over twenty years, both the authors (as well as Martin Weale) imbibed an enthusiasm for the dismal science which, bizarre as it may seem to some readers, has remained with us.

We owe a particular debt to two economists on whose work we have drawn extensively. Professor James Tobin was the originator of "q" (amongst economists, it is normally referred to, indeed, as "Tobin's q"): were it not for his pioneering work in this area, over thirty years ago, this book would lack its central idea. Professor Jeremy Siegel has done both economists and investors an enormous service in his work on historical returns, data on which he has very kindly allowed us to use in this book. We are especially grateful to both of them for discussing our ideas with us at various points over the past three years or so. Both displayed, in so doing, great intellectual generosity, since on a number of issues we have come to rather different conclusions.

We have also had valuable discussions, and have received advice from many other economists and practitioners. We thank especially: Charles Goodhart; Sushil Wadhwani; Peter Tinsley; Jeremy Grantham; and Barton Biggs.

In addition to those already mentioned we would also like to thank Jim Bianco and Professor Olivier Blanchard, who both generously provided us with data.

We hope that other authors receive as much help and encouragement from their editors as we have received from Kelli Christiansen of McGraw-Hill. Her enthusiasm has been unceasing.

All authors, except the saddest cases, thank their families; we now understand why it is quite right that they should. Ours have had to put up with all the usual tedious symptoms of authorhood, and have borne it patiently (or, in the case of Stephen's children, more patiently than could reasonably have been expected). So, special thanks go to Jill, Julia, Pelham, Kit, Lakshmi, Edmund, Hannah, and Rosa.

Authors' Note:

The Valuing Wall Street "Virtual Appendix"

This book draws heavily on underlying research that is rather technical in nature. Our original plan was to put this material (which for most people is not exactly a fun read) in a technical Appendix, to which enthusiasts for such things could refer. But as both book and appendix grew, it became evident that the book was in danger of getting too long. We therefore decided that, in the interests of the rain forest, we should instead provide a "Virtual Appendix," to which free access will be available via Smithers & Co's web site:

http://www.smithers.co.uk

The "Virtual Appendix" also allows access to some of the more technical material, both by the authors and others, cited at various points in the book. In addition, even those with less specialized interests may find some material helpful. In particular, we shall be providing regular updates of some of the key data series (most notably q) used in the book: these will be available both in graphic and spreadsheet form for those who wish to download the data.

PART ONE

THE CASE FOR q

In the four chapters that make up Part One we give an overview of the main themes that we shall cover in more detail in the rest of the book. Because we aim for brevity at this stage, much of what we say will of necessity be assertion. For supporting argument and evidence, you will need to look at later chapters. But these introductory chapters should give you a good feel for what q is about.

1

The Good News and the Bad News About *q*

THE GOOD NEWS

Most books about the stock market tell you how to make money. This one is different. It will show you how to avoid losing money. The most obvious part of the good news is that *q* can make investing in the stock market safer, by warning you of impending risks.

There is another, less obvious part of the good news. The idea at the center of this book, known as *q*, helps explain why, in ordinary circumstances, the stock market is such a good place to invest for the long term.

THE BAD NEWS

To balance the good news, there are two items of bad news, both relating to the immediate future. The first is the threat of large and prolonged falls in stock prices; the second is the threat of a major recession. The impact of the first can be avoided by investors who follow our advice. The impact of the second will almost certainly be harder to avoid.

The good news and the bad news depend on the same analysis. They come as a package and cannot be separated. You can't have the good news without the bad. But because of the good news you can avoid being hurt by the bad.

"q"

Both the good and bad news come from a simple idea known as q. The concept has been familiar to economists since Nobel laureate James Tobin first wrote about it in 1969. Recent research has established two new things about q. The first is that it works in practice, as well as in theory; the second is that does not work quite as expected. The result of these two developments is that q can be used to value the stock market objectively.

The ability to value stock markets is part of the good news, but it comes with the bad news, which is that the stock market is currently extremely expensive. As we enter the new millennium, the stock market is probably more overpriced than at any other for at least a century, including its previous peak in 1929.

q acts like a piece of elastic. It pulls the stock market back toward its proper value when prices get too high or too low. Also, like elastic, q has a stronger pull the more it is stretched. This makes the stock market a safer place for long-term investors.

In bear markets disgruntled investors often refer to the stock market as a casino. This is unfair. Under normal circumstances, the odds in the stock market are in your favor, and investing in stocks does not require you to take casino-type risks. The reason is simple. When you buy a stock, you are really buying the underlying assets owned by the firm. In the end it is these real assets that must generate the real returns you earn as an investor. The stock market would be much closer to a casino were it not for the q elastic, which stops the market from getting too far away from this fundamental value.

The risks in the stock market do, however, rise to casino levels when the elastic is, as at present, at full stretch. At current prices the odds are stacked against the stock market investor, to a greater extent than at any time in the past century.

EXCITEMENT AND CONCERN

The power of q is exciting from an intellectual viewpoint, but very worrying from a practical one. There is a grave risk that when Wall Street falls it will cause a major recession in the United States and quite possibly throughout the world. In the past, whenever there have been major overvaluations such as those in Wall

Street in 1929 or Tokyo in 1989, the subsequent crash has been a disaster for the economy as well as for the stock market.

VALUE AND *q*

The idea of value comes naturally to most people. As it is generally understood, the value of something is what its price should be, rather than what it actually is. If the way in which the word *value* is generally used has any meaning for the stock market, then stocks must have some fundamental worth that is usually different from their current prices. If people say that the stock market is overvalued, then they mean that prices are above their fundamental value. The ratio between actual prices and fundamental value measures the extent of the stock market's overvaluation.

It seems a matter of common sense that stock prices will not be correctly priced all the time. We shall show that this commonsense view is soundly based and that the best way to measure value is to look at the ratio known as *q*.

The risks in holding stocks are reduced because of the way *q* works, but they are not eliminated. The risks are much higher at certain times than at others, and *q* tells you when these times occur. When *q* is high, the risks are high, and when *q* is at an all-time high, the risks of losing a great deal of money are higher than ever. The rational response at such moments is to get out of stocks. As we write at the start of the new millennium, this response is what we strongly recommend.

THE BUY-AND-HOLD STRATEGY

The advice that we are giving runs slap up against the current consensus approach to investing, which is the buy-and-hold strategy. This basically says that price doesn't matter. Stocks are always the best investment, so the long-term investor should always be holding stocks. But we shall show that the buy-and-hold strategy is at odds with itself.

It has long been agreed that stocks should give better returns than other assets, such as bonds or cash on deposit. It is also agreed that the reason for higher potential returns is that stocks are more risky. In a world without free lunches, investors have a choice. They can go for better returns or for less risk. It is not to be expected that they can go for both. The evidence, however, is that stocks are less risky if held for the long term than if held for only a few years. This has helped provide historical support for the buy-and-hold strategy, but the real foundation for its popularity has been the long bull market. Claims that there is a free lunch out there have become very popular, and, for as long as the bull market lasts, such claims will remain widely believed.

We shall show, however, that the buy-and-hold strategy is at odds with itself because the strategy is inconsistent with its own success. The relative lack of risk involved in holding stocks for the long term is possible only because of q. It would not be possible if the buy-and-hold strategy were actually correct. Stock markets can be valued, and because they can be valued, the long-term risks involved in holding stocks vary from time to time. When stocks are cheap these risks are small, but when they are expensive the risks become very great indeed. In current conditions, the risks in holding stocks are too great to make them sensible investments. Therefore you should not buy and hold stocks, but buy and hold until too risky.

This approach is completely different from claiming that it is possible to know when the stock market has hit a peak or a trough. In our view, it is completely absurd to try to forecast the short-term direction of the stock market. If investors knew when to buy and sell stocks, they would act in advance and prices would rise or fall before the time forecast. All that the ability to value stocks provides is the ability to assess when holding them becomes too risky. Those who wish to know how to sell at the top will learn nothing from us, but then we think that there is nothing that they can learn from anybody.

Because stocks go up most of the time and, thanks to q, are not too unpredictable over the longer term, the buy-and-hold strategy is sound most of the time. Stocks do, however, become grossly overpriced occasionally. Even though you cannot know when the market will peak, it still makes sense to sell when the market becomes wildly overpriced, as at present. The risks you are running if you hold stocks in such circumstances are simply too great.

AN OVERSOLD STORY

Under normal circumstances, when the market is reasonably close to its fair value, the case for holding stocks is strong, but even so it has been dangerously oversold. A fact often cited in support of the buy-and-hold strategy is that investors have never lost money if they have remained fully invested in stocks for 20 years. This is a very important and interesting fact that we do not dispute. Indeed, we shall show that *q* helps explain it. But we shall also see that it offers very limited reassurance. The reason is that the long term, over which stocks become relatively safe, is simply too long for many, if not most, investors.

USING *q* INSTEAD

The good news is that, by understanding and using *q*, you can afford to hold more stocks, for longer, than investors who are wedded to the buy-and-hold strategy. You should therefore be able to get better returns with less risk. This is of course a funny sort of good news, because you can do so only by periodically taking note of the bad news that *q* is telling you, and getting out of stocks. We are, however, claiming only that a rational approach to the art of wealth maintenance is better than an irrational one. The buy-and-hold approach is irrational. It accepts one piece of evidence from stock market history and ignores another piece, even though the one cannot exist without the other. Once again common sense seems to be on the side of the rational. Common sense says that when you buy something, price matters.

INTERESTING TIMES

Bad news for the stock market is also likely to be bad news for the economy. On every occasion in the past that we can find, when a stock market has become as overvalued as Wall Street was at the end of the twentieth century, the consequences have been extremely bad for the economy as well as for investors. As evidence, we have not only the previous stock market bubbles in the United States, such as those of the late 1920s and late 1960s, but also those of Japan in the late 1980s and Southeast Asia in the middle 1990s. In every case the economies have subsequently experienced severe or prolonged recessions, and often both.

It is commonly assumed that the future management of the U.S. economy will be good enough to ensure that this bit of history is not repeated. Despite the historic evidence that such success would be unique, it is certainly a possibility. It rather depends on your view of how well the economy has been managed in the recent past.

There is currently a general belief that recent economic management has been brilliant. The long period of growth experienced by the United States is generally assumed to cast great credit on the Federal Reserve. But there is an alternative view, that the recent management of the economy has in fact been abysmal, and therefore provides a very worrying precedent for the future. When everything appears to be going swimmingly well, the views of those who claim the contrary are seldom popular, but on this occasion they will cause outrage. How, it might be asked, can it be possible to claim that Alan Greenspan is not doing a great job when the economy is doing so well?

One part of the answer to this question is to turn it around, and ask whether claims that Alan Greenspan was doing a great job would be nearly so common if the economy did *not* appear to be doing so well. But a more important part of the answer is the evidence of history, which suggests that allowing asset bubbles to develop is the greatest mistake that a central bank can make. Over the past five years or so the Fed has knowingly permitted the development of the greatest asset bubble of the twentieth century.

One of the interesting features of the next two or three years will be that events will tell whether the consensus view or the dissenting view of Alan Greenspan was right. We are, it seems, about to live in interesting times.

CHAPTER

On *q*

INTRODUCING *q*

Since *q* plays such an important role in this book, we thought that it should be quickly introduced. Its key attribute is that it measures the extent to which the stock market is, at any time, incorrectly valued. The stock market is overvalued when *q* is high compared with its historic average. It is possible to make such a statement only because *q* swings up and down around this average. Because *q* has this quality, which is called "mean reversion," it tells us about the future as well as the past. The fact that the market is overvalued means that there is a high risk that it will perform poorly in the future. When *q* is high, investors in stocks are set to lose a very great deal of money. We expect the stock market to fall back until stock prices will be less than half their level at the end of 1998.

Chart 2.1 shows how *q* has swung up and down around its average since 1990. At the end of 1998 *q* was higher than at any previous time in the century, which underlines just how overvalued the stock market had become.[1]

---

[1]At the end of 1998, the stock market was around 2.3 times its fundamental value and the Dow Jones Index stood at just under 9000. This means that Wall Street would have been fairly valued if the index had stood at around 3900. To know how over- or undervalued the market is at the time you read, you should get a pretty accurate answer, at least for the next year or two, by dividing the current value of the Dow Jones Index by 3900. (To do the equivalent for the more broadly based and therefore more representative S&P 500 Index, divide by 520.)

The idea behind q is basically very simple. It compares two different estimates of the value of U.S. companies. The first is what Wall Street says the companies are worth and the second is their "fundamental" value. As we shall explain in detail later, valuing the stock market as a whole is very different from valuing individual stocks. For the stock market as a whole, fundamental value is what it would cost today to replace all the assets of all quoted companies. Their value is what it would cost to create them, if we had to start from scratch and do it again. To calculate their fundamental value, we need to work out how much this cost would be. Their total value is thus the measure of what the companies are worth in terms of their assets, both physical and financial, minus their liabilities. This estimate is normally referred to as net worth.[2]

CHART 2.1

q: 1900–1999

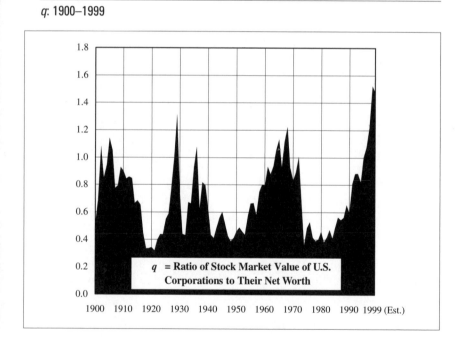

<hr>

[2]From 1945 onward these estimates are produced by the Federal Reserve and can be found in Table B 102 of the Z1 *Flow of Funds Accounts of the United States*. Figures before 1945 are our own estimates, derived from a number of public and private sources, which we describe in the Virtual Appendix.

To find *q*, we compare the net worth of the corporate sector with the total value that the stock market puts on corporate shares. The ratio between the two is *q*. The stock market's value is put at the top of the ratio and corporate net worth at the bottom; thus[3]:

$$q = \frac{\text{Value of Stock Market}}{\text{Corporate Net Worth}}$$

As a result, *q* has a high value when rises in stock prices increase the stock market valuation of corporations, relative to their net worth. This tells us that the stock market is overvalued. By the same token, a low value of *q* tells us that the stock market is cheap.

There are many points that we need to consider in order to justify such a claim, but at this stage we need to emphasize only a few key ones. A crucial characteristic is that *q* appears to be "mean-reverting." It doesn't wander all over the place, but tends to be pulled back toward its average. It thus reverts to its mean, or average. This average, in turn, appears to have been historically stable.

We shall discuss this aspect of *q* and other alternative ways of valuing the market in later chapters. Mean reversion is an essential feature of any valid way of measuring value, but it is by no means sufficient on its own. One reason lies in the ease with which statistics can be use to deceive rather than illuminate. As almost any user of statistics finds out sooner or later, it is all too easy to deceive oneself, or others, by looking at statistical properties alone. It is therefore vitally important that such properties be supported by a full understanding of the results. We shall therefore explain why economists expected *q* to be mean-reverting even before the supporting evidence was available. We shall also explain how this mean reversion comes about.

Because *q*, at the end of 1998, was higher than it had been all century, a fall-back from such an extreme level is virtually certain. Our statistical evidence shows a probability of well over 90% that *q* will fall back from end-1998 levels over the following

---

[3]We apologize to those who dislike mathematics for the intrusion of an occasional formula into the main text. We have generally sought to avoid this, but just occasionally it is unavoidable.

five years. Over even longer periods, the probability gets even higher.

q AND THE OUTLOOK FOR STOCK PRICES

The fact that q is extremely high is extremely bad news for stock prices. This is not only because q has always come down from such extreme levels in the past, but because it has always come down through a fall in share prices. We can write the definition of q in per share terms[4] as:

$$q = \frac{\text{Stock Price}}{\text{Corporate Net Worth per Share}}$$

If you look at the way that q is defined, you can see that it can come down only if share prices fall or net worth per share rises. This is because q is a ratio and its value can change when either the number at the top changes or the one at the bottom changes.

Because q mean-reverts, it is very important to know whether the elastic that pulls it toward its average value operates on share prices or on net worth. The only way that prospects for the U.S. market could look good would be if the elastic worked solely on the bottom of the ratio—on net worth. But we shall show that it is implausible for net worth to rise by enough, and rapidly enough, to bring q back to more normal levels. To do this we shall use arguments based both on statistical evidence and on economic reasoning. For the moment, however, we simply point to the historic evidence in Chart 2.2., which shows that the level of q has gone up and down with share prices. What has brought q back to its mean has not been changes in net worth, but changes in share prices. The evidence of the past therefore makes it highly probable that a high value of q will be followed by a fall in the stock market.

---

[4]In case this seems like sleight of hand, all that we have done is to divide both the top and bottom of the original ratio by the number of shares, which leaves the value of the ratio unchanged.

CHART 2.2

% Changes in Stock Prices and *q*

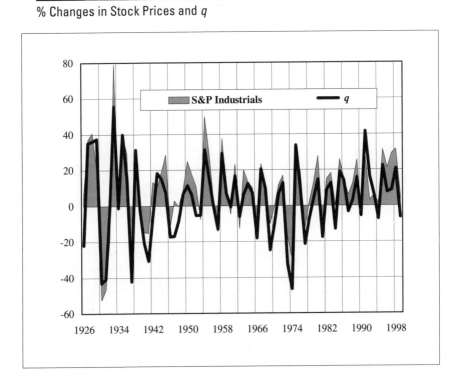

Table 2.1 shows that all major overvaluations, as measured by *q*, have been succeeded by major falls in prices.[5] We expect this to happen again when the current bull market comes to an end. Since *q* shows the stock market to be overvalued by more than twice, a fall of 50% to 60%, or more, is likely. This could easily bring the Dow Jones Index down to under 4000. While this would cause great alarm and would be an unfamiliar event to most investors, it would, as Table 2.1 shows, be similar to the previous falls that have occurred when the market has hit major peaks in the past.

---

[5]This is best illustrated, as here, by looking at the figures in real terms. Doing so draws attention to the loss of wealth involved, without the distortion that can readily be introduced by inflation. Historically this has often been very important, even though it is not obvious today when inflation is low.

Falls of similar size have also occurred in other stock markets. Table 2.2 shows that when international markets have had similar peaks to those of Wall Street, they have had similar falls. Table 2.3 shows the level to which the Dow Jones would fall if it matched its own historic falls or those experienced in other markets.

TABLE 2.1

Falls in Real Stock Prices after Peaks in q

Period of Fall	% Fall in Stock Prices, Peak to Trough
August 1929 to June 1932	82%
February 1937 to May 1938	49%
November 1968 to September 1974	59%

TABLE 2.2

Typical Falls in Real Stock Prices in Other Markets

Period of Fall	% Fall in Stock Prices, Peak to Trough
Japan[6] from end of 1989 to end of 1995	57%
UK[7] from mid-1972 to end of 1976	70%

TABLE 2.3

Implied Level of Dow Jones Index[8]

If Stock Prices Fell in Line With...	Implied Level
Historic Changes in U.S. Stock Prices after Peaks in q	
From August 1929	1620
From February 1937	4590
From November 1968	3690
Other Major Market Falls	
Japan from end of 1989	3870
UK from mid-1972	2700

---

[6] Nikkei 225 Index. At the end of 1998, the Japanese market was barely any higher—around 56% below its 1989 peak, in real terms. As we shall note later, it was probably still overvalued at this level!

[7] FT All Share Index. In real terms, the UK market fleetingly passed its 1972 peak during the course of 1987, but then took until mid-1993—a full 21 years later—to beat it on a sustained basis.

[8] Taking the end-1998 figure of 9000 as the "peak." Although, at the time of writing, it had passed this figure, we take the end of 1998 as the benchmark, since that already represented a record degree of overvaluation, as measured by q.

As we write, in the latter half of 1999, the Dow is in the range of 10,000 to 11,000, and to many people such values may seem unimaginable. But it is worth bearing in mind just how rapidly the stock market achieved those historic heights. As recently as 1995 the Dow was below 4000. History suggests that, with stock markets, the faster they rise, the harder they fall.

q AND THE EFFICIENT MARKET HYPOTHESIS: A RANDOM WALK ON WALL STREET?

Because *q* can tell us, in an entirely objective way, the extent to which markets have become incorrectly priced, it means that we can make soundly based and useful statements about the future of the stock market. This does not mean that we can make useful forecasts about whether the stock market is going to rise or fall over the next few months. But once we are able to measure value, it is possible to assess the probability of stocks rising or falling. The chances of the stock market rising or falling will be much stronger at certain times than at others, and these differences will depend on the level of *q*. Such a statement is fairly revolutionary, because it runs counter to the view, commonly found in textbooks on economics and finance, known as the "Efficient Market Hypothesis.

The Efficient Market Hypothesis is very important. It almost, but not quite, represents the standard view of economists about the stock market. It says something extremely simple, which is that shares are always correctly priced. In a world of perfectly efficient markets, stock prices change only because new information becomes available. New information has an effect on prices because it changes a rational assessment of the future. If this view is correct, all information on which share prices depend is immediately taken into account by the market. Thus, no reassessment of historic information will change prices, only new information. In such a world there can be no deviation from "fair" value, since financial markets arrive at prices that are always and everywhere automatically "fair." It follows that value cannot be sensibly discussed, for the only sensible way to measure value is by looking at current stock prices. No valuation criterion is worth using, since the market price itself is the best valuation criterion and cannot be improved upon.

Since we have claimed that q allows us to make useful statements about the future of the stock market, it is clear that q must fall afoul of the Efficient Market Hypothesis. A crucial part of our argument therefore needs to confront this issue.

The Efficient Market Hypothesis is a wonderfully simple and extremely powerful idea. Efficient markets are assumed to be efficient because if someone finds a new way to predict movements in prices, this is, in effect, a money machine. Efficient markets abhor money machines, just as nature abhors a vacuum. Any money machine that may occur will immediately be exploited by other traders, so rapidly and so thoroughly, that the money machine must cease to be a money machine.

Like all the best simple ideas, the Efficient Market Hypothesis can also be used to make clear predictions about how financial markets work. These predictions can be tested. It is no surprise, since economists have to have something to do to occupy their time, that vast numbers of tests of the Efficient Market Hypothesis have been carried out, on any imaginable market, in almost every part of the planet. Perhaps to the surprise of those who believe economists cannot come to conclusions, this work has led to some important areas of consensus.

One simple prediction which arose out of the Efficient Market Hypothesis is that stock prices should behave like a "random walk." Testing for a random walk is just testing whether stock price changes are at all predictable. If they were, this would imply the existence of a money machine, which efficient markets would abhor. It is now widely agreed among economists that the random walk version of the Efficient Market Hypothesis is very nearly, but crucially not quite, supported by the data. Over short time horizons, in well-developed markets, the theory works well. Over longer time horizons, even in well-developed markets, research shows that there are violations of the hypothesis. These violations are generally "statistically significant," but, crucially, they are not in general of the order of magnitude that would make it worthwhile to attempt to make money by exploiting them.[9]

---

[9]While the rejection of the random walk version of efficient markets is now pretty much uncontested, the suggestion that markets are not fully efficient remains more controversial. We deal with this issue in more depth in Chapter 28.

We shall show that our use of q as a valuation criterion falls into the same category. It tells whether markets are over- or undervalued, but it cannot be used to make big profits without big risks. Most of the time, when markets are neither extremely over- or undervalued, q is not very important, since it cannot be used to make strong predictions about future returns. It is only in times of extremes that it provides vital information. The end of the twentieth century is such a time. q tells you that you are running huge risks if you remain in stocks. It therefore tells you how to avoid these risks.

Thus, q is not a money-making machine, but it has vitally important things to say to the long-term investor. It measures the risk of being invested in the stock market and it tells us the direction in which share prices are likely to move in the longer term. We shall show that using this information can help the q-investor to make both higher and safer returns. Investors who understand and use q will, for example, make higher returns and run less risk, than those whose strategy is simply to buy and hold equities. The gains from using q come from avoiding losses, not from making a killing in the market. Understanding q will enable you to hold on to your wealth when others around you are losing theirs. But it would be very difficult and extremely risky to attempt to make serious money from q. We would be very surprised if anyone got rich by reading this book. But we hope that this book can help prevent you from losing a lot of money.

Both on a commonsense and on an intellectual level, we find this reassuring. We suspect that we would not have much chance of convincing either trained economists or experienced market practitioners of the validity of our point of view if we claimed that q provided a way to make money, without the risk of being arrested for forgery. Fundamentally we believe that the principle of efficient markets is sound. We shall show that the general principle of arbitrage, or buying low and selling high, which underpins efficient markets, also underpins our arguments on why q must mean-revert. Our qualification to the textbook Efficient Market Hypothesis is simply to insist that it be slightly modified to conform to the standard rules about the rewards from taking risks. Efficient markets are possible only if investors take risks, and investors will take risks only if the probability of making a reward matches that risk.[10]

---

[10]We stress that this idea is not in any sense a new one. There has been a great deal of theoretical research in economics, over the past two decades or so, discussing the nature of a feasible efficient market. We explain more about this aspect of q in Chapter 28.

CHAPTER 3

q and the Long-Term Investor

WEALTH PRESERVATION AND RISK

As we have already remarked, we do not expect investors to get rich from this book. Reading it should, however, greatly improve their chances of preserving whatever wealth they have. Since, in current conditions, preserving wealth is likely to be much more important than trying to make it, our analysis has great financial implications for the individual investor.

It also seems high time that long-term investors fully understand the risks they undertake when, as is often the case, the vast majority of their savings are placed in equity-based portfolios.

REDEFINING RISK AND RETURN

Only those who have been singularly unlucky or incompetent have failed to make splendid returns on their portfolios in almost every year of the 1990s and for most of the 1980s. This experience has transformed many investors' perceptions. People have become blasé about returns and risks. They expect much higher returns on their investments than before and they seldom know what it means to lose heavily.

Anecdotes provide telling evidence of the change in perceptions. One of the fund managers whom we advise recently got a call from a prospective private client. The potential client stated that they were not interested in quick returns, but wanted a safer strategy with only modest returns. They considered that a modest return would be of the order of 20% per annum.

Since most people base their expectations on their own experience, this definition of a "modest return" might appear perfectly understandable. Table 3.1 shows why. By the end of 1998 the returns from investing in stocks had been above 20% per annum for roughly five years.

A look at longer periods, however, sheds doubt on the idea that a return of 20% per annum can be considered modest. It is also instructive to look at the second column in Table 3.1, which shows how unusual it has been, in historic terms, to receive even the more modest 11% return recorded over the past 20 years.

In the coming chapters we shall examine the historical experience in more depth, but here we shall just state it as a fact: In historic terms, expecting 20% per annum turns out to be highly *im*modest. The average annual real return to the investor in stocks (before deducting any management costs, and assuming reinvestment of dividends) has been around 6¾%, which is only one third of the value that our prospective investor thought "modest."

In practice, the divergence between expectations and reality is even greater, since it is likely that future returns will, for many years, be well below this long-term average. The fact that q is so

TABLE 3.1

Real Stock Returns in 1998

Over the Past...	Compound Average Real Return on Stocks	Number of Years Since Returns Were This High
1 year	31.0%	40
2 years	28.1%	43
5 years	19.6%	69
10 years	13.9%	40
15 years	12.1%	34
20 years	11.1%	37

CHART 3.1

"Average Investor Returns" on the U.S. Stock Market, 1900–1998

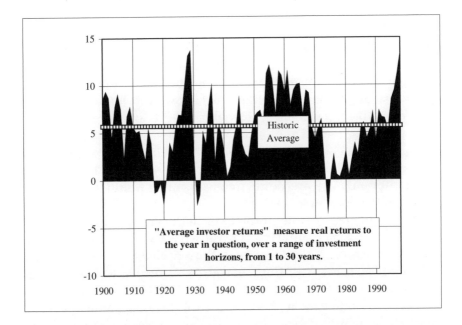

"Average investor returns" measure real returns to the year in question, over a range of investment horizons, from 1 to 30 years.

high is a warning signal that future returns must be low. The exceptionally good returns of recent years are highly likely to be followed by exceptionally poor returns over the next few years, which will probably bring long-term returns back close to the historic average. The high returns of recent years will in effect have to be paid for by bad returns in the future.[11]

Certainly this has been the pattern in the past. Chart 3.1 summarizes recent stock market performance by looking at the real returns earned by an "average" investor. Since different investors hold stocks for different amounts of time, the "average investor return" takes the average of returns over a range of horizons, from 1 to 30 years.[12] Returns are defined as total returns

---

[11]We should stress that our arguments for *q* do not depend on the implied mechanism that returns, as well as *q*, "mean-revert," but as we show in later chapters, there is a lot of evidence that they do.

[12]This is not the same as the commonly used 30-year rolling average return, but instead is an average of the 30-year, the 29-year, the 28-year, etc., down to the 1-year return. As we show in Part Two, long-period rolling returns significantly understate the degree of variation in returns experienced by the average investor.

(including reinvested dividends) measured in real terms, after adjusting for consumer price inflation, and, to make things more realistic, assuming that 1% per annum gets eaten up in management and transaction costs.

One thing is abundantly clear from the chart: In historic terms 1998 would certainly have been an exceptionally good year to have *sold* stocks. The typical investor would have earned an average of 13.6% per annum on an initial investment. To give a basis for comparison, the chart also shows the historic average return on the stock market, for which there are data for nearly two centuries, measured on the same basis. Hence the "typical" investor selling stocks in 1998 would have earned a total return over twice the historic average. Investors who had been in the market for only the preceding five years or so would, as Table 3.1 shows, have done even better.

The only other time in the twentieth century that investors enjoyed such spectacularly good returns was in 1929, with the late 1960s running a close second. Both periods were followed by extremely poor returns. Both, of course, coincided with very high levels of *q*.

At the same time as investors' expectations of stock returns have been rising, the concept of risk has been almost turned on its head. On August 7, 1998, after a fairly modest market correction, the *Wall Street Journal* ran a piece on an individual investor of relatively modest means who had prudently decided to liquidate his equity mutual fund investments and place the proceeds in money market accounts. Mr. Luis Giust had decided that the market was overblown, and since he was nearing retirement, he felt that he would prefer to sit on his very handsome gains rather than risk losing out in retirement. But even this rather prudent investor had clearly been affected to a great extent by the change in perceptions. When asked how he would feel if, after all, the market went on rising inexorably, he replied:

> "What Mrs. Giust and I did Tuesday took a helluva lot of guts... But we're firm in our convictions."

> And if they're wrong?

> "We'll roll with life's punches," he says.

The extent to which expectations have become bizarre is splendidly illustrated by these comments. It is not as if Mr. and

Mrs. Giust had much to fear from "life's punches." The risk they were running by liquidating their equity portfolio was not, after all, that of actually losing any money. At the time, the money market accounts they invested in were offering around 5¾%, which was 4% above the rate of inflation. Thus all the gains they had made in recent years not only were safe but would, for the foreseeable future, continue to accumulate at a respectable rate. The risk they were running was simply that they might have to sit on their six-figure lump sum, earning an otherwise very respectable rate of return, and watch other, less prudent investors earn an even higher return by holding onto their stocks.

Some previous generations of equity investors would have given a lot to wrestle with this kind of "risk." They had to face the actual fact of losing large sums of money, not just the risk of doing so. When market corrections arrive in earnest, losses are real rather than hypothetical. The real losses of the past had major effects on living standards. For investors on the verge of retirement, a major loss in the stock market—like the corrections shown in Table 2.1, in the previous chapter—means a loss of income of a similar magnitude for the rest of their lives.

THE OVERSOLD CASE FOR INVESTING IN STOCKS

As we noted in our introductory chapter, the benefits of equity investment have been dangerously oversold by harping on long-term returns, while failing to point out that this long term is simply too long for most investors.

The main reason people save is to have a prosperous retirement. Although most people work for around 40 years, many do not even begin to think about investing for retirement until well into their careers. This delay, coupled with the fact that their capacity to save normally grows as they get older, means that even the most prudent tend to save significantly more in the second half of their working lives than in the first half. So someone who saves regularly for 30 to 40 years effectively has an *average* investment horizon of 20 years or less. Over these shorter horizons, as we shall see in later chapters, the performance of stocks has been distinctly more uneven.

Once investors have retired, horizons effectively shorten even more. Those who hold stocks cannot benefit properly from their accumulated wealth unless they are regular sellers. Selling will be disastrous if they are faced with a major bear market. We do not wish to be unduly morbid, but it is an unfortunate fact that even newly retired investors cannot reasonably expect to live more than another 20 years. If they wish to spend their capital, they will therefore hold their securities for an average of about ten years. This is not long enough for it to be sensible to hold on through thick and thin to a portfolio based largely on stocks. As we have noted, a fact often cited in support of equity investing is that investors have never lost money if they remained fully invested in stocks for 20 years. But this is no help to those who will in all probability have died by then, and would prefer to live a little before doing so. The great economist John Maynard Keynes remarked, "In the long run we are all dead." If the long run means 20 years, this is not strictly true—only around a third of us are.[13] For the third of the adult population who will be dead in 20 years, however, such long-run considerations offer little consolation for making large losses in the stock market.

q AND THE BUY-AND-HOLD STRATEGY

The discussion in the previous section leads us naturally to a view of investing that has become dominant in recent years: the buy-and-hold strategy. The most convincing advocate of this view is Jeremy Siegel of the Wharton School. *Stocks for the Long Run*, Siegel's brilliantly argued and superbly documented book,[14] has at its center the proposition that the optimal strategy for any investor with a long horizon is almost always to hold equities. The basis for this proposition is the observation that over sufficiently long horizons, stocks have in the past been as safe as, or possibly even safer than, competing assets like cash and bonds.

We do not dispute the facts, but we show that the proposition needs to be carefully understood in two ways. First, as we have seen, the long term is far too long for most investors. Sec-

---

[13]We are making the rough-and-ready assumption that people under 20 do not think about such matters, and that the rest of us live to be 80. In 20 years, therefore, one third of "us" will be dead.

[14]We are extremely indebted to Professor Siegel for collecting, and allowing us to use, much of the long-term returns data we have used in this book.

ond, there are a few occasions, such as the present, when stock markets become so overpriced that prospective returns are poor however long your investment horizon.

There is also, as we said at the start, a good news/bad news aspect to our message on *q*. We have been focusing on the bad news thus far; the good news is less obvious at first glance, but just as crucial. We shall show that the behavior of *q* explains why the buy-and-hold strategy has usually worked. Indeed, if *q* did not work, and stock markets did not get pulled back toward their fundamental values, investing in them would be far too risky to be sensible. But the very quality that makes the stock market such a good place to invest, most of the time, means that it has to be a lousy place occasionally. One of these occasions is now.

We shall go into this at greater length in later chapters. Here the crucial feature of our argument is that the behavior of *q*, and the historic success of the buy-and-hold strategy, are two sides of the same coin. If the theory behind the buy-and-hold strategy were correct, stocks would logically be so risky that nobody in their right mind would want to hold them. But stocks are not this risky and *q* helps explain why.

WHEN BUY AND HOLD BREAKS DOWN

We support the buy-and-hold strategy in normal circumstances for long-term investors: those who are neither retired nor nearing retirement. Occasionally, however, *q* provides an essential guide for longer-term investors, however long their horizon. The conditions ruling at the end of 1998 and into 1999 seem set to be the outstanding example of the century. We can see why by imagining the investment decision of the most extreme case: those who, contrary to Keynes's maxim, *do* expect to live forever.[15]

We have already noted that stocks have given an average historic real return of around 6¾% per annum in the past. But this does not mean that investors today will get this average return if they buy stocks at current prices. Even for immortal investors, those who are going to hold on to stocks forever, the actual

---

[15]We do not defend this example on the grounds of realism, but simply because it makes the calculations a lot easier.

return will vary around this average depending on when they invest. At the end of 1998, q was roughly 2.5 times above its average value. An immortal investor who bought stocks then could expect only a 2.7% average real return over their infinite lifespan. This is because the average long-term return has to be divided by the factor of 2½, which is roughly the extent to which q is above its average level.

Investing in the stock market at the end of 1998 would therefore have been a bad policy for long-term investors, even if they were lucky enough to have an infinite time horizon. They could expect a real return of only 2.7% per annum from investing in stocks, whereas they could have locked in a real return of nearly 4% from buying indexed U.S. government bonds, where both the income and capital are protected from inflation. Immortal equity investors would thus be giving up more than 25% of their income, compared with investors in government index-linked bonds.[16] If stocks look this bad to investors who, in the long run, will *not* be dead, they look even worse to mortal investors, who do not have such a consolation.

THE q-INVESTOR

We have seen that in normal circumstances investing in stocks is too risky for investors who do not have sufficiently long time horizons. We have also seen that at times like the present it is too risky for anyone. At this stage we should remind you of the good news as well as the bad. Being a q-investor means that you can spot times when the market is too dangerous to be holding stocks. But the knowledge that you can get out of stocks at the particular times when it gets too dangerous means that, in general, investing in stocks becomes safer. Imagine how driving a car would feel if you knew that you had no warning light to tell you when your brakes were in danger of malfunctioning. You would be forced to drive far more conservatively and would be very likely to drive less. q can fulfill the same warning function for an investor in stocks.

---

[16]Tax will complicate the situation for many investors, but the difference in prospective returns is so big that it is unlikely to change the conclusion.

The payoff for being a *q*-investor is that you can hold more stocks, for longer. We shall show in later chapters that the rewards are a combination of higher returns and lower risk. Since the times when you have to get out of stocks are normally times of turmoil, using *q* should also allow you to get rather more sleep at night, and to lead a less stressful life. Being a *q*-investor is good for your health as well as your wealth.

THE QUALITIES A *q*-INVESTOR NEEDS

Not every investor is, however, able to act sensibly even when it is clear that stocks are poor long-term investments. To be a *q*-investor you need the following characteristics:

- You must have strong nerves, at least in the sense that Mr. Giust used the term.
- You must have an investment horizon longer than a few weeks or months.
- You must be interested in absolute returns, not in relative returns. You must not worry about outperforming other investors.

OTHER PEOPLE'S MONEY

All three of these characteristics automatically rule out most people who invest other people's money, such as the fund managers of pension schemes and mutual funds. This is not to imply any personal criticism of typical fund managers, but simply and realistically to acknowledge the constraints under which they operate. Using *q*, as we have already said, will not make investors rich, but it can help them preserve their past profits. The only way that investors can do so, however, is by having the nerve, at some stage, to stand on the sidelines of the stock market. This means taking money out of stocks and putting it temporarily into safer assets like money market accounts and bonds.

While this is possible for individual investors who have the necessary strength of mind, it is not realistic behavior for fund managers. For the individual investor, being out of an overvalued but still rising stock market is, as the case of the Giusts showed, never easy. But there is also the strong incentive of avoiding massive losses.

For fund managers, the stakes are different, and much higher. A failure to be fully invested in stocks can be professional suicide. The most dangerous position a fund manager can take is to run the risk of underperforming the average fund manager. As long as the market keeps rising, this is exactly what will happen if fund managers respond to the signals of overvaluation that q provides. So they have to ignore these signals. On the other hand, a fund manager who outperforms competitors in a bear market by, for example, losing "only" 40% of clients' money when the market falls by 50%, will probably, and reasonably, expect to get a bonus.

Many people (including one of the authors of this book!) who are, for example, locked into contractual savings schemes have no choice but to leave fund managers to do the best job they can with other people's money. But at a time like this, the long-term investors who do have control over their own investments, have the character attributes we have listed, and pay attention to the message q is providing are at a distinct advantage.

That this message has not thus far received widespread attention probably reflects the fact that most discussion of stock markets is still aimed at people who manage other people's money, and not their own. Or, even worse, the discussion is intended not to inform, but to persuade people to buy stocks—a topic we shall move on to in the next chapter. This book is intended to fill the informational gap.

CHAPTER 4

q Versus the Competition

q VERSUS ALTERNATIVE INDICATORS OF VALUE

Investing in stocks has been a rewarding business and, for the long-term investor, it is not normally too risky. We have argued that this combination has been possible only because prices are pulled back toward their fundamental value and that *q* gives the best indication of how far from fundamental value prices have gotten.

There are, however, other valuation criteria and some of them can provide useful insights into the level of the stock market. It would indeed be unfortunate if this were not the case, since for many stock markets the data necessary to construct *q* are not available. In practice, there are a number of alternative criteria which can be used when *q* cannot be constructed; indeed, they may be used in tandem with *q*, even when data for *q* do exist. We shall look at these criteria in detail in later chapters.

We do, however, make strong claims about the special nature of *q*, and *q* alone, as a valuation criterion. The claims are these:

- *q* provides a way of valuing markets with an objectivity that cannot be found by using other criteria.
- Thus where reliable data on *q* exist, it provides the best way to value the market.

- No useful indicator can give results that conflict with q.
- Any other indicator can invariably be made more useful by making it look more like q.

These are clearly large claims and they must therefore be carefully supported by argument and evidence. We shall provide both, building up the evidence in later chapters. A key issue in the debate is whether value can exist and if so how it can be measured. In Chapter 20 we consider carefully the properties of an "ideal" indicator of value. If you discuss an ideal, it is more than usually necessary to have both feet firmly planted on the ground. Being aware of the pitfalls in the path of those who discuss ideals, we will strive not to fall into them. Armed, we hope, with the necessary skepticism, we will consider the properties needed for any sensible measure of value. These will naturally be those than can stand investigation which is both theoretical as well as statistical.

We therefore look, in a succession of chapters, at a whole range of different indicators, aiming to cover all those that have received either serious attention or wide publicity. We then compare their properties with those of the ideal indicator. Since we have started the book with our conclusion, you will not be surprised that we conclude that q is the only measure that satisfies the requirements of the ideal indicator.[17]

THE FAILURE OF OTHER INDICATORS

We are not the only people who have looked at popular indicators of value and found them to be unsound. Part of the continuing, if half-hearted, acceptance of the random walk model of stock prices is the lack of alternatives. Economists have consistently found the criteria of value used by stockbrokers and financial journalists to be unsatisfactory. As we mentioned earlier, q is almost the only valuation criterion that arises from the work of academic economists. The other approach has been to try to overcome the

---

[17]Lest we appear to be falling into the trap of finding arguments to justify a conclusion we arrived at previously, we should stress that this was not the way the process worked. As we explain later, in Chapter 25, it was the process of dealing with the weakness of other indicators that led us to our conclusion that q is ultimately the only satisfactory one.

intrinsic weaknesses of other indicators by modifying them.[18] We shall show that the adjustments proposed in order to improve these indicators simply make them more like *q*. Indeed, we show that these measures become in fact identical to *q*, when properly adjusted. These adjusted indicators are in effect "*q*-equivalent."

AN EXAMPLE: *q* AND THE P/E MULTIPLE

Probably the most widely used alternative indicator of value is the price-earnings (P/E) multiple. It has, however, been an unsatisfactory indicator of value. To illustrate this, Chart 4.1 compares *q* with the P/E multiple over the course of the twentieth century. If both measures provided a satisfactory way of assessing stock market value, they should both tell us when the market

CHART 4.1

q and the P/E Multiple, 1900–1999

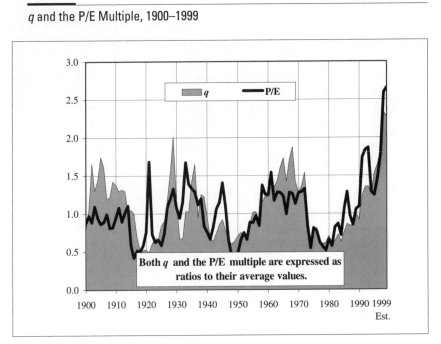

Both *q* and the P/E multiple are expressed as ratios to their average values.

---

[18]An example is in the work of Professors John Campbell and Robert Shiller, who have published many important papers in this area. Their paper "Valuation Ratios and the Long-Run Stock Market Outlook," published in the *Journal of Portfolio Management* (Fall 1998), comes to conclusions very similar to our own.

has been over- or undervalued. In each case this will be when either q or the P/E is markedly different from its historic average level. To illustrate, we show both indicators as ratios to their own average values.

A number of points are immediately obvious from Chart 4.1:

- q and the P/E often move in the same direction at similar times.

- Both appear to have the property of mean reversion introduced in Chapter 2: There is a piece of elastic that prevents either measure from getting too far away from its average value.

- Both were at exceptionally high levels at the end of 1998, and during much of 1999.

It is also clear, however, that the P/E multiple has occasionally given a disastrously wrong indication of value. A classic example was the early 1930s, when (as we shall show in a later chapter) the stock market was probably at the cheapest level of the century. At that time, profits were so depressed that the P/E multiple was extremely high. Anyone using the P/E as an indicator of value would have missed out on the best investment opportunity of the past 100 years.

It might appear tempting to use evidence like that presented in Chart 4.1 to say something like this: "q and the P/E multiple do not always agree, but at present both indicate that the stock market is massively overvalued. We can therefore be very sure that it is, because we have not just one, but two signals to confirm it."

Such an approach would, however, be both intellectually dishonest and decidedly shaky in practical terms. From an intellectual viewpoint, we need to understand the reasons that different indicators sometimes give different signals. From a practical stance, no indicator that showed the market to be expensive at its all-time low can be considered satisfactory.

Since both q and the P/E have price as the number on the top of their respective ratios,[19] the occasions when the two indicators give different results must be due to differences in the number at the bottom of the ratio. In the case of q this number is

---

[19]Most other valuation criteria can be expressed in this form.

based on assets, and in the case of P/E multiples it is derived from profits. The fact that the signals given by *q* and P/E differ from time to time indicates that profits and assets do not always go up and down together. The fact that the P/E multiple can give a very misleading signal, as it did in 1932, means that P/E multiples need to be adjusted in some way if they are to be used as guides to value.

There are a number of reasons why such adjustments to the P/E multiple might be needed. Probably the most crucial are:

- Profits may be incorrectly measured.
- Even when correctly measured, profits may fluctuate greatly around some normal level. Since profits will tend to revert to this level, P/E multiples will give poor indications of value either when profits are depressed, as they were in 1932, or when they are high.
- There is no economic theory available to tell us what the normal value of the P/E should be. Because the P/E has moved around its historic average of around 13 for so long, there is a natural tendency to assume it will continue to do so. We think that this assumption is reasonable and will probably be justified at some stage by the development of a satisfactory theory to explain it. Until this happens, however, it is fundamentally unsound to assume that it will. We cannot therefore assume that the average P/E will continue to be 13 in the future.

"STOCKBROKER ECONOMICS"

As we have already indicated, our approach (with some new features) basically conforms to that taken by academic economists when they address the question of how to value stock markets. It is therefore in sharp conflict with the approach taken by most stockbrokers.

Economics is a difficult subject. The result is that economists find it hard to make up their minds, disagree with one another endlessly, and seem to get bogged down in minor details or excessive abstraction. But there is one thing that all economists should share and almost all do. They should at least try to address their subject in a scientific manner. The consensus view of the scientific approach is that it proceeds by (1) formulating a hypothesis, (2) testing it against observation, and then, if the data reject the hypothesis, (3) discarding the hypothesis. Economics is difficult because formulating simple hypotheses that can be tested and conclusively rejected is difficult in a complex world. The principle is nonetheless there.

The concept of q is in fact an unusually good example of the scientific approach. When James Tobin proposed the concept in the 1960s, he did not have the data to test his hypothesis, which required that q must be a mean-reverting series. Since then, the data have become available and his theory has been put to the test in a true scientific way. We would not be writing this book if the theory had not proved robust under testing.[20]

We shall show that the reverse is the case for "stockbroker economics." Whereas a scientist rejects a hypothesis if it is inconsistent with the data, stockbrokers habitually reject data that are inconsistent with their hypotheses. The difference in approach derives from different motivation. Scientists who discard data that conflict with their hypotheses are despised and rapidly become unemployable. (Given the nature of the academic world, unemployable does not always mean unemployed, but normally it does.) A stockbroker's "hypothesis" is that stocks are wonderful. Any stockbroker who discards this hypothesis will rapidly become both unemployable and unemployed. (In the case of stockbrokers, the two are definitely the same thing.) Scientists are paid to pursue truth; stockbrokers, to sell stock.

Stockbrokers may of course draw on evidence from valuation criteria of all kinds, but if the evidence is in conflict with the "Stocks are Wonderful Hypothesis," it cannot make commercial sense for a broker to use it. For this reason, a number of indicators that are the regular tools of the trade for stockbrokers are inconsistent with value analysis in both theory and practice.

---

[20]Statistical evidence of a technical nature supporting this claim has been presented in a paper for academic economists, by one of the authors, Stephen Wright, cowritten with a Cambridge colleague, Donald Robertson. The paper, entitled "The Good News and the Bad News about Long-Run Stock Market Returns," is available as University of Cambridge Department of Applied Economics *Working Paper* no. 9822. It can also be accessed via the Virtual Appendix.

More trustworthy measures may of course get used on occasion, but only if they happen at the time to support the "Stocks are Wonderful Hypothesis." As a result, stockbrokers have steadily discarded the valuation criteria they used to use, as the stock market has become more and more overvalued. Examples include the dividend yield and the P/E multiple. These measures have been discarded, not because they are less reliable than they used to be, but because they no longer give the answer "stocks are wonderful." *q*, which showed the stock market to be overpriced by a factor of 2½, is thus deeply unpopular with stockbrokers. The same is true for P/E multiples, which suggest similar or even greater degrees of overpricing. Of course, once the stock market falls to more sensible levels, we must expect *q* and other discarded indicators of value to come back into favor again. Flexibility is the essence of stockbroking.

Like fund managers, therefore, stockbrokers have a profound conflict of interest between doing their job and valuing the stock market. Unsurprisingly, self-interest usually wins. The fact that it does not always do so reflects great credit on the minority.

WHAT MOTIVATES US?

Since we have questioned the objectivity of information provided by stockbrokers, on account of the motivation that drives them, it might quite reasonably be asked why anyone should pay any attention to us. We conclude these introductory chapters by giving an answer to the following question : What is our motive in writing this book?

This question is indeed something that is worth asking of almost anyone who writes a book on investment. The most obviously suspect are those, too numerous to mention, who offer a new way to get rich quickly by investing. Although we have noted our reservations about the Efficient Market Hypothesis, we have also said that we believe it to be fundamentally sound as a guiding principle. "Get Rich" books clearly violate this fundamental principle. A book that genuinely offered you a sure-fire way to get rich significantly faster than the average investor would, in effect, be offering you the keys to a money machine. Why would the authors provide you with the keys instead of using the machine themselves? Even in the exceptional case of an author who was motivated by sheer benevolence, the publication of the secret would destroy its value.

We are not open to this criticism. As we have already said, this book can help you avoid losing money, but it would be very difficult to become seriously rich by reading it. What, therefore, motivates us to provide you with this information?

Believers in conspiracy theories might imagine that we are hoping that our book will be so influential that our predictions about the stock market will be self-fulfilling, at which point we shall make a killing on option trades which allow you to make money by, in effect betting against the market. Strangely enough, even though the conspiracy theorists would be wrong about our motivation, they would be half right about the rest: Yes, we (or at least Smithers & Co., the London-based company we both work for either full- or part-time) do stand to make a modest profit (if not quite a killing) on "put" options that bet against the U.S. stock market. But these options are really only a hedge—in other words, an insurance policy. This book is another.

To explain: Smithers & Co. derives its revenues from selling research to fund managers. There is a paradox here, in that such revenues are probably most at risk if we are correct in our assessment of the future of Wall Street. Making money in financial research requires two things: clients who are interested in what you are saying, and clients who can afford to pay. When we are proved right about what is going to happen to the U.S. stock market, clients will no doubt be extremely interested in what we have to say next. Unfortunately, a significant number of them will probably not be able to pay to listen to our advice. Bad times for the stock market are always bad times for anyone who works on Wall Street, or in the City of London. Such bad times as we expect will almost certainly mean that even those firms that manage to survive will be forced to slash their research budgets. So our pleasure at being proved right is likely to be tempered by the knowledge that our business will probably suffer.

On the other hand, new as we are to the publishing business, it seems reasonable to assume that being right about the U.S. stock market will help along sales of this book nicely. The royalty payments we receive, together with the proceeds of our option trades, are unlikely to be enough to offset the impact of lost business, but they should at least be a step in the right direction.

TWO

STOCK MARKET RISK AND RETURN

Having introduced you to the main ideas behind q, we now need to build up our arguments more systematically. In Part Two we temporarily suspend discussion of q itself to consider why the long-term investor should be interested in q at all. We argued in Chapter 3 that the exceptional behavior of the stock market in recent years has distorted expectations. It has become difficult for investors to take a balanced view of what reasonably to anticipate in terms of future returns and their associated risks. Part Two aims to restore the balance. Our main themes will be:

- To remind you what historic experience of return and risk has been over longer periods.
- To point out that the case for stocks, as it is usually presented, is heavily oversold. It ignores the way most investors save, or, indeed, why they save.
- To show that although stocks have played an essential role for the long-term investor, there are periods in life (most notably retirement) when stocks are much less suitable; there have also been important occasions when *all* investors would have been much better off getting out of stocks.

CHAPTER **5**

The Power of Compound Interest (or How to Oversell Stocks)

THE REWARDS FROM INVESTING IN STOCKS

In recent years, as we have noted, investors in stocks have led a charmed life. As a result, it has been very hard to retain a sensible perspective on what to expect in the future. In the next few chapters we aim to restore some balance by looking at the risks as well as the rewards from investing in stocks. To do this, we look back, not just a decade or two, but at the entire twentieth century.[1]

We start, in this chapter, by looking at the case for stocks as it is often argued: that over long enough periods stocks have always yielded higher returns than competing assets.

We have already stressed that this differential has not been anywhere near as great as that witnessed in recent years. The very long-term average return has been around 6¾% per annum in real terms (before costs). It is a point of considerable interest, which we will consider in detail later, that the real return on stocks

---

[1] In this book we shall often stress the importance of looking at all the data available, not just at selected bits. Reasonably good data on the stock market are available for the past century and some for the past 200 years. In some later chapters we shall look back over the whole period for which data can be found, which is almost to the beginning of the nineteenth century.

appears, like q, to be mean-reverting. Returns may fluctuate greatly in the short term, but average returns over longer periods never stray far from this stable average value. The average return of 6¾% therefore provides a suitable benchmark for the return that investors can reasonably expect over the long term, in the future as well as the past.

Small differences in returns mean large differences in final results, if they are extended over long enough periods. This quality has been used to exaggerate the benefits of equity investment. The power of compound interest is so great that even 6¾% per annum over a long time can compound into huge figures. In this chapter we look at two examples that demonstrate how easy it is to push the logic of this argument into the realm of absurdity.

Much of the hyperbole surrounding the benefits of holding stocks is based on erroneous assumptions, which are encapsulated in the very name of the "buy-and-hold strategy." As we shall see in the next chapter, investors do not usually buy stocks on just one occasion, but on a repeated basis. Even more crucially, they do not buy stocks in order to hold them. The ultimate objective is, of course, to spend. Both of these features of real-world investors significantly limit the gains from the power of compound interest. Although the case for stocks is strong, it tends to be oversold.

The other crucial point is that the happy experience of recent years has led many investors to forget the inevitable link between risk and return. Recently they've had the return, but they have not yet had to wake up to the risk. In the last chapter of Part Two we shall show that the risk is very real.

THE POWER OF COMPOUND INTEREST

Compound interest is a wonderful thing. If you wait long enough, it can turn any trivially small sum into fabulous wealth.

Every U.S. schoolchild is familiar with the story of how Dutch traders bamboozled the Native North Americans into selling Manhattan Island in 1624, for a measly $24 worth of trade goods. Myth and legend aside, the degree to which the Native Americans were bamboozled is, admittedly, rather overstated by forgetting about inflation: In terms of real spending power, $24 in 1624 was probably roughly equivalent to around $800 at 1998 prices.[2] But even that amount would buy you only a few square inches of modern Manhattan.

There is a school of thought, however, that says that the Native Americans were not bamboozled at all. According to this view, the sellers of Manhattan were paid a price that was perfectly fair— or even generous. If only the Native Americans had invested their $24 wisely, it is claimed, they would by now be able to buy back Manhattan.

Such a claim relies on two things: the power of compound interest, and an assumption that those Indians had an almost infinite supply of another even more important commodity, patience. The first of these is undeniable, the second much, much more debatable. We shall come back to the sale of Manhattan in due course, but we turn first to an example that is somewhat, though not much, closer to home.

YOUR FOUR GREAT-GRANDFATHERS

Most people have had four great-grandfathers.[3] Let us suppose that you are like most people in this respect, but unlike most people in that all four of your great-grandfathers were exceptionally forward-looking. Indeed, they were the investing equivalent of the great eighteenth century gardener Capability Brown, who planted tree-lined avenues that took more than a century to mature. Only his great-grandchildren could ever hope to see them in their full beauty.

One fine day you receive four letters, from four different lawyers. Each writes to inform you that one of your great-grandfathers had set up a trust fund, just for you, way back at the start of

---

[2]"Roughly" is definitely the right word to use here. The only available long runs of (wholesale) price data go back to 1720 (these come from G.F. Warren, F.A. Pearson, and H.M. Stoker's *Wholesale Prices for 213 Years, 1720 to 1932*); for the 100 years before that we had to resort to extrapolation, using a price series for Great Britain, constructed by the Bank of England. The major changes in prices were, of course, in the twentieth century: while prices probably only roughly doubled between 1620 and 1914, they increased seventeenfold, in the USA, between 1914 and 1998.

[3]Four is a maximum. The actual number will depend on the extent to which cousins have married each other in your family.

the twentieth century. All the wills provide that you were entitled to the money at the end of 1997, but the lawyers have only now, with suitable legal delay, got around to telling you. In all four cases, fund management and, thank goodness, lawyers' fees have been taken care of, so that all the proceeds from all four funds are yours.[4] In all four cases, dividends or interest payments have been reinvested continuously since 1900, so the power of compound interest has really been able to get to work.

The first great-grandfather invested $100 in 1900. He put the money into stocks, and the portfolio turns out to have tracked precisely the general index of total stock returns used by Jeremy Siegel in *Stocks for the Long Run*. With all the dividends having been reinvested, you are now slightly more than $1 million better off than before you opened the letter. In other words, your great-grandfather's initial investment has increased a little more than 10,000 times.

The next letter turns out to be something of a disappointment. This great-grandfather was as well off as the previous one, and also invested $100 at the outset. But he was more cautious, and rather than investing in stocks, he asked the lawyers simply to keep the cash on deposit with a reputable bank.[5] As a result, you are not better off by another million dollars, but by significantly less. This fund pays out, with reinvested interest, slightly less than $4000. This rich-but-cautious great-grandfather's investment has increased, not 10,000 times, but only 40 times.

"Ah well," you sigh, "better luck next time." and open the next letter. The news is distinctly better than that of the previous letter, but in an interesting way. The next great-grandfather was not as well off as the previous two. He did not have $100 to invest on your behalf. Instead, he invested the rather curious sum of $5.28. This turns out, by some mysterious chance, to be the equivalent of $100 in today's prices. So what you get out of this fund will be the equivalent of a real return on an initial $100 investment in today's money. Fortunately for you, this poorer great-grandfather had faith in stocks. As a result, although he invested about one twentieth of what your rich-but-cautious great-grandfather

---

[4] This last element in the story is probably the one that stretches credibility the most.
[5] To estimate the interest you would have received we use the return on Treasury bills.

did, this fund actually ends up paying out around $58,000. Since the initial investment was equivalent to $100 in today's money, the fund has increased more than 500 times in real terms, compared with 10,000 times in nominal terms. You are thus powerfully reminded that the apparent multiplication of your wealth was overstated 200 times by the effect of inflation and that much of the apparently fabulous gain on your first great-grandfather's legacy was illusory, since it was needed simply to keep up with inflation.

The final letter verges on the pathetic. Your fourth great-grandfather was as poor as the third, and also invested $5.28, or the equivalent of $100 at 1998 prices. But he was poor and cautious, which is the worst possible combination from the point of view of his descendants, so he put the money into the bank. The fund pays you only $216. In real terms, this fund has only just doubled over the course of nearly a century.

The power of compound interest, over a very long time period, explains the enormous differences between the sums you received. Table 5.1 shows the four amounts together with the four associated compound average returns that generated them.[6]

TABLE 5.1

The Power of Compound Interest

	Invested in Stocks	Invested in Bank Deposits
Value at the end of 1997 of $100 invested in 1900	$1,099,015	$4,092
Value at the end of 1997 of $5.28 invested in 1900	$58,028	$216
Implied compound average: nominal returns	9.96%	3.86%
Implied compound average: real returns	6.68%	0.75%

[6]Compound average returns tell you what constant rate of return would have produced the figure you have at the end of the period, starting with the figure you had at the start of the period. For example, the formula that gave you the compound average growth rate of stocks in nominal terms was:

$$\frac{1,002,931.31}{100} = 1.0996^{97}$$

Once you take into account the impact of seemingly minor differences in compound interest, it is very easy to make stocks look, not only better, but staggeringly better than competing assets. But in fact the example is as absurd as it is mathematically correct. To see why, look again at the even more extreme example of the Native Americans who sold Manhattan.

THE SALE OF MANHATTAN REVISITED

Given the power of compound interest, it is even possible to make our Native Americans rich enough to buy back Manhattan, just as long as they were patient enough. But given the time period involved, the difference made by different interest rates becomes so great that all that this does is bring out the absurdity of the exercise. Table 5.2 shows the calculations.

TABLE 5.2

What the Native Americans' $24 Would Have Been Worth by 1998, Depending on the Assumed Real Return on Investments

Assumed Real Return	Lump Sum Value
1%	$32,984
2%	$1,313,921
3%	$50,492,512
4%	$1,873,155,522
5%	$67,127,858,289
6%	$2,325,404,711,912
7%	$77,917,999,432,506

If interest rate differences were important in the case of your four great-grandfathers, the impact there is dwarfed by the figures shown in Table 5.2. If the patient Native Americans had only managed to earn an average of 1% per annum on their investments, all that patience would have been rewarded with little more than the price of a second-hand limousine, in which their descendants could drive around their former property. But had they earned 6% per annum, they would have ended up with $2.3

---

[7]They would by necessity have owned it by this stage anyway.

trillion, which would have bought them roughly one fifth of what Wall Street said U.S. corporations were worth in 1998 (we would not of course have advised them to make such a purchase at this time!). By earning a mere 1% more per annum on their investments, the $77 trillion they would have ended up with would have bought them pretty much everything salable in the entire world.[7]

But, as we have said, both examples are as absurd as they are mathematically correct. They demonstrate the fundamental weakness of arguments based on the power of compound interest, which all assume that the purpose of investment is to get rich, but never to spend the money. The primary purpose of saving and investing, however, is to be better off in the future. The money that we can't touch does not make us better off.

It is quite striking how historically based arguments for the buy-and-hold strategy almost invariably involve an application of the power of compound interest, or, as we should perhaps call it, the Patient Native American model of investment. Such notional investors live to save; they do not save to live. They are, of course, purely imaginary. In the next chapter, we look at what differences in return can do for more realistic investors. We also look at how return differentials based on the experience of the twentieth century overstate the relative performance of stocks. Taking both points into account, we shall see that the case for stocks, although strong, becomes much less striking.

CHAPTER **6**

The True Impact of Stock Returns

THE BENEFITS OF SMALL DIFFERENCES ARE OVERSTATED

The examples of the previous chapter tell us very little about how important differences in returns really are. In fact, the benefits of small differences are overstated—for three important reasons.

- Real investors do not invest for such long periods. They usually spend at least part of their capital in retirement. The altruistic who invest purely for the benefit of their children, let alone their grandchildren or great grand-children, are rare. People who inherit wealth often work, but they tend to spend their investment income as well. People who save on a regular basis don't have much money to invest until they have saved for a good number of years.
- Once you look at the shorter periods of time over which investments are really made, the gains from higher returns look far less exciting.
- The average differences between returns on stocks and returns on competing assets over the twentieth century almost certainly exaggerate the extent of the differential in normal circumstances.

A MORE REALISTIC COMPARISON: THE REGULAR INVESTOR

Most people save in a way that bears only a very limited relationship to the examples of your four great-grandfathers, or the patient Native Americans. Rather than setting aside a single lump sum, they save on a regular basis, throughout their lives, in order to accumulate enough to live on in retirement. Regular saving limits the gains made from differences in returns, for two crucial reasons.

The first is that only the money saved in the first year will benefit fully from the power of compound interest. Suppose you save $100 a year for 30 years. The first $100 will get the benefit of 30 years' compound interest, the second will get only 29 years' worth, and so on. On average, each of these $100 payments will earn interest only for half the total saving period. There is a very large difference between investing for 15 and for 30 years. Using the same returns as we used to illustrate the great-grandfather legacies, then over 15 years the investors in stocks would be 2½ times better off, but over 30 years they would be 5½ times richer.

The second reason is that most people's income, and hence their capacity to save, rises throughout their working life. Furthermore, they do not save at a constant rate each year, but tend to save more, even in proportion to their rising incomes, as they get older.[8] This is exactly the wrong way around to maximize the impact of compound interest, since it is the payments early in life that multiply up the most.

Chart 6.1 shows how different returns affect the size of the lump sum that investors will accumulate when the saving is made over different periods of time.[9]

As indicated, higher rates of return clearly increase the size of the lump sum, and the impact increases with the length of the saving period. The chart also illustrates, however, that even though the gains are substantial, they are a long way from being as spectacular as might otherwise be expected from our previous long-term examples.

---

[8]Only as people get older do they appear to worry enough about the need to save for retirement.

[9]For ease of comparison, we assume that if you earn a zero real return (in other words, all you do is preserve the real value of the amounts you save), this gives you a lump sum of $100. We also assume that, whatever the period you save over, you make a contribution that is some constant proportion of your income, which we assume to grow at 2.5% per annum (roughly the growth of GDP).

CHART 6.1

The Impact of Different Rates of Return for a Regular Saver

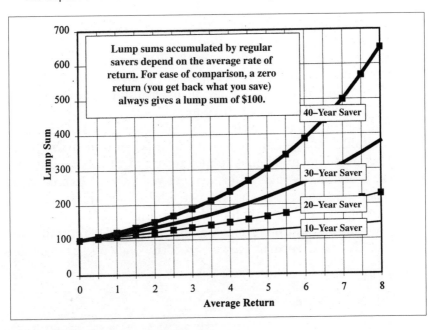

Lump sums accumulated by regular savers depend on the average rate of return. For ease of comparison, a zero return (you get back what you save) always gives a lump sum of $100.

THE EXAGGERATED DIFFERENTIAL

When we look at the impact of higher or lower returns, it is also very important to have an appropriate basis for comparison. There are three reasons why stocks have appeared to be such especially good investments in the twentieth century, and in the postwar period in particular.

- The first, to which we have already alluded in earlier chapters, is that at the end of the century the market was so overpriced that this affected average returns even over the century as a whole.
- Return comparisons usually ignore the fact that holding a portfolio of stocks is much more expensive, in terms of management and brokerage costs, than holding government bonds or cash on deposit.
- Because of the impact of inflation, the twentieth century, and especially the postwar era, has been an exceptionally poor period for bonds and cash, in contrast to stocks.

None of these factors imply that the return differential in favor of stocks disappears, but it does become distinctly less marked. Table 6.1 illustrates the impact of the three factors on the rates of return that generated the massive differences in value among the legacies of your four great-grandfathers.

The first adjustment allows for the fact that, in our estimate, the U.S. market was close to being twice overvalued at the end of 1997. Even spread over 97 years, the overvaluation takes nearly ¾% off the annual average return since 1900.

The second adjustment is very rough and ready, but assumes that portfolio management costs eat up 1% per annum of the value of a stock portfolio, and hence reduce returns by that amount. We assume that the average difference between the return on cash on deposit and the return on Treasury bills (for which we have historic data) would be only half this amount.[10]

The third adjustment is also rough and ready, but quite important. The weak returns earned by both bonds and cash on de-

TABLE 6.1

Adjustments to Real Returns

	Stocks	Cash	Differential in Favor of Stocks
Actual real returns	6.68%	0.75%	5.93%
Impact of overvaluation in 1997	−0.7%	n/a	
Portfolio management and other costs	−1.0%	−0.5%	
Impact of stable inflation		+1.25%	
Adjusted real returns	4.98%	1.5%	3.73%

[10]Research into the typical costs of managing stock portfolios, even large ones, suggests that the assumptions that we have made are conservative and most investors are likely to pay more than we have assumed that they will. See, for example, Keith P. Ambachtseer, "The Economics of Pension Fund Management," *Financial Analysts Journal* (November–December 1994). The spread between bank deposit rates and Treasury bills is harder to estimate, although there is evidence that our figure would be an overestimate in the more recent past. It is highly likely that both the spread and equity fund management costs will have fallen over the course of time, but we assume that these reductions in effect cancel out in terms of the return comparison.

posit during the twentieth century on average were significantly affected by the period, running roughly from the 1940s to the end of the 1970s, when inflation was much higher than expected for most of the time and the returns from bonds, or cash on deposit with a bank, were close to zero or even negative in real terms. Since that time, in a period of much more stable inflation, returns from cash on deposit with a bank have been around 2% per annum in real terms and from bonds have been around 3.5%.[11]

The net effect of all these adjustments is to reduce the differential in favor of stocks quite markedly.

Such adjustments make a big difference to the outcome of investing in stocks versus other assets. Table 6.2 shows that the regular 30-year saver would be twice as well off in stocks if the only alternative were to put money into bank deposits that paid only enough interest to keep up with inflation. But if the alternative was to hold bonds that yielded 3.5%, stocks would produce only 25% more. The comparison shows that today's excessive faith in stocks is partly a hangover from high postwar inflation.

The comparison with an alternative that pays 3.5% in real terms is particularly appropriate at the time of writing. The U.S. Treasury currently issues index-linked bonds that are the ultimate safe asset, since the government not only guarantees repayment, but does so in real terms: Both principal and interest

TABLE 6.2

A Comparison of Gains to a Regular Saver in Stocks

Saving Period	% Difference in Lump Sum	
	Compared with Bank Deposits Paying 0%	Compared with Bonds Paying 3.5%
10	24%	6.8%
20	59%	15.3%
30	102%	25.1%
40	157%	36.1%

[11]These figures are also very similar to those in a few countries, most notably Germany and Switzerland in the postwar era, which have not experienced major inflationary surprises.

are guaranteed to be uprated in line with the consumer price index. Such bonds are currently yielding rather more than our assumed rate of 3.5%.

The differences in return clearly do have an impact, but the payoffs are a lot less than the usual "Stocks are Wonderful" story would have you believe. This underlines two important points. The first is that stocks are best for really long-term investors. You need to be investing for at least 20 or 30 years to get the real benefits. The second is that the power of compound interest has been misused to oversell stocks, even over long periods.

ANOTHER REALISTIC COMPARISON: THE RETIRED

For retired investors who have accumulated savings for their retirement, the rewards for investing in stocks are even more limited.[12] This is because those who have retired are the exact opposite of these Patient Native Americans. Having saved all these years, the time has come to achieve the ultimate objective, which is, after all, to spend the money. Even the most prudent retiree is unlikely to wish to accumulate additional capital and must aim to run it down, albeit slowly. This process seriously limits any further gains from higher stock returns, unless the investor proposes to start retirement early or finish it late (both of which require pretty good luck, though in rather different forms).

One option at retirement is for investors to buy annuities. This step ensures that they get the full value of all their savings, leaving nothing for their children. The income from these annuities will depend on the return that the insurance companies can make on their investments. Comparing the different levels of income that annuities provide, at different rates of return on the investments, is thus a simple way to illustrate the relative lack of importance of higher returns for those who have retired.[13] In prac-

---

[12]We will also show later that the uncertainty of these potential rewards makes it very tricky to actually get the benefit from any higher returns.

[13]This comparison can now be made much more clearly than used to be possible, given the existence, already noted, of indexed bonds. It is therefore possible for a life insurance company to offer investors annuities protected from inflation, and based on real rates of return. One of the authors has an annuity that is protected against inflation and which he purchased on retiring from investment banking at the tender age of 52. This was, however, in the UK, where "index-linked" bonds have been around for much longer than they have in the USA.

tice, for reasons we explain later, it is not possible to buy annuities that yield equity returns, but the results may be calculated
on a hypothetical basis.

Table 6.3 shows that the impact of higher returns is modest
for those who have retired, even assuming that they could buy
annuities that yielded equity returns. Despite all that you may
be told by mutual fund sales representatives or stockbrokers, high
returns, at least on a feasible scale, are simply not that crucial
once you are retired. Only those who retire early, or die late, can
really reap significant benefits.

TABLE 6.3

Difference in Average Retirement Income Earned from Stocks Compared with
Index-Linked Bonds

Life Expectancy	% Difference in Income
10 years	6.1%
15 years	9.2%
20 years	12.2%
25 years	15.1%

For a retired investor with a life expectancy of ten years, the
increase in average income from an annuity giving an equity return, rather than one based on indexed government bonds, is less
than 10%.[14] But we must stress that this figure treats the average return from stocks as if it were a guaranteed one. We have
skated around the risks involved in this strategy, in terms of the
variability of the income around its average value. We deal with
this issue in the next chapter.

THE OVERSTATED CASE

We have seen that, for regular savers, there is a strong case for
stocks as the dominant instrument in normal times. The longer

---

[14]This assumes that the index-linked bond yields 3.5% and that stocks yield their
historic average real return. At the time this book went to press, the actual
return on index-linked bonds was nearly 4%, and it seemed highly improbable
that future yields from equities would be anywhere near their historic ones. In
practice, therefore, at the time of writing we expect an investor who chose index-
linked bonds over equities to have a much better income in the future. But at this
stage we are focusing on the comparison under average conditions.

the period over which they save, the stronger is the case, thanks to the power of compound interest. It is true that over reasonable time horizons compound interest cannot work the fabulous magic for you that it did for your great-grandfathers' legacies, or the patient Native Americans, but it can nonetheless do a lot. The closer you get to retirement, however, the less compelling the case for stocks becomes, even if you look only at returns and ignore risk. The sensible investor does not, however, ignore risk, which we shall therefore consider in the next chapter.

CHAPTER

Stock Market Risks: Some History

RISK ALWAYS GOES WITH RETURN

The rise in the stock market has led many investors to forget the inevitable link between risk and return. This is probably because they've had the return first and have yet to wake up to the risk. We shall show that the risk is very real. If history is anything to go by, and there is no alternative guide available, it is likely that Wall Street will fall sufficiently to affect the living standards of most of today's investors in a major and permanent way.

Those who emphasize the high returns that have come from holding stocks usually fail to draw equal attention to the risks. This is tantamount to ignoring one of the most fundamental ideas of economics, most commonly summarized in Milton Friedman's much-quoted principle that there is no such thing as a free lunch.[15] Markets do not give something for nothing. In the case of financial markets, higher returns always reflect higher risk.

During bull markets the principle that there is no free lunch is easily forgotten. Almost by definition, a bull market is a period in which investors get high returns with little, if any, apparent

---

[15]This vies with Keynes's "In the long run we are all dead," which we have quoted already, for the honor of being the most famous thing an economist has ever said. Despite our background in Cambridge, UK, we cannot help but acknowledge that Friedman's is the deeper of the two.

risk. This readily leads to the assumption that there never was any risk in the first place. The true conclusion is that investors have been lucky, as even the briefest glance at a longer period of history will reveal.

THE VARIABILITY OF STOCK RETURNS

To get high returns on stocks, investors must be prepared for large fluctuations in value. Because of these fluctuations, the returns vary a lot from one period to another. The more stock prices fluctuate, the less certain investors can be about the return that they will actually receive. There is thus a trade-off between the returns that stocks give on average and the probability that the actual return investors get will be very different from that average.

In the past, the returns from holding stocks have, as we have seen, been significantly greater than returns from holding cash on deposit. But those who hold cash on deposit all get roughly the same return, independent of when they need to spend their money. This is, however, far from the case for investors in stocks. Their average returns are better, but the risks they run of not getting such returns are much greater. The extent to which returns fluctuate around their average determines the risk that investors have to take to get those returns.

Chart 7.1 shows the real returns that equity investors received in each year of the twentieth century. To illustrate just how variable returns have been, the chart also shows the range of values within which they fall 90% of the time. We shall also show, in Chapter 17, that the variations in stock returns remained much the same in the twentieth century as they were in the nineteenth.[16]

---

[16]For presentational clarity, we have used log returns, multiplied by 100, rather than the usual percentage return. This gets around the problem that normal percentage rises and falls are not symmetric in their impact. For example, using percentage returns, a negative return of 20% needs a 25% positive return to get you back to where you started. With log returns you get symmetry, but for smaller changes the two measures of returns are virtually identical. Using this definition of returns allows you to see an additional important feature of the data: In terms of the impact on the investor there have been more very bad returns than very good returns.

CHART 7.1

The Short-Term Variability of Stock Returns in the Twentieth Century

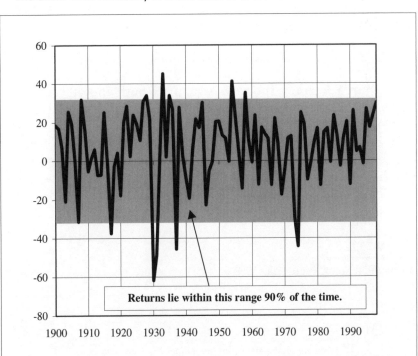

Returns lie within this range 90% of the time.

This large variation in short-run returns gives some idea of the uncertainty that investors have to accept when investing in stocks. But it does not obviously translate into an impact on what really matters, which is individual living standards. To get a feel for this we shall, in the next chapter, investigate how variability of returns affects the two examples we discussed previously: regular savers and investors who have retired. First of all, however, to put this in context, it's worth looking briefly at some history.

REAL STOCK PRICES OVER THE TWENTIETH CENTURY

As a first step we look at what has happened to stock prices. Their twentieth-century history, in real terms, is shown in Chart 7.2. There is a strong case for requiring this chart to be attached to any publicity material for mutual funds, in the same way that graphic public health warnings are put on cigarette packs. The chart might be more effective than the usual disclaimer, which is normally something along the lines of:

Stock prices can fall as well as rise

Chart 7.2 shows the real stock price both on a normal scale and a log (logarithmic) scale. We shall use log scales a lot. It doesn't matter if you can't quite remember how logarithms work. The only important thing to understand is that log scales allow the eye to assess the significance of price changes without distortion. On the normal scale, for example, a rise from 100 to 200, which is a 100% rise, looks the same as a rise from 200 to 300, which is only a 50% rise. This is obviously misleading. The problem is

CHART 7.2

The Real Stock Price, 1900–1998

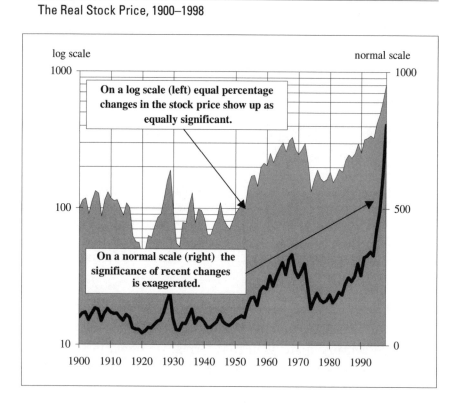

avoided by using a log scale, where a rise from 100 to 200 looks the same as a rise from 200 to 400 (both 100% increases).[17]

In future chapters, we shall look in more detail at the story behind Chart 7.2, but for now, we shall focus on a few major features that are crucial from an investor's point of view:

- It is certainly true that stock prices can fall as well as rise. This is a statement not just about short-term volatility, but every bit as much about price movements over substantial periods.

- If you cover the first part of the chart, so that only the period after 1950 is visible, you will get the idea that it is perfectly sensible to expect to make real capital gains from stocks. If, however, you look only at the first half of the century, you will get the idea that the real stock price had no clear trend. This doesn't mean, however, that holding stocks has been more rewarding in the second part of the century than in the first. In fact, the total return on stocks, which includes dividends, was much the same in both periods. The difference was that dividends supplied most of the return in the first half, whereas capital appreciation became much more important in the second half.[18] But since capital values fluctuate much more than dividends, the increased reliance on capital gains has increased the importance of stock price volatility.

- The chart makes it very clear that, at various stages throughout the century, there were prolonged periods when stock prices were falling. In broad-brush terms, these were (1) the 15 years from 1906 onward, (2) the 25 years or so from 1929 onward, ignoring the brief recovery in prices in the mid-1930s, and (3) the 15 years from 1968 onward. In other words, roughly a third to a half of the century could be characterized broadly as "bear markets."

---

[17]For this reason the gridlines marking off 200, 300, 400, and so on get closer together as they approach 1000, since the implied percentage changes get progressively smaller.

[18]We shall see in a later chapter that the counterpart to this has been a lower dividend yield.

These were not simply periods of short-term volatility; they had a major impact on longer-period returns and hence on the living standards of investors in stocks.

- If you look back to Chart 2.1, you will note that each of the above periods came after a peak in q. In other words, each of these bear markets followed a period of major overvaluation.

- In terms of the real stock price, the recent bull market has been as big and lasted as long as the previous record bull market. This was the immediate postwar market, which finally ran out steam at the end of the 1960s.

- Because it is so much discussed, it is worth mentioning a red herring or, for Sherlock Holmes enthusiasts, a dog that did not bark.[19] The most recent "crash" in popular mythology, that of October 1987, barely appears on the chart at all. For the stock market historian, 1987 does not register as a serious bear market. Newspaper articles have referred to 1987 as a terrible crash that is unlikely to be repeated. Such comments show an abysmal ignorance of history. Investors have comparatively little to fear from small blips like 1987. For all the scare stories associated with that crash, investors should be aware that the most recent period to look back upon with dread, lest history repeat itself, is not 1987 but the disastrous decade of the 1970s.

The key point to remember from Chart 7.2 is that for over one third of the twentieth century, we have been living in bear markets and that each bear market followed a peak in q. We shall show in the next chapter that investors who lived through these periods would have found that these bear markets had a large negative impact on their living standards.

TOTAL RETURNS (THE PATIENT NATIVE AMERICANS REVISITED)

Of course, Chart 7.2 tells only part of the story. Investors in stocks receive dividends as well as making capital gains in the good times.

---

[19]The reference is to the clue given by the dog that did not bark in the story "Silver Blaze."

This is shown by an index of total return, which compounds up not just real capital appreciation, but additional capital accumulated through dividend reinvestment.

In some ways total return indices give a more accurate picture, since the importance of dividends is undeniable. But in another important way they also give a distorted picture. For total return indices are telling you what would have happened to the Patient Native Americans' investments or your great-grandfathers' legacies, by showing how the values would have changed over time, rather than just their values today, as we did in Chapter 5. As such, you would expect total return indices to give a distorted picture (since, as we have observed, the Patient Native American model of investment is far from being realistic), and to magnify relatively small return differences to an extent that does not reflect their true impact on real investors.

CHART 7.3

Total Real Return Indices, 1900–1998

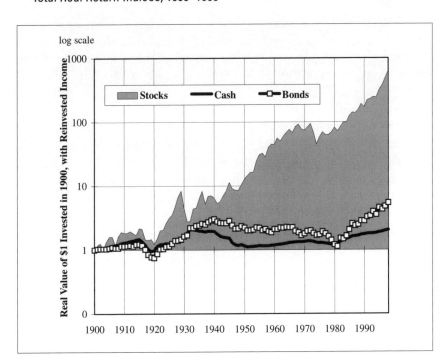

As Chart 7.3 shows, this is exactly what happens. The chart shows the total return index for stocks alongside equivalent measures for cash on deposit and long-term government bonds. All are measured in real terms and, like Chart 7.2, use a log scale.

Chart 7.3 offers a marked contrast with Chart 7.2. The most striking feature is exactly what we were expecting: the overwhelming magnitude of the cumulative total return on stocks compared with returns on alternative assets. But the chart has a number of other interesting, if less arresting, features. The most important of these is the way in which the relatively higher return on stocks is so much less evident over shorter periods than over very long ones.

The marked divergence in the relative performance of stocks, bonds, and cash on deposit, over longer rather than shorter periods, becomes even more evident in Chart 7.4. This shows the relative returns of stocks over bonds and cash (represented again by the return on Treasury bills) rather than the actual returns from each type of asset. Look at the line marked "stocks vs cash," for example. In periods when this line was rising, stocks outperformed cash and when the line was falling, cash was the better investment.[20]

These indices of relative returns show that stocks barely kept pace with either bonds or bills, not only in all the three bear markets previously discussed but also in other periods, such as from 1980 to the mid-1990s. These were periods when bonds either matched or even exceeded returns from stocks, even though stocks performed well.

We noted, when looking at Chart 7.2, that the bull market of the 1980s and 1990s looked similar to that of the 1950s and 1960s in terms of real capital appreciation. Chart 7.4 shows, however, that in terms of relative performance, the earlier period was much more impressive. In both periods stocks gave similarly high returns. The difference was in the poor returns offered by cash and bonds in the 1950s and 1960s.

---

[20]More precisely, whereas Chart 7.2 showed the cumulative value of an initial notional $1 invested in each of the assets in 1900, in Chart 7.3 the line marked "stocks vs cash" shows the ratio of the amount cumulated from stocks to that from cash on deposit. It therefore in effect shows how many times greater was the legacy of the great-grandfather who invested in stocks, compared with the one who invested in bank deposits.

CHART 7.4

Relative Return Indices, 1900–1998

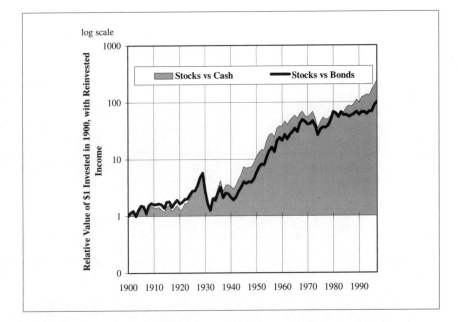

Another very important feature brought out by Chart 7.4 is just how long the periods have been in which investors would have done significantly better by moving out of stocks into either bonds or cash on deposit.

The most obvious case is the period immediately following the peak of August 1929. An investor who had switched out of stocks into cash at the peak could have waited 15 years for investors who had stayed in stocks to catch up.[21] If the investor had switched into bonds, the equivalent period would have been 21 years. But such prolonged periods were not just a feature of the post-1929 period. Investors who switched into cash in 1968 would have kept ahead of investors in stocks for the next 15 years.

In the next chapter we go on to examine the impact of these features of the history of stock market in the twentieth century on real savers, as opposed to Patient Native Americans.

---

[21]This was despite the fact that, in a number of years during the course of the 1930s, interest rates went to zero in dollar terms.

CHAPTER **8**

Stock Market Risks:
The Impact on Investors

RISKS TO REAL INVESTORS

In the last chapter, when we looked briefly at the history of the stock market over the course of the twentieth century, we saw that the average performance we had looked at in Chapters 5 and 6 concealed enormous variations. Although stocks outperformed assets on average, there were long periods when the reverse was the case. In this chapter we examine the impact of these fluctuations on typical investors.

THE REGULAR SAVER

We noted in Chapter 6 that most people do not follow the Patient Native American model of investment, simply putting by a single lump sum. Instead, they are regular savers, over the course of a number of years. In previous chapters we have looked at the wealth that such savers could expect to accumulate if they received the average returns that have been historically available from stocks. We were implicitly assuming that these returns were available to investors every year, and were therefore ignoring the element of risk that comes from market volatility. To illustrate the impact of risk on regular savers, we now look at the actual gains they would have received in the past.

Chart 8.1 shows these figures assuming the following:

- The amount shown for any year represents the lump sum you would have accumulated by saving in the 30 years leading up to that year.
- The amount saved in each year grows at 2.5% per annum.
- As before, the figures are set up so that, if the real return was zero (you got back just what you paid in), you would have got a real lump sum of $100.
- For the purposes of comparison, the chart also shows the equivalent lump sums accumulated by regular savers who invested in bonds, or simply held cash on deposit.
- Management costs per year are 1% for stocks, but only ½% for cash and bonds.[22]

CHART 8.1

Lump Sums Earned from Regular Saving: 30-Year Saver

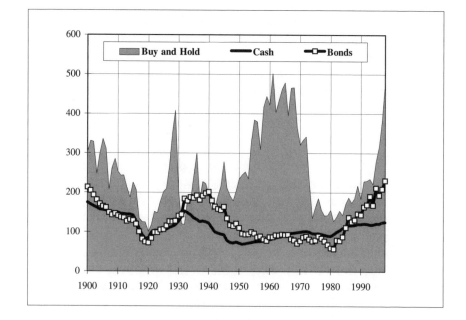

---

[22]The figures used here are consistent with our discussion in Chapter 6.

The most striking thing about this chart is how much the implied lump sum you would have accumulated both from stocks and other assets has varied over the course of the twentieth century. On the positive side, there was not a single year in which 30-year investors did not get back what they invested, though it was a pretty close shave at times. There were also relatively few years when stocks did not provide better returns than other assets. But the gap has varied markedly, often over quite short periods. Thus, for most of the 1960s, the regular savers could hope to get back, from stocks, four or even five times what they had invested in the first place.[23] Yet, within only a very few years, the amount accumulated would have been only a little better than the amount initially invested.

The low point for this process was 1974, in which year an unfortunate generation of 30-year investors would have ended up with only 30% more than their initial investment. This is a daunting figure, since such investors would have been saving for the 30 years since 1944, which was, in general, an outstanding period for stocks. As we have already shown, this very poor result arises from two key features of regular saving. First, the average period over which the money is invested is not 30 years but less than half that time; second, the amount available for investment rises as time goes by. The power of compound interest to work wonders over long periods becomes less wonderful when it has relatively little money to work on.

A further point relates to the timing of returns. Clearly, if you save over the course of 30 years, every one of the returns in individual years will have some impact on the amount you accumulate. But, for a 30-year regular saver, the real return in the last year is 30 times more important than the return in the first; the return in the penultimate year is 29 times more important; and so forth. The intuition for this is quite straightforward. Think of the amount that the 30-year saver accumulates as being 30 different lump sums, one for each year. Only one of these, the first, is affected by the return in the first year; but all 30 are hit by the return in the last. As we showed in Chart 7.2, 1974 was a particularly dreadful year for stocks. The real stock price fell by

---

[23]A similar amount would have been earned by 30-year savers who were sensible enough to cash in their stock market investments at the end of 1998.

nearly 40%, after falling by nearly 30% in the previous year. In other words, even for the long-term investor, relatively short-term developments had a drastic effect.

The impact of stock price volatility on living standards is dramatically underlined by the difference between those who retired in 1968 and those who retired in 1974. Even though both groups were very long-term savers, and the period over which both groups saved was substantially the same, the first group would have been 3½ times wealthier than the second.

Not everyone, of course, is sufficiently organized and forward-looking to be a 30-year saver. Charts 8.2 and 8.3 show the comparison of lump sums for 20- and 10-year regular savers, respectively. As might be expected, the relative performance of stocks looks far less impressive. Over both 10- and 20-year periods, there were several years when investors would have ended up with less money than they had invested. The comparison with lump sums earned from alternative assets is also less clear-cut. There are more instances of stocks underperforming competing assets and, reflecting the strong performance of bonds in the 1980s,

CHART 8.2

Lump Sums Earned from Regular Saving: 20-Year Saver

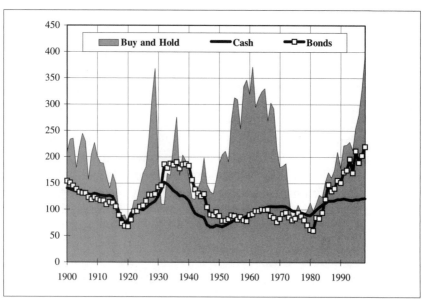

CHART 8.3

Lump Sums Earned from Regular Saving: 10-Year Saver

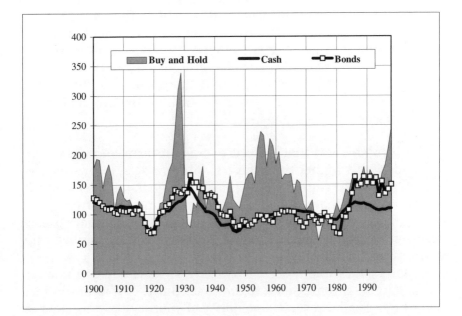

there is little to choose between the lump sums accumulated from bonds and stocks in that period.

AFTER RETIREMENT

We showed earlier that the annuity value of higher returns is fairly limited over the period of investors' normal life span after they retire. But even that improvement assumes that the extra return is readily available, which in practice it isn't. The principle of risk and return means that you cannot get the long-term real return on stocks in the form of a guaranteed income. If you want the higher return, you have to pay the price in terms of a riskier income.

This relationship is hard to capture in a simple chart or table, because it is so very hard to do in the real world. Different strategies offer different combinations of return and risk, but none can escape from the risk entirely.

- One simple strategy might be to ignore risk, presumably in the hope that, over the course of your retirement, the ups and downs of the market will cancel out. At the start of your retirement, you would calculate the amount of income you can withdraw from your investments as an annuity value—based on historic average rates of return and the length of time you expect to live. From then on, you would simply treat that dollar amount as if it were a fixed income, running down your investments as necessary to achieve this income.

Since we know that historic average returns on stocks have been distinctly higher than those on other assets, it must be the case that such a strategy would provide a higher, though not much higher, income than could be earned by buying a risk-free annuity. A glance back at Table 6.3 reminds us that the gains are pretty modest, as long as the safe annuity offers a positive implied rate of return.

This policy might seem attractive since it appears to offer both a stable income and a higher one. But the risks are in fact very high. If all or even the majority of your assets were held in stocks, and you assumed that the income you had calculated was there to be spent, you could soon be in deep trouble. You would have to sell more shares in bad years than in good ones, in order to maintain living standards. In many periods this would simply wipe out all your assets. Assuming that the anticipated return was there to be spent would be too risky to be sensible.

- An alternative approach would be to amend the previous strategy to take account of what was happening to the market. Hence if the market rose or fell, you would recalculate the income you could afford to maintain.

Such a strategy might reduce the risk of running out of assets, but at a very significant cost. All being well, your average income would match that in the first strategy, but it would become enormously more variable. If the market fell by 50% (which we have shown is not at all inconceivable given historical experience), so would your income. Imagine having an income that tracked the path of the real stock price shown in Chart 7.2. It would be a pretty bumpy ride.

In addition, such a policy would not entirely eliminate the risk of running down your assets to zero, for a very straightforward reason. Very few of us can plan with any precision to die at any particular point in time. Living longer than you expect, though a pleasant surprise, runs the risk of running down your assets or eating into whatever you were hoping to leave to your children. It is worth noting that there is no comparable dilemma if you buy an annuity. Although you cannot be certain when you will die, an insurance company can effectively treat your life expectancy as if it were known with certainty. Insurance companies have the "Law of Large Numbers" on their side. If you live longer than expected, another customer is pretty much guaranteed to die early, leaving their profits unaffected.

- Another approach might therefore be to maintain your capital intact, and spend only the actual return achieved in any given year.

But while this strategy is perfectly possible if you hold your wealth in an asset that gives you a guaranteed return, like bonds, it is completely impracticable with stocks, for which the return can be—and, as we have seen, frequently is—negative. If you tried it, your standard of living would simply track the real return on stocks. In down years you would not only have nothing to live on; you would have less than nothing.

- The only even remotely feasible policy, therefore, would be some hybrid of the first three, in which you held back more assets than you would strictly wish to, for precautionary purposes, eating into these assets in bad years, and building them up again in good years.

Although such an approach might avoid the particular pitfalls of the other three, it is worth pointing out that it also runs the risk of defeating the object of the exercise. The idea of being in stocks is to get a higher average income; but holding on to assets for precautionary reasons inevitably must lower the income you can actually use. Suppose you expect to live for 15 years after retiring, but you hold back assets equivalent to an additional 3 to 4 years' income. At historic average returns, the average income you will end up with will almost precisely match what you would get from a safe annuity.[24] If you held back more money for precautionary reasons, you'd actually be better off with the annuity.

There is no escaping the conclusion that, for retired investors who have all their assets in stocks, there is no satisfactory compromise. Holding stocks on a continuous basis is simply too risky for investors who wish to spend their savings in retirement. Indeed, if a compromise were possible, then insurance companies could sell annuities giving the same returns that have historically been available to investors in stocks. They do not, because they cannot.

It follows that investors in retirement cannot optimize their standard of living if they invest only in stocks. For this reason most people in retirement have had diversified portfolios, containing perhaps bonds and annuities as well as stocks, or they have company pensions, which are annuities. They have a lot less risk, but they cannot expect to get equity-type returns. As we have seen, however, returns (when at historically normal levels) are not in any case that important to the retired. Thus, it is very questionable why the retired should actually bother with stocks at all, if the best they can do is use the buy-and-hold strategy.[25]

Increasingly, however, many retired investors have gone to the other extreme. They have been seduced by the prospect of high returns into taking the inordinate risk of putting most, or even all, of their assets in the stock market. For those who have retired, even more than the regular investor, being aware of the risks involved in holding stocks is crucial. If they fail to recognize

---

[24]If the underlying rate of return for safe annuities is 3.5% in real terms.

[25]For example, suppose you invest only one third of your assets in stocks and the rest in safe annuities that yield a real return of 3.5%. At historic average returns, if you have a life expectancy of 15 years, this would on average raise your income by less than 5%. But in a bad bear market—if, say, stock prices halved—your income would fall by one sixth, or nearly 17%.

these risks, they are likely to find that they suddenly have to cut back sharply on their standards of living.

STOCKS ONLY FOR THE LONG RUN?

We have seen in the last few chapters that there is a strong case for stocks as the dominant instrument of the regular investor. But the closer you get to retirement, the more dangerous it becomes to be fully invested in stocks—unless it is possible to recognize when the market has become overvalued. Otherwise there is no escape from the fundamental principle that high returns reflect high risk.

If it is possible to spot a market that is overvalued, it is less risky to be more fully invested in normal times. But two conditions must be satisfied to make this a sensible policy. First, it must be possible to recognize an overvalued market; second, investors must act on that knowledge by selling stocks. This strategy is risky in the sense that Mr. and Mrs. Giust perceived risk in Chapter 3. There is a risk of losing out on further gains if an overblown market becomes even more overblown. But it is not risky in an absolute sense. Preserving wealth has normally been possible and, with the availability of index-linked bonds, is much easier today than ever.

The power of compound interest is a wonderful thing, but its benefits to the investor in stocks, though significant, can easily be exaggerated. Few, if any, investors can wait long enough to achieve gains as fabulous as might appear possible from looking at long-term total returns.

- The power of compound interest is often overstated because most people save regularly over long periods, rather than starting with a single lump sum which then accumulates.
- At historic rates of return, a 30-year regular investor in stocks might on average expect to end up 1½ times better off, or at best twice as well off, as the regular investor in competing assets. Over shorter periods, the relative benefits are considerably more modest.

- For those who have retired, the gains from higher returns are even more limited.
- Higher returns on stocks in any case must reflect higher risk. Risk is not just a short-term phenomenon. Roughly a third to a half of the past century has been made up of bear markets, when the general tendency in stock prices was downward, or at best flat, in real terms.
- These fluctuations in real stock prices have had significant effects on the living standards of investors. This is true not only for those who have retired but also for those nearing retirement.

Neither group of investors can therefore really afford the risk of being fully invested in stocks unless they can tell when markets have become overvalued. This is the issue to which we turn in Part Three.

THREE

q AND THE VALUE OF WALL STREET

In Part Two we showed that investing in stocks can bring significant gains to the long-term investor, but only at the cost of considerable risks. These risks have not been restricted to the short term. There have been prolonged periods when being out of the market would have saved investors from making major losses. In Part Three, we turn to the central issue of this book, which is whether *q* can enable investors to spot such periods in advance. We conclude that there is strong evidence that it can, on the grounds of both historical experience and, equally important, common sense.

CHAPTER **9**

The Meaning of
Stock Market Value

THE STORY SO FAR

We have shown in Part Two that the significant gains to be derived from long-term stock investing come at the price of considerable risks. Understanding these risks is important for investors, but it is not enough. For, despite the risks, *never* investing in stocks cannot be a good investment strategy either. For those who can take a long-term view, the power of compound interest is too important to be ignored. Similarly, always being invested in stocks is too risky for investors who are approaching retirement or who have already retired. Paradoxically perhaps, only those investors who can recognize when stocks are overvalued can afford to be fully invested in normal times.

Of course, when stocks are extremely overvalued, no one can afford to be fully invested. Such occasions are rare, but the end of the twentieth century was one of them. Poor returns into the new century are virtually inevitable. So far we have not substantiated this assertion, but it would hardly have been worth making if we could not do so. We shall now explain how the stock market can be valued, and how you as an investor can make use of this information. In doing so, we need to deal with a number of separate but crucial issues, which we shall address in several different chapters. The first of these, which we consider here, is the question of what we actually mean by stock market value.

If you are of a practical disposition, you may wonder whether such an examination of principles is really necessary; but we would assert that it is. The concept of value is so crucial to this book that we cannot use the term without first explaining carefully what we mean by it. Having done so, in the rest of Part Three we revert to more practical matters. If you are impatient to investigate these, by all means skip this chapter and come back to it later if you feel the need.

EVERYDAY VALUE

Value as it relates to the stock market is actually very closely related to value in everyday life. We can get some quite useful insights into the notion of value by thinking about it first of all in this way.

The simplest version is the value that we get when we buy a "bargain." If we are very lucky, we know at the moment we buy something that it represents good value. If a store has gone bankrupt and is selling off stock at low prices, and if (quite a big if) we can be certain that the goods in question are not of inferior quality, then we have got something that indeed represents good value. We also know, or think we know, when we are being ripped off—if, for example, we pay $10 for a cup of coffee.

But such simple cases, when we can assess good or bad value at the moment we make the purchase, are actually quite rare. Most of the time, the concept of value is forward-looking and hence uncertain. Thus if you buy a used car, you may hope that you are getting good value, but you can make that assessment only in relation to the car's subsequent performance, not only for you but for future owners. Future owners matter, because you may need to sell the car at some point. Hence you can assess value only in relation to two things: first, the services the car will provide while you own it and, second, the price you expect to sell it for. "Good value" implies that the price you pay is low, in terms of the total returns you are going to get in the future. This includes the services the car provides while you own it and the capital gain or loss you make when you sell it. Since the quality of the service you will get from the car and the price you will receive when you sell it are both uncertain, so is value.

However, you *can* assess value once you have the benefit of hindsight. When you sell the car, you can figure out whether the original price was "good" or "bad" value, by comparing the sale price with the original price, and by taking into account the benefit you derived from the car in the meantime. This is what we call "Hindsight Value."

If you own the car for the rest of its working life, you can still assess Hindsight Value. Indeed it is actually in principle a more exact calculation, since if you had sold the car, then there would still have been uncertainty about whether the price you received from the next owner had been fair value. This uncertainty disappears only on the day the car is scrapped. At this point you could, if you wanted, sit down and calculate Hindsight Value by comparing the price you paid with the services the car gave you over its working life. If you wanted to do a really thorough job, you could compare this with what other car owners paid for similar cars and with the services they received. With all this information, you could in principle calculate Hindsight Value fairly precisely.

Value is therefore something you can never know for sure until you have the benefit of hindsight. If you buy a cheap car, it may turn out to have been good value; but it may just have been cheap. The ambiguity of the term "cheap" points to another key issue relating to value. In everyday speech, it is often said that "you get what you pay for." Economists, who, like all specialists, cannot resist inventing their own jargon, call this the Efficient Market Hypothesis. The language and context may be different, but the key concepts are identical.

What does the Efficient Market Hypothesis, which we examined in relation to stocks in Chapter 3, say about everyday value? If you can buy goods at lower prices in one shop than in another, can you really be certain that the goods are comparable? Very often you cannot, since the low price may reflect the dubious origin of the cheaper goods. But if you can be certain that there is no difference in quality, then the Efficient Market Hypothesis would suggest that, even though you may sometimes really get "good value," this is likely to be a rare event and the extent of the good value will be limited.

The reason lies in what economists call arbitrage. If identical goods are selling at one store at sufficiently lower prices, compared with the other store, then this opens up an opportunity for arbitrage. Someone who was interested in making a quick buck, at little risk, has a clear incentive to buy up the cheap goods, and sell them at a profit. The most obvious candidates here are the owners of the two shops. If neither of them do in fact carry out the arbitrage, then there are two likely possibilities. Either the goods are not in fact identical or the arbitrage is simply not worth the trouble. Only if the latter is the case can you be really sure that you are getting good value. In these circumstances, you and all the other customers who buy up the discounted goods effectively do the arbitrage yourselves.

The concept of arbitrage can also illuminate our other everyday examples.

It can, for example, help explain why you might manage to buy a used car that, with the benefit of hindsight, turns out to have been "good value." If the true value of a used car were obvious, then a car dealer would have a clear incentive to buy it from the owner at the low price, and sell it at a profit. But the price difference may not be sufficiently large to be worth exploiting. More crucially, the price at which the car could be sold in the future may be far from certain. Seeking to profit from arbitrage is therefore a risky activity.

Arbitrage is also relevant to the question of whether a $10 cup of coffee is really bad value. It is certainly expensive, but a night club owner would no doubt argue that you are in a fancy night club and are paying for the music and the décor at the same time. However, if you find it difficult to believe that anyone ever received a fairly priced cup of coffee in a night club, your instincts are probably correct. Someone with a coffee machine and a cart would, no doubt, be very pleased to come into the club and sell you a cup for a dollar. This would effectively be another form of arbitrage. The fact that the owner of the night club is most unlikely to allow this to happen illustrates the important point that, for arbitrage to work properly, there has to be competition. By impeding competition on a permanent basis, the night club owner can get away with prices that may well represent permanently bad value. Fortunately for the consumer, competition cannot normally be suppressed to this extent.[1]

We shall see in due course that the idea that departures from "fair" value can arise only if arbitrage does not take place, or is restricted in some way, is a crucial element in understanding how stock markets work.

A final feature to note about value, which is so fundamental that it is easy to forget, is that it must clearly be a relative concept. The goods in one store are cheap only compared with goods in another store. The cup of coffee in the night club is expensive relative to a "normal" cup of coffee. The used car that miraculously holds up for 10 years is cheap compared with the average car.

When we are comparing like with like, things are relatively straightforward. But can we make sense of any claim such as "coffee in general is expensive," or "used cars in general are cheap"? The answer is, yes, of course we can, but it does make things more complicated. Coffee in general can be expensive relative to common alternatives such as tea or soft drinks. Used cars can in principle offer better value than new cars, allowing for the obvious differences. But evaluating "how much better" is more complicated than if we were comparing like with like.

It's also worth bearing in mind that, even when we are comparing the relative value of what economists call "imperfect substitutes," we cannot ignore the idea that "you get what you pay for." If we assert that used cars offer better value than new cars, would we not expect people to respond to this differential by buying up used cars and thereby eliminating the differential? The process would be just another form of arbitrage, but one with a particularly demanding need for full and accurate information,

---

[1]We should stress, in case we are besieged by indignant night club owners, that, as long as the night club business is sufficiently competitive (which we have every reason to believe it must be), the total experience of going to a night club *should* represent "fair" value. The prices of certain elements, like cups of coffee, may represent bad value, but competition between night club owners should ensure that this only offsets other elements in the package that may actually represent good value. For example, night clubs do not charge directly for the experience of being surrounded by flashing lights or shimmering glass balls.

since we are not comparing like with like. We might therefore
expect this form of arbitrage to be considerably less reliable than
that between similar goods.

What have we gathered from this brief look at the concept of
value in everyday terms? The key conclusions are these:

- Value is normally forward-looking. "Good" value implies
  that you are paying a low price for the benefits you
  expect from your purchase, including any cash you may
  receive from subsequently selling it.
- Since value is normally forward-looking, at the time of
  purchase, value is almost invariably uncertain.
- Value can nonetheless be calculated, with some precision, with the benefit of hindsight.
- Departures from "fair" value are likely to occur only if
  someone does not have sufficient incentive to exploit
  them. In the economist's terminology, the limits of
  arbitrage represent the limits of "market efficiency."
- Value is always a relative concept. It is easier to assess
  and hence easier to exploit via arbitrage, when comparing like with like.

STOCK MARKET VALUE

The key ideas outlined above all have clear parallels when we
deal with stock market value.

We should start, however, by considering what you are buying when you buy stocks. There are two distinct ways of looking
at this. Both are true and must therefore be mutually consistent,
but they can appear to be very different.

The "official" story is that buying stocks in a given company
means that you become a part owner of the company, and hence
of everything it owns. The idea underlying this interpretation is
the "corporate veil," whereby companies, as such, do not exist—
there are simply people who own the firm.

But what, in practice, does it mean to own a firm in this
way? As a shareholder, you have a vote at the annual general
meeting. In principle, this means that if you buy enough shares,
you can actually control what the company does. You can hire or
fire chief executives or set the dividend. There are individuals

who do this, but they are rare and they are highly atypical, both in character and in wealth. For the average investor, the right to vote in the annual general meeting is, most of the time, nothing more than a notional right, which is probably barely ever exploited. Thus typical shareholders do not feel like part owners, even though this is their legal status.

For typical shareholders, therefore, buying stocks is like buying any other financial asset. The only difference is the nature of the financial asset that is bought.

If the right to vote at annual meetings has no practical importance, then when you buy stocks, you simply buy the right to receive dividends and the right to be paid the same price as other investors in the case of liquidation or takeover. You have, of course, no guarantee that you will ever actually receive any dividends. There are plenty of examples of corporations that start up, trade, and close without ever paying out a cent. You do, however, have a very reasonable expectation that the average firm will pay out dividends in the future. The value of stocks depends on this expectation.

Value in the stock market is thus, like everyday value, forward-looking, but more so than is the case for almost anything else you can buy, since, barring liquidation, the benefits that investors derive from corporate stocks are effectively expected to last forever.

DIVIDENDS VERSUS CAPITAL APPRECIATION

The dividends you receive on a stock are like the services you receive from a car while you own it. The stock's value is similarly dependent on these dividends and on the price at which the stock is sold. The key difference is that in effect stocks last forever, whereas cars last only a decade or so. While those who own a car for a decade are mainly interested in the benefits they get from using the car, and are relatively unconcerned with the resale price, the reverse is true for investors in stocks. If you buy stocks, the resale price is often far more important than the income you expect to receive while you own them.

Nonetheless, in the end stocks have value only because of the dividends they will pay. This is actually quite hard to bear in mind at times like the present, when dividends are so low in comparison with prices. The average stock in the Dow Jones Index in 1999 had a dividend yield of well under 2%. This means that investors receive less than $2 per year in dividends for every $100 they invest in stocks. They would receive more than twice as much from a money market fund, so it is obvious that, unless investors are completely irrational, they must be holding stocks mainly for some other reason. The other reason, of course, is the expectation of a capital gain. It is the total return, dividend plus capital gain, that makes an investment worthwhile. Stocks, it might seem, cannot possibly be worthwhile investments just for the dividends.

In a fundamental sense, however, investors *do* own stocks just for the dividends. Each investor plans in due course to sell to another investor, who must in turn have a reason to buy. If everyone is rational, each investor's motivation must be the same. Everyone will hold the stock for the dividend they receive, plus the anticipated capital gain. This process has to go on forever.

But how can everyone involved in this process expect the price to rise indefinitely? The only possible explanation is that, even if dividends are low in relation to the value of the stock, they are expected to grow. In order to see why, let us adopt a standard technique used by mathematicians and assume the contrary. Suppose that dividends did not grow. Then, if prices continued to rise, dividends would gradually become a smaller and smaller percentage of the price of the stock until, in the end, they effectively vanished. At that point, the only reason to hold the stock would be the expectation of capital gain. But in this case, the stock price would be simply pulling itself up by its own bootstraps, a situation that no one could rationally expect to go on indefinitely.[2]

---

[2]This is the relatively cheap version of the proper mathematical proof. In interwar Budapest, there was a cafe where impoverished mathematicians would meet up and exchange ideas. The going rate was a cognac for a proper proof, whereas a counterexample, like this, merited only a cup of coffee. Unless the counterexample is general enough to include all possible alternative possibilities, and generates a clear logical contradiction ("1=0" or "black is white," for example), it can only suggest that what you are asserting is correct; it does not prove it to be so. Hence we can claim only that the above argument represents a true proof of our claim if we are prepared to make the supplementary assumption that rational investors will see the instability of any alternative, and rule it out for that reason.

On the other hand, dividend growth solves this apparent puzzle. The simplest case is when both the share price and dividends grow at the same percentage rate. In this case, the dividend yield would remain constant. As long as everyone involved in the process believes that this growth will go on indefinitely, then everyone's motivation is the same and the process is sustainable. Each person in the chain of owners of the stock pays more than the last, but since dividends will have grown in line with prices, the rise in dividends will be just enough to make the new owner as happy to buy the stock as was the person before.[3]

WHAT IS THE BENCHMARK FOR STOCK MARKET VALUE?

We have already observed that value in the stock market is forward-looking, to a much greater extent than in most everyday examples. It is also clear that, if value is uncertain in everyday terms, it is much more uncertain when we look at the stock market.

The basis for assessing value in the stock market is, as we have shown, basically the same as for assessing everyday value, although the process is less certain and thus more difficult. We shall now show how, in spite of these difficulties, the stock market may be valued.

Value is always relative: but relative to what? We need to distinguish very carefully between the value of one share, compared with other shares, and the value of the stock market as a whole. Valuing individuals stocks and valuing the stock market overall pose very different problems, and this simple fact is the cause of much confusion.

Valuing individual stocks is by no means easy, but compared with the problem of valuing the market as a whole, it is relatively straightforward. At least with the benefit of hindsight, we can easily establish whether one stock was a better or worse value than another, simply by looking at whether the total return on the one was higher than that on the other.

---

[3]Whether the assumed perpetual growth rate of dividends is plausible at present is another question, discussion of which we shall postpone until later chapters.

For the market as a whole, we cannot do this, so we need an alternative benchmark.

AGGREGATE STOCK MARKET VALUE

We have seen that we can draw quite close analogies between measuring stock market value and measuring value in a more everyday way. Since shares effectively last forever, stock market value is about as forward-looking as anything can be. Because the fundamental basis for stock market value is the highly uncertain level of future dividends, stock market value must be uncertain too.

But we have so far skated around perhaps the most fundamental issue. We noted earlier that value must be a relative concept. We need a benchmark by which we can assess value. Here it is worth emphasizing the distinction between the value of an individual share and the value of the stock market as a whole.

If we want to assess the value of an individual share, we do so in relation to other shares. But, as noted earlier, when we look at the stock market as a whole, we cannot do this. We have already looked at two alternative benchmarks. One of these is alternative investments and the other is the history of the stock market itself. Both have their attractions, which we shall consider. But because alternative investments are both very different in nature to stocks and are not clearly constant in terms of their properties, we shall focus more on the latter.

In Chapter 11, we shall look at value in this way, exploiting the fact that, while value is always uncertain at the time you make a purchase, it becomes much less uncertain once you have the benefits of hindsight. Then, in Chapter 12, we shall start to look at q, and show that it provides an alternative benchmark against which to compare value, but one that turns out to be very closely related to Hindsight Value.

Before we look at this issue, however, we pause in Chapter 10 to address an important issue, which is whether it is more important to pick good stocks, or whether it is being in or out of the market as a whole that matters.

10

Stock Picking or Aggregate Value?

"PICKING WINNERS"

If you looked at a random selection of books on investing, it would be easy to conclude that by far the most important part of the problem is deciding how to pick the individual stocks that you hold in your portfolio. In fact, nothing could be more misleading.

The message attracts because it is so easy, after the event, to show examples of stock picking that would have yielded not just good returns, but spectacularly good returns. The argument usually starts with this sort of claim: "If you had bought ten Microsoft shares when Bill Gates started out, you would now be a multizillionaire." The writer then goes on to explain how you can pick the Microsofts of the future. In terms of practical investment advice this is about as useful as saying, "If you had bought the winning ticket in the state lottery," and then explaining how to pick the winning numbers in the future.

The problem with arguments based on the principle of "picking winners" is that they imply that investors picking stocks can be like the children of Lake Wobegon, who are all, it is well known, smarter than average. "Picking winners" implies picking out shares that outperform the average share. But, by the law of averages, for every winner, there must be a loser: There must be shares that underperform the average. By definition, however, the average investor must end up holding the average share, or the average portfolio of shares.

Saying this does not, of course, refute the possibility that stock picking can yield above-average returns, if you have above-average luck or possibly skill as a stock picker. There are individual investors who have regularly done better than the average and it may be due to skill. In the end, though, it does not matter whether skill in stock picking is possible. The Lake Wobegon principle must imply that it is simply impossible for the *average* investor to benefit from stock picking.

HOW MUCH DIFFERENCE DOES STOCK PICKING REALLY MAKE?

The average stock and the average portfolio, will, by definition, yield the average return for the market as a whole. Investors therefore need to weigh the relative importance of worrying about which individual stocks to pick or being concerned about the value that is offered by the market as a whole. The evidence on this score is both clear, and, for most investors, unfamiliar. Investors should pay far more attention to the market as a whole than they do to stock picking.

There are three well-documented reasons. The first is that getting good or bad returns from a reasonably well-diversified portfolio of stocks is far more dependent on the performance of the average than it is on the variation of such a portfolio from the average. The second is that there is quite a lot of evidence that beating the average by stock picking depends on luck rather than skill.[4] The third reason, which is the central message of this book, is that even though successful stock picking is very hard, it *is* possible to tell when the stock market as a whole is over- or un-

---

[4]If you took a random sample of investors who all picked stocks by sticking pins into the relevant pages of the *Wall Street Journal*, you would find that some performed better than others. It is very difficult, or even impossible, to say whether individual successful investors have reached this position by luck or skill. If skill is important, however, you would expect that there would be more people who do consistently better than average than there would be in a random sample. Tests, however, have persistently shown that this is not so, and the rational conclusion that skill in stock picking is at best very rare has resulted in the growth of index funds. Burton Malkiel's recently revised classic *A Random Walk Down Wall Street* (New York, W.W. Norton, 1996) provides plenty of evidence on this score.

derpriced. The implication of this is that the crucial thing is not which stocks you pick, but whether you should hold stocks at all.

We can demonstrate this quite easily with a sequence of charts. Chart 10.1 shows returns on ten stocks of large U.S. corporations, chosen pretty much at random, apart from the aim of providing a reasonable cross section of the market.[5] For ease of comparison, the chart shows the value of a notional initial $1 invested in each stock, and assumes that all dividends paid out on any given stock are reinvested in the stock itself. The assumption makes it easier to compare returns on stocks in corporations with different dividend policies. As in all our charts, we show returns in real terms, after adjusting for inflation.

At first glance, the diversity of the experience of the ten stocks is striking. A dollar invested in the highest-performing stock in

CHART 10.1

Real Returns on 10 Stocks, 1973–1998

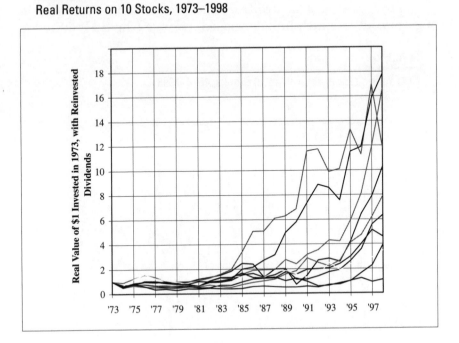

---

[5]For the record, the ten stocks were American Express, Chase Manhattan, Du Pont, Johnson and Johnson, Kellogg, General Electric, General Motors, Eastman Kodak, IBM, and PepsiCo.

1973 would, including returns on reinvested dividends, have increased nearly eighteenfold in real terms by the end of 1998, whereas the real value of a dollar invested in the worst performer would barely have risen at all. But this is, of course, what we would expect. As we have already noted, it is the sheer diversity of experience that explains the attraction of trying to "pick winners."

However, if we look at year-on-year returns, shown in Chart 10.2, we can see that, despite the divergent tendencies in the individual prices over long horizons, there is a pretty strong common tendency in the short run. Many of the stocks move by similar amounts in any given year.

What happens when we allow for the fact that the typical investor holds a portfolio of stocks? Chart 10.3 shows what happens if we assume, completely arbitrarily, that the initial portfolio gave equal initial weighting to the ten stocks. There are two striking results.

First, even such an arbitrary choice of portfolio ends up looking very like a much broader-based average (the S&P 500). We

CHART 10.2

Real Year-on-Year Returns on 10 Stocks, 1974–1998

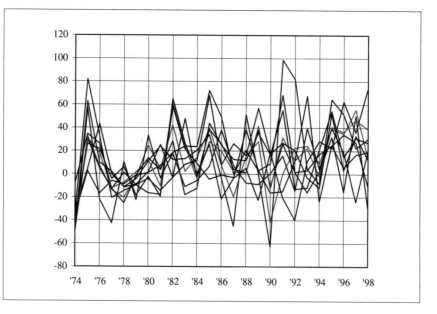

CHART 10.3

Total Real Returns: Average of 10 Stocks Compared to S&P 500

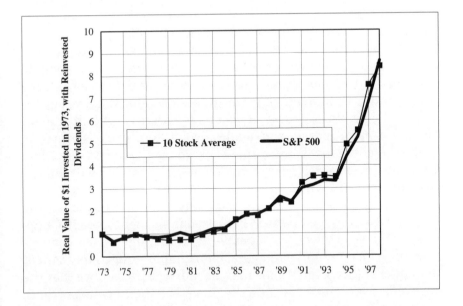

have deliberately not done anything more sophisticated than simple averaging; but you can rest assured that if we had attempted to derive an "efficient portfolio," as set out in almost any introductory text on investing or finance theory, we could have produced a closer match to the index, even using only ten stocks, than we have here.

Second, although this averaging significantly reduces the variability of returns, compared with that on the individual stocks, it does not eliminate return variability. What is left over, once you have found a portfolio that looks pretty much like the broad-based index, is generally called "nondiversifiable risk," which is the risk associated with the stock market as a whole. As Part Two has shown, there has historically been plenty of this kind of risk.

STOCK PICKING VERSUS THE MARKET DECISION

Two different types of decision are involved when investing in stocks: first, deciding whether to be in or out of stocks and second, if you are in stocks, deciding which ones to pick. The charts show that even for the smartest or luckiest of investors the first of these, the market decision, is extremely important. We have also seen that it tends to get neglected. But for the average investor, of course, *only* the market decision is important.

At this stage, you may wish to interject a rather fundamental question. Do not our arguments about averages also apply to the market decision? Can choosing whether or not to be in stocks give a better than average performance even for the average investor? Logically, of course, if we include all investors, it cannot, though it might possibly give a less volatile return.[6] If everyone took note of what we say in this book and got out of stocks when they were overvalued, prices would not get out of line with fundamentals to begin with.

In this instance, however, the individual investor is not the same as the average investor. For reasons we mentioned in Chapter 3, it may well be that people who manage other people's money—pension fund managers, for example—effectively cannot get out of stocks, even if they may, as individuals, believe that the market is overvalued and, as individuals, sell their holdings.[7] Since financial institutions dominate the market, this limits the degree to which they can adjust to an overvalued market. It therefore gives the individual investor an opportunity to get out at the expense of fund managers.

When it comes to stock picking, however, the individual investor has no such advantage, and some disadvantages. Fund managers who are paid by results have a clear incentive to seek out information on corporations, and will be rewarded well if they pick winners. Classic arguments in favor of the division of labor would suggest that, if there is anything to be had from stock picking, it might as well be left to the specialists. That is, of course, a very big if. If you distrust the specialists even in this area (and there is quite a lot of evidence that you should), when you decide

---

[6] We are careful to say "might" rather than "would," because a less volatile stock market might simply lead to higher leverage, which would simply restore the original volatility. If this did not occur, then the return from the stock market should actually fall to reflect the lower volatility.

[7] We believe that it is currently commonplace for professional investors to be fully invested for their clients, but liquid in their own portfolios.

to hold stocks, it may well make just as much sense to put your money into tracker funds, which simply mimic the performance of a broadly based market index. Or pick stocks out of a hat.

As we have seen, however, the decision on whether to be in stocks at all is far more crucial. To this we now turn.

11

What Hindsight Tells Us About Stock Market Value

THE INSIGHTS FROM HINDSIGHT

Value, as we noted in Chapter 9 , must always be uncertain. This is particularly true of stock market value. However, as this chapter will explain, we can considerably reduce or even eliminate such uncertainty once we have the benefit of hindsight. We shall of course have to do without this benefit when we look forward in later chapters. But we can look forward at all only through knowledge gained by studying the past, so we need to understand the past as well as we can, and this involves making full use of hindsight.

We focus here on identifying critical times for the stock market in a rather different way from our approach in previous chapters. We look at returns over a wide range of horizons, representing the sorts of horizons in which the typical investor is interested. We show that it is possible, with the benefit of hindsight, to identify, from the point of view of the long-term investor, critical times which were clearly good and bad years to have bought stocks. We shall show that we can learn quite a lot from the characteristics of these critical years.

In the good years, by implication, stocks were undervalued; in the bad years they were overvalued. We should stress that this is not just a matter of opinion, it is a matter of fact. Since we are working with the benefit of hindsight, we can measure with reasonable precision how over- or undervalued the stock market was at these times. We can summarize this information in a useful statistic, which we call "Hindsight Value." We then show, in the following chapter, that q can help identify bad years and good years, without the benefit of hindsight.

DIVERSITY OF RETURNS AND THE BUY-AND-HOLD STRATEGY

The case for the buy-and-hold strategy is that all years are, at least without the benefit of hindsight, equally good years. Buy-and-hold enthusiasts do not seek to deny the possibility that returns in any given year can be negative. They simply hold that it should not matter too much, for the long-term investor, if stocks give negative returns in one year. Provided that investors are patient, poor years will be offset by higher returns in later years.

To demonstrate the weakness of the buy-and-hold strategy, we show that there are long periods when this simply does not happen. Since investors do not hold stocks forever, the buy-and-hold strategy can have very unpleasant results indeed if stocks can be bad investments for periods of ten years or more.

To examine the first of these two crucial issues, we look at stock returns in the twentieth century from a rather different perspective, in contrast to the straight historical approach we have taken so far. In the normal way of things, a good rule of thumb is that, if you want to convey information in a chart, you do it best with two, maybe three lines—perhaps a maximum of four. We have generally tried to stick to this rule in this book, but just occasionally there are justifiable exceptions. We hope that you will find Chart 11.1, which contains 97 different lines, is one of them.

Each of the 97 lines in this chart provides a summary of whether each of the 97 years from 1900 to 1996 was a good or bad year to have bought stocks. Each line shows the total real return you would have earned on an investment in stocks in that year, depending on how long you held on to that investment. Thus the first point in each line is the return in the first year, the second is the average return over the first two years, and so on. We extend this out to an investment horizon of 50 years. All figures are shown as average returns, to make them comparable to each other.

The chart shows a highly distinctive pattern of returns over different horizons. Although there is tremendous variation in short-term returns, the degree of difference between different years diminishes steadily as the horizon increases. This is, of course, the basis for the buy-and-hold strategy. Even if you bought stocks in a year with a very bad one-year return, future years are likely to have included some good years. Once you average out by calculating returns over more than one year, the differences between good and bad years become less significant. As the horizon over which you calculate the return gets longer, different years look more and more similar, until, by the time you look at the 50-year horizon, returns are concentrated into a solid mass.[8]

CHART 11.1

A Century of Stock Returns, by Investment Horizon

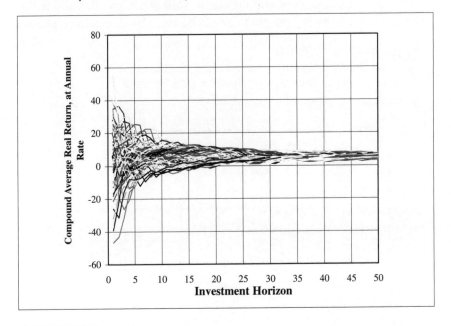

---

[8]This is partly of course because they actually are very similar. For example, the 50-year returns from 1900 and 1901 both contain the return from 1901 to 1950—the two differ only to the extent that the return in 1901 differed from the return in 1951. The fact that the returns over long horizons overlap, and hence use almost the same data, means that care must be taken when drawing conclusions from them. Thus, for example, the chart cannot show two entirely independent 50-year returns. We discuss this issue further in Chapter 17.

The differences between different years do not, however, disappear, particularly over the time periods in which most investors are interested. Fifty years is, of course, far too long for mortal investors (who wish to benefit from their savings) to be wholly invested in stocks. We showed in Part Two that even if regular savers invest over a 30- to 40-year period, the average period over which they hold stocks is normally less than half as long. On the other hand, most regular savers should not be overly worried about very short-run returns. For this reason, it is worth zooming in on the chart, focusing on horizons of more immediate interest to the long-term investor. In Chart 11.2 we cut off both ends of Chart 11.1, and thereby allow you to see rather more detail, by looking only at returns over a narrower range of horizons, from 5 to 30 years.

On the positive side, Chart 11.2 shows one feature that is often cited in support of the buy-and-hold strategy. Beyond a 20-year horizon, in every single year of the twentieth century, stocks

CHART 11.2

A Century of Stock Returns, Long-Term Investor Horizons

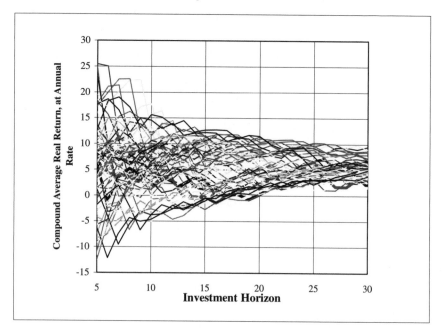

yielded a positive real return. This is a feature of stocks that is well worth bearing in mind. As Jeremy Siegel points out in *Stocks for the Long Run*, over sufficiently long horizons, stocks have effectively been a safe asset, but only in the limited sense that there has been no risk of actually losing money, in real terms. Far from wishing to deny this important fact, we shall show in a later chapter that it is actually a feature that q helps to explain and that, to the best of our knowledge, it is not explained by any other theory of value.

Twenty years, as we noted earlier, is roughly the average horizon of interest to someone who saves regularly over a 40-year period and whose income does not rise over time. It is therefore simply too long a time period for most investors. An average return of zero over 20 years means you simply get back exactly what you have saved. Even those few investors for whom such a long time is relevant would be disappointed, to say the least, by such a performance.

The zero return over this worst 20-year period contrasts sharply with the best, over which investors received an average annual real return of around 11.5%. A dollar invested in stocks over this 20-year period would have increased in value nearly nine times. The difference between retiring on a lump sum of $900,000 as opposed to just $100,000 is too large to support the idea that over the long term it doesn't matter when you choose to sell or buy stocks.

Of course many investors, most notably those who have already retired, cannot wait anywhere near 20 years to cash in their investments. Chart 11.2 shows that over shorter horizons the range of variation is much larger. Even for those who are content to wait for 5 to 10 years, there have been many years in which investment in stocks have produced substantial losses in real terms.

TEN GOOD AND BAD YEARS TO HAVE BOUGHT STOCKS

What Chart 11.2 cannot show, since the lines are still so jumbled together, is whether there were some years that were either consistently bad or consistently good, in the sense that most, or even all, returns over different horizons were below or above average.

In principle and indeed in practice, years that were particularly bad or good over the short term might have turned out to be pretty much average years over longer horizons.[9] But if returns over different horizons for certain years turn out to be consistently bad or good, we may have some reason to label these particular years good and bad years to have bought stocks.

One simple way to see if there were such years is to take each of the 97 years in Chart 11.2 and put them in order of the average return over a range of different horizons. We then pick out the ten worst and ten best years and see if they have any common features.

This method of ordering may seem arbitrary, but is in fact quite easy to explain in terms of the regular saver we considered in previous chapters. Let's assume[10] that all savers save for 40 years, that all savers start saving at the same age, and that there are an equal number of savers of different ages. Then, in any given year, 1 in 40 savers will be just starting out saving, and will therefore be interested in the return over 40 years; another 1 in 40 will have been saving for just one year, and will therefore be interested in the return they will get over the following 39 years; etc., etc., down to a final 1 in 40 savers who have already been saving for 39 years, and are about to cash in their savings—these savers will be interested only in the one-year return. Thus taking an average of the returns over horizons 1 to 40 will give a reasonable measure of the return to a "representative" regular saver.[11]

---

[9]Subject to the obvious constraint that, say, a bad return in the first year followed by average returns in succeeding years would still imply a somewhat subnormal return over longer horizons. We deal with this issue in more depth in Chapter 17.

[10]Whenever an economist asks you to assume something, it is reasonable to be on your guard. We usually do it to simplify our arguments; but not all assumptions are innocuous. (An economist, a priest, and a lawyer are trapped in a lifeboat with only canned food, and no can opener. The priest responds by praying for divine intervention; the lawyer issues a writ for damages to the shipping company; the economist says, "Assume we have a can opener....") The assumptions here, however, do seem reasonably innocuous. We could derive a more "realistic" way of averaging, but it would be needlessly complicated, and would end up telling us pretty much the same thing.

[11]Even this method arguably places too much weight on the longer horizons, since it takes no account of those who are retired. Taking 20 years as the average expectation of life on retirement, this group will have time horizons of 1 to 10 years.

We show the results of this exercise in Charts 11.3 and 11.4.[12] In both charts, as well as the individual years, we also show a line with a benchmark return, which is the long-run average return of around 5¾% after management, custody, and transaction costs have been deducted (implying a return before costs 1 percentage point per annum higher). The charts suggest that, despite obvious differences, there is quite a lot we can learn from the bad and good years to have bought stocks.

We begin by focusing on the bad years. This is not from a natural inclination to focus on bad news, but simply because the whole basis for using value in the stock market is that investors need to know how to respond to the risk of bad rather than good years.

CHART 11.3

Ten Bad Years to Have Bought Stocks

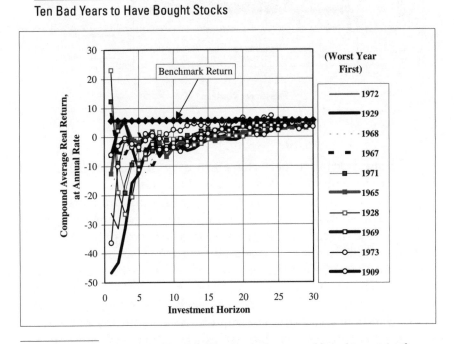

[12]If we were going to compare like with like rigorously, we would need to restrict the charts to show only years for which we could calculate full 40-year returns, ruling out any year since 1957. To avoid this, we calculate average returns as far as we can, but to a minimum horizon of 20 years (hence we exclude all years since 1977). Inevitably, however, we cannot be so confident of hindsight with reference to more recent years.

CHART 11.4

Ten Good Years to Have Bought Stocks

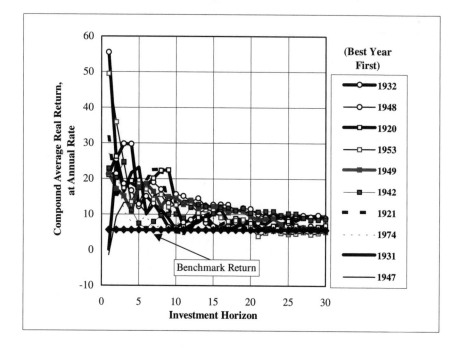

In one crucial respect there are very important differences between the bad years. Not all were bad years in terms of one-year returns. Indeed, a couple of them initially appeared to be good years—notably, 1928. Looking over longer horizons, however, we find much more in the way of a common pattern. For all but one of the 10 years, subsequent returns were negative at 10 years, and well below the benchmark return even at a 20-year horizon. Thus the bad years had effects that clearly took a long time to disappear. Most strikingly, at horizons longer than one year, in only one case did subsequent returns at any horizon exceed the benchmark. The bad years were thus, with only one exception, pretty uniformly bad.

It's also worth looking down the list to note the actual years in question. Although no one would be surprised to see 1929 among the bad years, it is noteworthy that the worst year for stock investors in the twentieth century, on this criterion, was 1972. (We anticipate that 1998 or 1999 may well win this booby prize when the information is available, but you will have to wait for the fifteenth edition of this book to have that fact confirmed with any certainty, given the need for large quantities of hindsight.) All the years but one come from two periods, which are the late 1920s and the late 1960s to early 1970s. We shall note in due course that both periods shared a number of characteristics with the recent past, the most obvious being that there was near universal agreement, at the time, that things were going swimmingly, with the economy in excellent shape.

The single exception to this characterization is, rather obviously, 1973, which most people at the time felt to be rather a bad year. But 1973 is also the single exception we have already noted to the general pattern of the bad years, in terms of returns. The return in the year following, 1974, was an appalling minus 36%, and it takes a long time for the impact of such a fall to be wiped out.[13] Despite this, 10-year returns from 1973 were well into positive terrain, and by the time you look at it on a 15- to 20-year horizon, 1973 looks pretty much average.

In terms of the patterns of returns, the experience following on the good years, shown in Chart 11.4, is initially almost as diverse. The difference is that all first-year returns were positive, or so close to zero as to make no difference. The implication is that all the good years were, unsurprisingly, "troughs." Beyond a one-year horizon, the pattern is more diverse. Although almost all horizon returns lie above the benchmark return, the difference is less striking than for the bad years.

In terms of the historic timing of the good years, there is much less clustering. But they shared one characteristic that mirrors that of the bad years. Good years to have bought stocks were invariably years that seemed at the time to be either pretty bad or more often downright terrible. The best year of all 97 in which to have invested in the stock market was 1932, which is generally regarded as being, for the U.S. economy, the most disastrous of the twentieth century.

---

[13]Bear in mind that a fall of 36% is *not* reversed by a subsequent rise of 36%. In order to undo the effect of a return of –36%, you need a return of +56%.

A SUMMARY INDICATOR OF HINDSIGHT VALUE FOR THE U.S. STOCK MARKET

How can we summarize the range of information in Charts 11.1 to 11.4? Chart 11.5 shows two ways, which are highly complementary: Indeed, visually they look almost identical. Remind yourself, incidentally, why the chart stops in 1977: We can evaluate Hindsight Value only if we have some hindsight to go on! So the chart cannot, of course, tell us anything directly about value in the much more recent past. However, as we shall see in the next chapter, it can tell us something very useful in an indirect way.

The line on the chart is simply the average of the returns on the U.S. stock market on an investment in the year in question, over horizons from 1 to 40 years. This was, of course, the criterion we chose to sort through the first 97 years of the century, in order to find the Ten Best and Worst Years to Buy Stocks. We show it using an inverted scale. Thus, the higher the average horizon return, the lower the number on the chart. If this seems perverse,

CHART 11.5

Hindsight Value

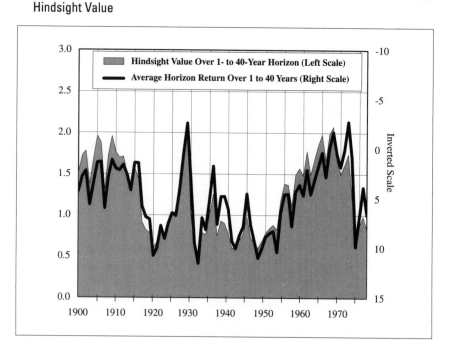

we should remind you of the way we are trying to assess value. The stock market represented good value when subsequent returns turned out on average to be unusually high; it was expensive when they turned out to be unusually low. Since we think of good value as a low price, and bad value as a high price, it makes sense to use an inverted scale.

If you prefer to think of value in terms of prices rather than returns, the series shown as a shaded area, which we call "Hindsight Value," actually gives an indication of the implied extent of the mispricing. A figure of 1.0 shows that the market was "fairly valued," with the benefit of hindsight, while a figure of, say, 1.5 implies that it was 50% overvalued. This approach has the advantage of aiding intuition, but the slight disadvantage of being rather harder to calculate.[14]

Looking at the chart, we can locate our Ten Best and Worst Years to Buy Stocks historically. The bad years are at or near the peaks, and the good years are in the troughs (both as measured by the line showing the average horizon return[15]). The chart helps show why the historical spread of the good years has been wider: There have simply been more troughs than peaks, in historical terms. These were occasions when the market recovered and then fell back to a historic low despite being undervalued.

Hindsight Value shows how misvalued the U.S. stock market was at any given time. In 1929 the market was, with the benefit of hindsight, a little more than twice overvalued, which is roughly equal to our q-based estimate of market overvaluation at

---

[14]The implied calculation for Hindsight Value is somewhat complicated. We assume that a set of representative investors in this century, over the same range of investment horizons, were expecting the benchmark return of 5¾%, after transaction costs based on the realized return over the previous century. Having observed the actual returns on the stock market, these investors would have been prepared to pay for the ability of being able to invest in a given year. By taking an average of the bids that they would rationally make, we produce an indicator of Hindsight Value. This allows us to quantify how overvalued the market was at any point in time.

[15]Enthusiasts may observe that the two series shown, although they track each other very closely, do not agree entirely about the misvaluation in every year. The line showing average horizon returns implies that 1972 was the most overvalued year, whereas the area showing estimated overvaluation by price puts it at 1929. No practical problem is created, since the degree of disagreement is slight.

the end of 1997. By 1998, and into 1999, *q* implied that the market was more overvalued even than at its peak in 1929.

Of course, we can measure the degree of overvaluation in 1929 with the benefit of hindsight, but for more recent years this is clearly impossible. So in the next two chapters we bring *q* back into the picture, and show how well it fits in with Hindsight Value.

12

A Closer Look at q

q AS COMMON SENSE

All prices—whether they are the prices of shares, goods, or services—are basically determined in the same way. Competition drives the prices of goods and services down toward their cost of production.[16] It is the same with corporations. If goods and services can be sold for more than they cost to produce, it will pay to increase production—and the prices of those goods and services will then fall. If corporations can be sold for more than they cost to create, then existing ones will expand and new ones will be created until the price of corporations falls. In the end, in a competitive world, corporations, like goods and services, are worth what they cost to create. This is just what q means.

The principle applies, of course, just as much to companies selling services as to those selling goods. Stockbrokers, however, like to deny this. They are fond of saying that q applies to manufacturing companies but not to service companies, on the grounds that service companies need less capital. As we shall show later, in Chapter 30, the claim that service companies need less capital than manufacturing companies is not supported by the data. The important thing, however, is that it would not matter even if it

---

[16]Treating a competitive return on the capital employed as just another cost.

were true. If services gave higher returns than manufacturing, investors would pour their money into services until profitability was the same. What matters is competition. If profits are above average in either a service industry or a manufacturing industry, then they will fall quickly back to average if the business is a competitive one.

This is another of those instances where stockbroker economics differs from the real thing. The claim that *q* is relevant for manufacturing but not for services implies that the returns on capital are relevant for one but not the other. This is nonsense. Economists have long established that the issue is competition. In a competitive economy, the value of goods, services, and companies will all depend on the cost of production. For companies, the difference between the cost of production and the cost of buying them in the stock market shows how over- or underpriced they are—and this is quite simply measured by *q*.

THE CONFUSION BETWEEN STOCK MARKETS AND COMPANIES

While cynics may think that it is natural for the stock market to reject common sense, there are less perverse reasons for it. Investors tend to concentrate on individual companies rather than on the stock market as a whole, despite the fact that, as we showed in Chapter 10, it is really the stock market as a whole that matters far more. It's a classic case of failing to see the wood for the trees. The same holds for the prices of goods and services. The cost of production determines prices in general, but it is much less relevant to the prices of individual products. This is because the effect of competition is pretty constant in general, but it varies a lot with regard to individual products.

Since companies in general are worth what they cost to create, their value cannot depend on how profitable they are. This principle obviously does not apply to companies individually, so it is necessary to use a different technique in each case. Not only can individual companies benefit or suffer from the cyclical swings in the economy, but at any one time different companies will be making above- or below-average returns for a variety of reasons.[17]

---

[17]Companies with above-average returns will justify a premium over those with below-average returns. This will make no difference to the average value since those with above-average returns must exactly balance those with below-average returns.

Companies in general, however, can suffer only from cyclical problems. They are not all going bankrupt.

Stockbrokers of course want to have it both ways, and the result can be most amusing. At the close of the twentieth century, Japanese profits were low and U.S. profits were high. It was regularly claimed, in both countries by the same brokerage firms, that in each case this justified high P/E multiples.

Profits matter only when valuing one company, not when valuing all of them. Companies individually are small relative to the economy, but companies in the aggregate produce the major part of all economic output. A single company's output can grow much faster or slower than the economy as a whole, but companies in general must grow at the same speed as the economy. One company's profits can also grow much faster than the average, but those of companies in general obviously can't.

WHY q IS NEW

Since q is rooted in common sense, it might seem surprising that it has only recently become widely used and discussed. There are two main reasons for this.

The first is that, until recently, economists have been rather shy of studying stock markets. The key theories on which our understanding of markets is based, such as the Efficient Market Hypothesis and the Capital Asset Pricing Model, have all been developed over the past 30 or 40 years. James Tobin published his paper on q in 1969.[18] It is therefore quite an elderly piece in terms of most work on financial markets. It is also worth noting that in his paper Tobin generously referred to early nineteenth century economists who had pointed out the commonsense attributes of q. None of this detracts from the value and originality of Tobin's work, since he was the person who first showed q's great significance.

The second point of importance is that when Tobin first wrote about q, no data were available to test his theory. This is not because the data are difficult to produce, but because no one had thought that it was important to do so. Official data have now

---

[18]In his paper Tobin defines q slightly differently from the way used in this book. This does not affect the conclusions in any way. The differences are explained in the Virtual Appendix.

been compiled for the USA since 1945 and we, and other economists, have constructed reasonable data going back to the beginning of the century.

It was only when long-term data became available that it was possible to test Tobin's theory. To test whether *q* reverts to its mean, you need several cycles of peaks and troughs. Since the stock market has become seriously overvalued on only five occasions since 1900, many years of data were needed before *q* could be seriously tested. We seem to have been the first people to suggest that there were now enough years' worth of data to test Tobin's theory.[19] Under testing, the theory proved gratifying robust. The outcome led to a research paper examining the results with full academic rigor[20] and to this book.

COMMON SENSE IN ACTION

Because *q* is the commonsense approach to stock market value, we should be able to see it working in practice. Value is not going to have any real meaning, and *q* is not going to be of any use, unless it tells us something about the future. Since investors will normally and correctly want to invest in the stock market, the most useful thing *q* can do is tell them when they should be careful. This is just what *q* can do for you.

We shall show the importance of *q* as an indicator of value in two ways. First we shall show just how well it would have done to make you money in the past. This is *q*'s "Hindsight Value." Had a few investors in the past understood *q* and used it, they would have been outstandingly successful. But this might have been a statistical fluke. In order to show that it is not one of those pieces of data mining, of which we so strongly disapprove, we will also take a severely statistical approach and show that *q* is a "statistically significant" factor in predicting future stock prices and returns, when all reliable data are used.

In the next two chapters we focus on *q*'s Hindsight Value and show how it could have been used to help the *q*-investor save a lot of money, and even more stress, by avoiding the historic pitfalls that have made past investing an occasional nightmare.

---

[19]In a report to Smithers & Co. clients in 1997.
[20]See our reference to the paper by Robertson and Wright in footnote 20 in Chapter 4.

13

What *q* Could Have Told Investors About Value in the Past

q AND HINDSIGHT VALUE

We saw in Chapter 11 that hindsight can tell us not only the historically good or bad times to have bought stocks, but also how misvalued the stock market was on these occasions. The catch, of course, is that however valuable hindsight may be in understanding the past, we need a measure of value that looks forward rather than backward.

Chart 13.1 revisits our measure of Hindsight Value from Chapter 11, and shows it alongside *q*. Bear in mind that the chart has to stop at the end of the 1970s, because we do not have enough subsequent data to tell us about Hindsight Value for subsequent years. The message of Chart 13.1 is pretty clear. Historically at least, *q* would have been a wonderful indicator of market value.[21]

When anything looks as good as this, it is sensible to be skeptical. The chart looks a bit too good to be true and in a limited sense it is. If value has any meaning at all, then the market will become more expensive whenever it goes up sharply. This means that other valuation ratios, apart from *q*, may also appear to in-

---

[21]Remember that we can say only that it "would have been" a wonderful indicator of value, rather than that it actually was: The data were not available for investors to use. Had they been, we cannot say what the outcome might have been.

CHART 13.1

q and Hindsight Value

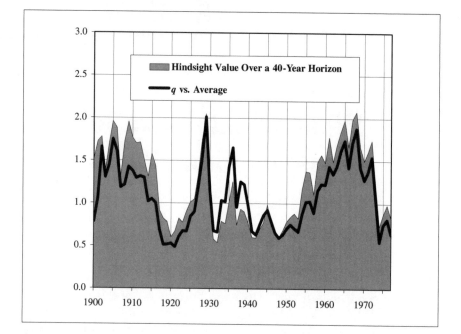

dicate whether the market is getting cheaper or more expensive. All that is required is that the measure of fundamental value (which sits on the bottom of any valuation ratio) be more stable than the stock market.

But the chart shows that *q* does more than this. Stability is not a sufficient quality, though it is a necessary one. We also need the property we alluded to in Chapter 2: mean reversion. We likened this property to a piece of elastic that prevents the market from getting too far away from its fundamental value. Over the longer term there would be nothing to stop a stable but bogus valuation criterion from drifting gradually apart from the market. This does not happen with *q*.[22]

These two features taken together—stability of the fundamental, and mean reversion—are essential in making *q* such a good indicator of Hindsight Value.

---

[22]By construction, Hindsight Value has both of these properties, but is not of course a usable measure of value except with reference to the past.

ALTERNATIVE INDICATORS AND HINDSIGHT VALUE

The excellence of *q*, judged by Hindsight Value, is best shown by comparing it with two alternative valuation criteria. The most obvious is the P/E multiple, which is based on the assumption that earnings, which are profits measured after interest and taxes, can be used as an indicator of fundamental value. Chart 13.2 shows how much less effective the P/E multiple has been as an indicator of hindsight value.

A comparison of the two charts reveals some similarities, as we would expect, given our comparison between *q* and the P/E in Chapter 4. On many occasions, the P/E multiple and hindsight value move together, and, as we have seen, the P/E does appear to be mean-reverting. At a number of crucial points in the twentieth century, however, the P/E failed the test of stability of the fundamental, because the bottom part of the ratio—E, for earnings—has been too volatile.

CHART 13.2

The P/E Multiple and Hindsight Value

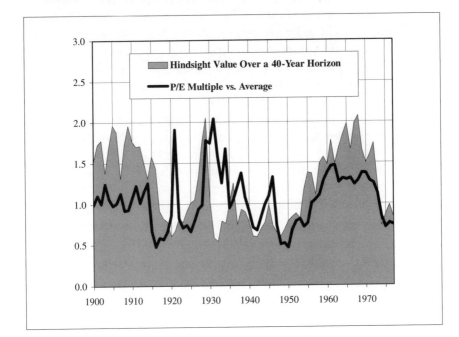

Just to pick out the extreme examples, as we noted in Chapter 4, the P/E multiple indicated that the market was very expensive in 1932, when hindsight tells us quite the opposite: The market was clearly, and unambiguously, extremely cheap. Looking back at Chart 13.1, you will see that q would have told us so. Similarly, q was a much better guide to overvaluation before World War I and in the late 1960s and early 1970s. The explanation in all these cases is what was happening to profits. In 1932, in the depths of the Great Depression, profits were extremely low for cyclical reasons; in the 1960s and before World War I, they were extremely buoyant. In all these cases, purely cyclical movements caused the P/E multiple to give extremely misleading signals on value. We shall come back to this issue in more detail in Chapters 22 and 23.

An alternative comparison shows that mere stability is not enough either. Chart 13.3 does the equivalent comparison for dividends, which are much smoother than earnings.

A brief word of explanation on the measure shown in the chart, which we call "dividend value." Normally the measure of dividends used to value the market is the dividend yield, or dividends per share, divided by the price. A purely presentational difficulty with this measure is that, in contrast to q and the P/E multiple, the dividend yield shows the market as cheap when the yield is high, and expensive when the yield is low. Our measure of "dividend value" deals with this presentational problem by turning the dividend yield upside down, and comparing the resulting value with its historic average.

Chart 13.3 shows that dividends meet the condition of stability much better than earnings. For this reason, dividend value is a good indicator of what is happening to value in the short term. Chart 13.3, however, shows that it has problems over the longer term. It is far from clear that using dividends results in a valuation criterion that has the property of mean reversion: The elastic that links prices to dividends is either nonexistent or so weak as to be useless.

Thus dividend value appears to drift upward over the course of the century (the counterpart of a downward drift in the dividend yield). The resulting measure of value implies that the market pretty much always looked "cheap" in the first half of the

CHART 13.3

"Dividend Value" and Hindsight Value

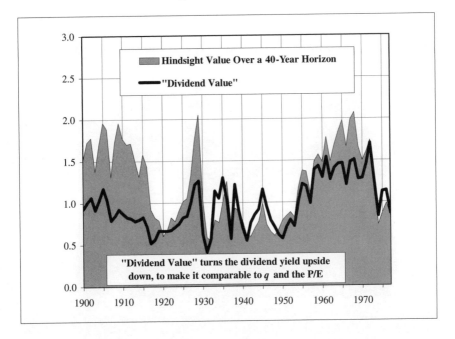

century (even at the peak in August 1929), and nearly always looked "expensive" in the second half. We shall also look at this issue in more detail later, in Chapter 21.

Both of these comparisons show us that in the past *q* did significantly better than the two most commonly used alternative indicators of value at spotting when the market was over- or undervalued. In the next chapter we ask whether, if data on *q* had been available, the *q*-investor would have been able to exploit this information.

14

q as an Investor Tool

TRADING RULES FOR THE *q*-INVESTOR

We saw in the last chapter that *q* has, in the past, given excellent signals on market value. In this chapter we shall show that investors who used *q* would have been highly successful. This is hardly surprising in view of the clear evidence shown in Chart 13.3.

Before considering just how successful, it is sensible to recall that no twentieth-century investor could actually have used *q* as an investment guide, since the data simply weren't available. Had they been, then the history of stock prices might have been rather different.

Using *q* as an investment tool is basically simple. Because it shows when stocks are cheap and when they are expensive, *q* enables investors to sell high and buy low. There are a number of different ways to express this in terms of trading rules, but they are all based on this simple principle. It is, of course, exactly the same principle that underlies the general process of arbitrage that we introduced in Chapter 9.

When investors are not in the stock market, they have to hold something else. For the sake of simplicity, in the examples we give below, we shall assume that there are only two assets that the investor could have held: cash on deposit, represented by 3-month Treasury bills, or a representative portfolio of stocks.[23]

We assume that the only choice the investor could have made was whether to be in or out of the market. Professional investors, of course, have additional weapons that they can use. They can gear up and sell short, but these involve additional risks and are not part of the armory of the ordinary investor.

Not being fully invested all the time offers the investor an added advantage: The additional returns are achieved at less risk than would be involved by following the buy-and-hold strategy, since the periods of being out of the stock market always imply lower risk.[24] Lowered risk should improve investors' chances of getting a good night's sleep, so, as we have already noted, q could be said to provide health benefits as well as wealth benefits.

q-BASED TRADING RULE 1: THE AVERAGE RULE

The simplest rule is to hold stocks when q is below average and hold cash when it's above. We shall see that this would by no means have been the best way to use q in the past century, but the results show that even such a simple rule would have been a distinct improvement on being fully invested all the time.

Chart 14.1 illustrates how this rule would have performed. In this chart, and in the next two, the returns from the trading rule, and from the buy-and-hold strategy, are expressed relative to the returns from holding cash on deposit. Thus when either strategy is doing better than holding cash, the relevant line will be rising; when it is doing worse, the line will be falling. In the case of the buy-and-hold strategy this occurs straightforwardly, when stock market returns are better or worse than returns on cash. In the case of the trading rule, things are slightly more complicated. When the rule implies staying in stocks, movements in the line will track movements for buy and hold. However, when the rule implies getting out of stocks, we assume a switch into

---

[23]We use the index constructed by Jeremy Siegel in *Stocks for the Long Run*.
[24]This has the added advantage that investors who had some unexpected need for
   money would have had much less risk of having to sell stocks at depressed prices.
   We deal with this issue in greater depth in Chapter 18, when we note that such
   unexpected needs tend often to occur when stock prices are weak.

CHART 14.1

Trading Rule No. 1: When *q* Goes Above Average, Switch to Cash

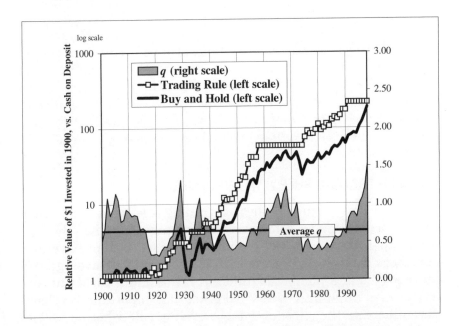

holding cash. At such times, the return to the rule will obviously equal that on cash, and so the line is horizontal.

It is these periods, when the strategy implies being out of the market, that must make or break such a trading strategy. If the strategy is out of the market mainly when the stock market is weak, and hence falling relative to bills, the strategy will outperform buy and hold; if, however, it implies holding cash too often in rising markets, it will underperform.

Chart 14.1 shows that the positive features of even such a simple trading rule clearly offset the negative ones. Over the period as a whole the returns from the trading rule are marginally (0.2% per annum on average) better than from buy and hold.[25] But what is more significant is that *q*-investors would have earned

---

[25]Though this comparison is arguably biased against the rule, since we are measuring the gains to buy and hold at what must be very close to a market peak. As the chart shows, at almost all points before 1998, the trading rule offered better returns.

these returns with far less risk. They would thus have been far less liable to have lost their nerve and sold out at the wrong time.

Simply getting out of stocks when they are expensive is however unlikely to be the best strategy, because the average return on stocks is higher than the average return on cash. Hence even below-average returns on stocks may still be better than the return on cash. The rule therefore does not efficiently exploit one of the great virtues of stocks, which is their high long-term return relative to cash. Investors using this rule would have been holding stocks less than half of the time. This is excellent for risk reduction but it is less than optimal for increasing returns.

q-BASED TRADING RULE 2: THE 50% RULE

One simple way to modify the first trading rule is not to sell when shares are expensive, compared with average, but when they are very expensive. Instead of getting out when q is above average, investors could wait until it is 33% or 50% above average. We have looked at a number of different ratios and it turns out that the precise value of the threshold is not that important. We therefore illustrate the effect of using a trading rule where investors hold stocks until they get 50% overpriced.

Chart 14.2 shows the results of using q in the 50% Rule. Here the gains are significant in terms of both return improvement and risk reduction The rule would have earned an average return 1.5% per annum better than buy and hold. Even over ten years this improves the value of an investment by 20%. Once again, the benefit is achieved with the added advantage of less risk to investors. On this basis q-investors would hold cash only 17% of the time; but the period represents very bad times to be invested in stocks.

The performance of the 50% Rule is clearly much better than the Average Rule, but it is still pretty easy to see how investors might do better.

- The rule implies getting back into stocks whenever q falls below the threshold value. This appears to go against common sense, since it means investing in stocks again when they are still overvalued.

CHART 14.2

Trading Rule No. 2: When *q* Goes 50% Above Average, Switch to Cash

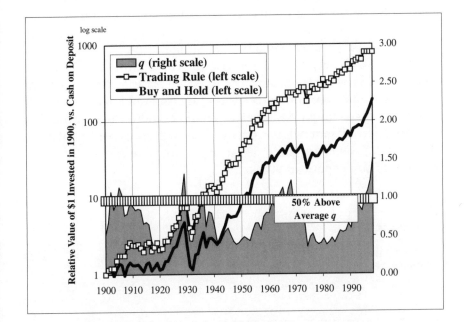

- The rule often implies buying into a falling market, since, once *q* starts to fall, it has (historically, at least) tended to carry on falling.

Both these characteristics are reflected in the rather high proportion of time spent in stocks. The rule implies being out of the market only 17% of the time. Yet, as we saw in Part Two, stocks underperformed other assets in about one third of the years in the twentieth century. The final rule we look at deals with these problems.

q-BASED TRADING RULE 3: THE DOUBLE THRESHOLD RULE

A relatively simple way to deal with the problems associated with the two previous rules, while drawing on the insights from both, is to base a rule on two thresholds, rather than just one. The idea is simple: Wait until *q* reaches a level that indicates a reasonably significant degree of overvaluation, then sell and, crucially, stay out until the market appears to be fairly valued.[26] In principle the high threshold need not equal that in the previous rule, nor need the low threshold equal the average, but for simplicity we use the same figures.

Chart 14.3 shows the outcome of using the Double Threshold Rule. It clearly dominates the previous two. It produces a markedly higher return than the Average Rule, with an average return 1.7% per annum better than buy and hold over the whole period. It also clearly does better than the 50% Rule, through a combination of somewhat improved return and significantly reduced risk. The latter effect is largely a function of the lower proportion of time spent in stocks.

CHART 14.3

Trading Rule No. 3: When *q* Goes 50% Above Average, Hold Cash Until It Goes Below Average

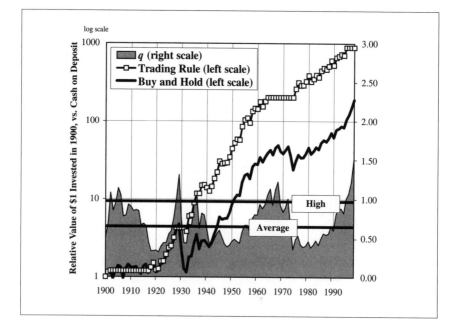

---

[26]These types of rules can also be shown on theoretical grounds to be an optimal response both to uncertainty and transactions costs. Economists call them *Ss* rules.

Under the Double Threshold Rule, investors are out of the market for roughly the same amount of time as stocks have underperformed other assets.[27] This point should not be overemphasized, however, since there were many years when the rule was in or out of stocks at the wrong time. It is this characteristic, as we shall see shortly, that is the principal drawback of the Double Threshold Rule. The need to hold your nerve would be very demanding if you applied this rule rigidly.

THE TEN BEST AND WORST YEARS TO BUY STOCKS REVISITED: WOULD OUR RULES HAVE SPOTTED THEM?

In Chapter 11 we picked out ten years that, on the basis of subsequent returns, were unambiguously bad years to have bought stocks, and ten more years that, on the same basis, were unambiguously good. An obvious question to ask about the three *q*-based trading rules is whether they would have spotted these years at the time.

Given the close correspondence between *q* and hindsight value, which we showed in the last chapter, it should not be surprising to find that they do. In the Virtual Appendix we show that all rules score 10/10 for the good years, as do two out of the three rules for the bad years. Only the 50% Rule fails to get a perfect score for the bad years as well as the good years. This accords with the rule's principal defect, which is that it leaves investors holding stocks for too much of the time.

WHAT'S *q* WORTH? QUANTIFYING THE GAINS FROM *q*-BASED TRADING RULES

One way we could in principle quantify the gains from using *q* would be to calculate the value of a lump sum invested at the start of the century, and calculate the cumulative benefits from each of the rules, compared with buy and hold. This, however, falls afoul of the criticisms we applied to the Patient Native American model of investing. There are simply no investors who actu-

---

[27]Indeed, it almost precisely matches the proportion of time spent out of stocks by someone who could actually see into the future.

ally behave like this. Instead, we prefer to quantify the benefits of the *q*-based strategies to the typical regular saver as set out in Part Two.

We again assume that regular savers add a constant proportion of their growing incomes to their cumulated savings every year. To exploit the trading rules, savers would then need to decide once a year whether to put all the accumulated surplus from the past stocks or hold it as cash on deposit.

Chart 14.4 shows that all three rules would have provided investors with higher average lump sums, at almost all times, than the buy-and-hold strategy. In the case of the Double Threshold Rule, the averages are, over some periods, very significantly higher. There are, however, a few periods when even the trading rules cannot avoid significant losses in real terms. A prime example is the 1970s, when even holding cash on deposit did not protect the real value of investors' wealth. There were several years when interest rates paid on cash on deposit did not keep pace with inflation.

CHART 14.4

Lump Sums Earned by 30-Year Regular Saver: Buy and Hold Versus *q*-Based Trading Rules

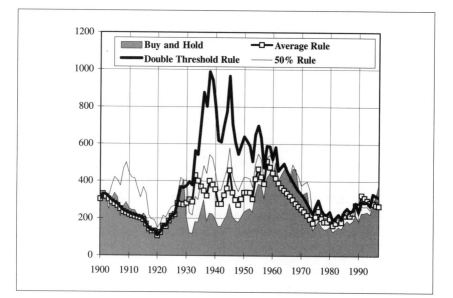

THE VALUE OF HOLDING YOUR NERVE: THE ASYMMETRIC GAINS FROM *q*-BASED TRADING RULES

We would hate to give you the impression that using *q* as a guide to investment would have been straightforward. Apart from all the caveats already mentioned, a *q*-based investment strategy would have required very strong nerves.

There is a simple reason for this. Our trading rules can help investors only in the relatively infrequent periods when returns are seriously negative. Times when rules point to investors holding cash, even though stocks are still rising, can be most uncomfortable times to be a *q*-investor. Any practical rule will usually mean selling out before the market reaches its peak. Hence the time when it is most important to get out of stocks will also be the time when getting out of stocks is likely to be penalized most heavily, at least in terms of the relative kind of risk that so worried Mr. and Mrs. Giust in Chapter 3. These might be termed the periods of the Giusts' Dilemma.

The charts have shown that the periods of being out of stocks bring benefits to *q*-investors overall, but these gains have to be set against the periods when *q*-investors underperform, because the market continues to rise despite being overvalued. Clearly *q*-investors don't actually lose money during these periods. They simply get richer more slowly than those who stay invested. Their reward comes when the market crashes and they are unaffected by these debacles. Nonetheless, it must be recognized that the periods of underperformance are uncomfortable periods to live through.

The penalty gets worse, the more extreme the bubble. Recent years would have penalized a *q*-investor more heavily than at any time in the twentieth century—first because the magnitude of the rise in *q* was almost unprecedented, and hence unpredictable; and second because the rise lasted longer than any previous bubble. To *q*-investors who sold out of stocks in 1996 or 1997, life would have seemed pretty discouraging by the end of 1998. True, they would have been freed from the stress while the market fell in the second and third quarters of that year, but by the end of the year they would have missed out on the even sharper rebound.

Faced with such a turn of events, the *q*-investor might well have been tempted to ignore value and reenter the market. The experience of the past ten or so years would have supported such action, since looking back with this very limited amount of hindsight appears to suggest that investors can ignore value entirely. But the experience based on a longer time horizon, coupled with a good dose of common sense, would have suggested that reentry was thoroughly unwise. Any long-term view tells us that 1998 and 1999 would unquestionably have been extremely good years to sell stocks, and disastrously bad years in which to have bought them.

Armed with the hindsight that informed our analysis of the past, *q* provides us with many reasons for pessimism about the near term. We deal with these in Part Four, when we examine the future of Wall Street. It is perhaps worth stressing at this point, however, that the reasons for both short-term pessimism and long-term optimism about investing in stocks are dependent on the same reasoning.

FOUR

q AND THE FUTURE OF WALL STREET

As we have said from the start, q conveys both good news and bad news about the future of Wall Street. In Part Four we focus first of all on the bad news, simply because this is a more immediate issue, given Wall Street's record level of overvaluation. While we do not make any claims to predict the future with precision, in Chapter 15 we show that the past tells us a lot about the balance of probabilities for the future. It is clear that the odds are currently stacked heavily against investors in stocks.

It is also important to understand why. In Chapter 16 we show how high levels of q have already set in motion economic forces that, in the end, must prove unstoppable.

When we look further forward, however, we need to remind you of the good news. At some point in the not too distant future, stocks will again offer fair value. Experience suggests that the next time this happens, stocks will be deeply unpopular. We show in Chapter 17 that, since q helps explain the past success of the buy-and-hold strategy, it will also provide the q-investor with the confidence to get back into the market when stocks are immensely unpopular. An even more important point is that a proper understanding of q will allow investors to invest more of their wealth in stocks, and with less risk, than would be prudent if their only alternative was the buy-and-hold strategy.

15

The Bad News About Stocks as Investments for the Long Run

WHAT q CAN AND CANNOT TELL YOU ABOUT FUTURE STOCK RETURNS

It should already be clear that the high value of q at the end of the twentieth century points to a very a gloomy outlook. This doesn't mean, however, that we can predict when the stock market will fall. As we will stress throughout this book, it cannot be possible to make reliable predictions about when the market will rise or fall. If it were possible, the market would respond in advance and it could not then rise and fall in the way it does. The fact that market timing must be unpredictable, but that investors nonetheless clamor to know when things will happen, is probably the single main reason why so much nonsense is written about the stock market. It is an old English adage that if you ask a silly question, you will get a silly answer.

What q can do is to tell you what will probably happen. A lot of the most certain things that we know are of this type. An example is playing roulette or craps. The odds are in favor of the house. We know that gamblers will lose if they play long enough, and we know the probability that they will lose. We cannot, however, predict very much about any individual spin of the ball or roll of the dice.

We shall show in this chapter that at the end of 1998, *q* implied roughly a two-thirds chance that the stock market would fall in real terms over the course of 1999. With such a modest balance of probabilities in the short term, the fact that the market rose, rather than fell, during 1999 comes as no great surprise. But as with predictions of who will win at the roulette wheel, the predictions generated by *q* become stronger over time. Thus there was approximately an 85% chance that the market would fall, in real terms, over the next ten years. The result of each spin of the wheel is highly uncertain, but the odds against continuing to beat the house grow rapidly as the number of spins increases.

HOW OVERVALUED?

The nature of economic data means that valuation cannot be a precise science. Thus, although we can say that *q* was very high at the end of the twentieth century, we cannot be sure exactly how high. There are two main kinds of uncertainty in valuation.

The first form of uncertainty, and the easiest to deal with, relates to that crucial property of *q*, to which we have alluded already in Chapters 2 and 13, which is mean reversion—the strength of the elastic that pulls *q* back to its average. The stronger the force of this mean reversion, and the more data we have to measure its force, the more precisely we can gauge the degree of overvaluation. (Imagine watching a ball being bounced up and down on a piece of elastic, but not being able to see either the elastic or the base to which it is attached. The base would be like the "fundamental." The longer you watched the ball, and the more regular its motion was, the better you would be able to figure out precisely where the base was, just by watching the motion of the ball.)

The extent of this type of uncertainty can be measured, by showing a range within which we can be confident (up to some degree of precision) the true figure lies. The more certain you wish to be, the wider the range. For example, if you need to be 95% certain, the range will need to be wider than if you are satisfied with just being 90% certain. Statisticians call these ranges "confidence intervals."

TABLE 15.1

A Comparison with Previous Peaks in q

Peak Period	Upper Estimate of Overvaluation of q	Lower Estimate of Overvaluation of q
End 1905	1.88	1.62
August 1929	2.17	1.87
End 1936	1.78	1.53
End 1968	2.02	1.74
End 1998	2.51	2.17

Table 15.1 show confidence intervals for the extent of over-valuation at the end of 1998[1] and at previous market peaks. If the stock market had been fairly valued, the range would have been on either side of 1, and the range covers 95% of the probable values on each occasion. So while we cannot be absolutely precise about the extent of overvaluation, we can be more precise about the probabilities, based on the mean reversion properties of the data. The data suggest that there is a 95% probability that the degree of overvaluation at these points lays between the two values shown. This means that we can say that there was roughly a 95% probability that the stock market was between 2.2 and 2.5 times overpriced, at the end of 1998.[2]

The range of uncertainty in Table 15.1 deals, however, with only one form of uncertainty, and thus must overstate the true degree of precision with which we can measure the extent of the market's overvaluation. To be more precise in our measurement, we need to know how confident we can be in the reliability of the data.

Many of the criticisms we have encountered of the use of q rest on the claim that the data are unreliable. We address these claims at greater length in Chapters 25 and 30, but at this stage we merely point out that the data on q are drawn from the same sources as a wide range of economic data, such as those for gross national product, which are normally regarded as being reason-

---

[1]The last year for which we have complete data.
[2]To arrive at these probabilities we need to make certain assumptions about the statistical properties of the data (technically, that innovations to the process driving q are normally distributed in logarithms), but these do not appear inconsistent with observation.

ably trustworthy. Those who claim that data on *q* are unreliable do not make similar claims about the unreliability of the data on which *q* is based. But, in reality, it is not the reliability of the way that *q* is measured that is being questioned; it is the fact that those who are in the business of selling shares do not like their business being undermined by the message that *q* conveys.

In order to change the data on *q* enough to change this message in any significant way, it would be necessary to produce a radical rewrite of the history of the U.S. economy over the past 10 to 15 years. Since other figures produce a consistent story, and hence are mutually supportive, such a rewrite would strain credibility to breaking point. So, while we do not claim that the data for *q* are perfectly reliable, we do believe that *q* has the same claims to reliability as other economic data that are drawn from the same generally accepted official sources.

We should also point out that the very property of mean reversion is in itself supporting evidence of the accuracy of the data, since, as we noted in Chapter 4, this is exactly what economic theory predicts.

THE FUTURE OF *q*

Although such a high value of *q* has very strong implications for what *q* is going to do in the future, these can be stated only in terms of probabilities. Since we have nearly 100 years of data, we can use these probabilities to track out how *q* will be most likely to move in the future. We show this in Chart 15.1.

Like Table 15.1, the chart gives a confidence interval—a range of uncertainty for future values of *q*. Continuing the analogy of the bouncing ball, the chart shows the area in which the short-term bouncing could be expected to stay for 90% of the time. Only 5% of the time would we expect *q* to "bounce" into a range below this, and only 5% of the time above it. We can thus be 95% certain that *q* will lie below the top limit of the range.

There is a distinct contrast between the short-term and longer-term outlook. Because stock prices, and hence *q*, are highly uncertain in the short term, the fact that *q* is starting from such a high value certainly does not rule out the probability that it will rise further in the short term; but the chances of this hap-

CHART 15.1

What the History of q Says About the Future of q

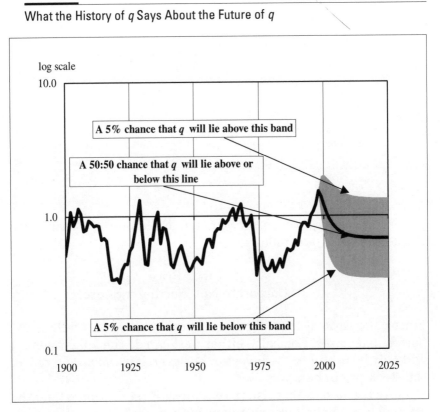

pening become less and less over time.[3] At a 5- to 10-year horizon, the likely range is clearly below the end-1998 value. Table 15.2 shows that, at the 20-year horizon, it becomes a near statistical certainty that q will fall back.

WHAT BRINGS q DOWN?

Thus far we have restricted our attention to q, but clearly the long-term investor must be interested in the implications for stock

---

[3]At the time of this writing, in the latter half of 1999, it looked as if q would probably show a modest fall in 1999; but as the band shows, a further rise in the short term would not have been surprising.

TABLE 15.2

Probabilities of Falls in *q*

Horizon	Probability That *q* Will Fall from End-1998 Level
1 year	67.7%
2 years	78.0%
5 years	90.4%
10 years	95.9%
20 years	97.4%

prices, and hence returns. As we noted in Chapter 2, we can write the definition of *q* as follows:

$$q = \frac{\text{Stock Price}}{\text{Corporate Net Worth per Share}}$$

Since *q* is a ratio, it can fall because either the top part falls or the bottom part rises. Logically, either part can do the adjustment. *q* will only be useful to the investor, however, if it warns of a risk of the stock price changing.

We can assess this risk in two ways. First we can extend the approach we have already taken with *q* by looking at historic patterns and using them to estimate the probabilities of falling stock prices. This is our focus in the remainder of the chapter. But *q* will only be satisfactory if, in addition, we understand how it works. So we turn to this issue in the next chapter. Both answers are mutually reinforcing, as indeed they should be.

THE RISKS TO STOCK PRICES

The property of mean reversion means that when *q* is high it is likely to fall back, and when *q* is low it is likely to rise. Hence *q* contains information about future *changes* in *q*. Chart 15.2 brings out the other half of the message in its simplest form: It shows clearly that changes in *q* and changes in stock prices are strongly correlated. When *q* rises or falls, stock prices normally rise or fall. These two properties, taken together, tell us that q can provide information, not just about its own future, but also about the future of stock prices. What can be seen by eye in this way can also be verified by more thorough examination. In statistical terms there is clear evidence that q does provide such information.[4]

This short-term relationship becomes even stronger over longer horizons. This was, of course, implicit in the strong relationship that we noted between q and Hindsight Value in Chapter 13, since Hindsight Value in any given year captures, in summary form, what happened to subsequent returns. The link

CHART 15.2

Percent Changes in Stock Prices and q

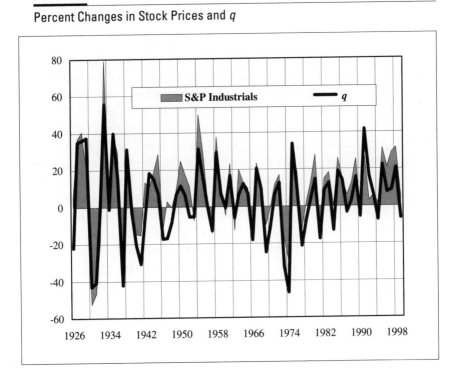

---

[4]We provide some technical evidence of this claim in the Virtual Appendix. In statistical terms, we show that q "Granger-causes" stock prices, which is a rather grand way of saying that q is a useful leading indicator of changes in the stock price. The research paper previously referred to by Stephen Wright and colleague Donald Robertson deals with this issue in greater depth.

between *q* and Hindsight Value therefore showed the strength of the information *q* conveys about long-term, as well as short-term, risks to stock prices and returns.[5]

We also saw in Chapter 2 that past peaks in *q* have been followed by major price adjustments. These have ranged from falls of around 50% in more recent adjustments, both in the United States and elsewhere, to over 80% in the aftermath of 1929.

We can capture all these features in summary form, in terms of the risks to the stock price. The statistical approach involved is rather complex, although the ideas behind it are simple. In essence we assess the risks to future stock prices by looking at the pattern of the relationship between *q* and stock prices in the past.[6] The approach is very similar to the one we used to derive Chart 15.1 and Table 15.2. But, whereas these told you about prospects for *q*, they could not tell you directly what the implied prospects were for prices. Chart 15.3 does so, however.

Chart 15.3, like any statement about the future, is really a statement about the past. The band summarizes prospects for the real stock price in the future, assuming that movements in stock prices and *q* match the average patterns of the past.

The pattern of uncertainty for stock prices shown in the chart is very similar to that which we showed for *q* in Chart 15.1, although the actual extent of the uncertainty is greater. Prices and *q* have normally moved together in the past, but they have not done so exactly. Looking back at the ratio that defines *q*, not all of the adjustment has come in the top half of the ratio, which is the stock price. A small amount has come from the bottom, via changes in net worth. So there is an additional element of uncertainty about prospects for stock prices, as opposed to *q*.

On the other hand, Chart 15.3 conveys one message that Chart 15.1 cannot: The range of values within which the stock price can be expected to move for the next 10 to 20 years is pre-

---

[5]We use prices and returns pretty much interchangeably here, since almost all the uncertainty about future returns relates to uncertainty about future prices. The dividend component in returns is fairly predictable, and, of course, at present, also insignificantly small.

[6]The techniques draw heavily on the academic paper previously cited by Stephen Wright and Cambridge colleague Donald Robertson, to whom we are very grateful for his indirect, but valuable contribution to this book. We provide a summary of the approach in the Virtual Appendix.

CHART 15.3

What *q* Says About Risks to the Real Stock Price

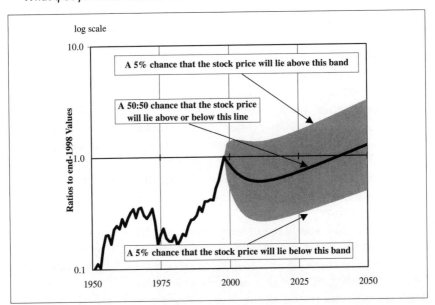

dominantly below its level at the end of 1998. The chart says that it is possible that the stock price may *not* fall, but not very probable. Table 15.3 gives the probabilities of falling stock prices over coming years.

TABLE 15.3

Probabilities of Falls in Stock Prices,[7] as of the End of 1998

Horizon	Probability That Stock Prices Will Fall from End-1998 Level
1 year	66.1%
2 years	71.7%
5 years	80.0%
10 years	84.5%
20 years	81.2%
30 years	69.3%

---

[7]As throughout the book, we are talking about stock prices in real terms, adjusted for CPI inflation.

We have already drawn the analogy between investing in stocks and playing roulette. There is, of course, an important difference between the stock market and roulette in normal circumstances, when *q* is at or near its average. Usually stock investors have the odds stacked somewhat in their favor. As *q* rises, however, the odds gradually worsen, until at today's extreme levels, the odds are heavily stacked against investors. The table shows that the probabilities of prices falling over the course of the next five to ten years are distinctly higher than over one year. This follows directly from the analogy with roulette. There is always a chance of getting lucky, but the chances of a sustained run of luck get smaller the longer you sit at the table.

Beyond around ten years the probabilities start to fall again, albeit only gradually. This happens because, as we noted earlier, over long enough horizons, the odds are usually much more strongly in the stock investor's favor. As time goes by, the bad prospects for the near term are gradually offset by the positive prospects for the longer term. Thus, in Chart 15.3, the band covering the range of probable returns gradually drifts up over time. But, as we also noted earlier, very few investors will be able to wait long enough to be reassured by this.

IMPLICATIONS FOR THE INVESTOR

Even though there is always some chance that the stock price will *not* fall, this offers very little consolation. Without capital appreciation, the only return you get out of the stock market is your dividend income. At current extremely low dividend yields, in a "sideways market," when prices neither fall nor rise, investors would be very much better off holding alternative assets.

Chart 15.4 zooms in on the band of future values of the stock price from Chart 15.3, and shows how unlikely it is that stock prices in the future will grow at the sort of rates to which investors have become accustomed over the past two decades. As the chart shows, even these highly immodest returns are possible in the short term, given the volatility of stock price movements. It also shows, however, how poor these chances are. There is less than a 5% chance of stock prices growing at 20% per annum for more than one year or growing at 10% per annum for more than three.[8]

By now it should be abundantly clear that the chances of stock prices growing at 10% per annum or more on a sustained basis are a near statistical impossibility. Since surveys suggest that average investor expectations are generally higher than 10%, the chances that investors will soon become disillusioned with stocks seems a near certainty. Once this occurs, *q*-investors can look forward to the stock market becoming once again a worthwhile place to invest. But since a major collapse in stock prices

CHART 15.4

q-Based Estimates of Stock Price Risks vs. Alternative Scenarios

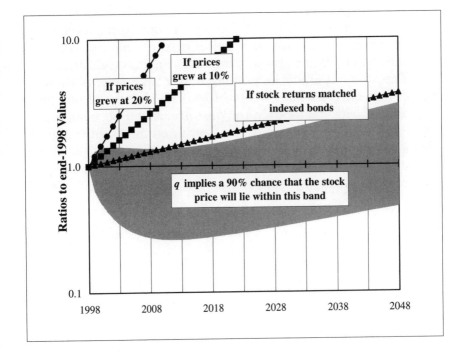

[8]These are the number of years shown on the chart in which the 20% and 10% lines are within the band of 90% probability. There is, however, an equal chance of being outside this band on the downside as well as the upside, which leaves the chance of doing better, once the line is outside the band, at less than 5%.

will be a necessary part of the process of disillusionment for the average investor, only *q*-investors, who will of course be out of stocks at the time, will be able to view the opportunity with real pleasure.

The third line in Chart 15.4 shows what would happen to prices if they continued to grow at their historic average rate of around 2½% per annum in real terms. In the past, this rate of capital appreciation has been sufficient to provide a total return on stocks, before costs, of roughly 6½%. This was only possible, however, because the average dividend yield, at around 5%, was so much higher than it is today. With dividends yields currently only around 1%, the return on stocks would fail to match the return of over 3½% currently available on safe indexed bonds, even if the prices of stocks were to rise at 2½% per annum. Chart 15.4 shows that even this much more modest return is highly improbable on any long-term basis. Fifteen years out stocks have a less than 5% chance of proving to be better investments than the U.S. government bonds that protect investors against inflation.

The chances of stocks proving better investments than indexed bonds are set out in Table 15.4. The chances of matching average returns on stocks in the past are, of course, even worse. This backs up the arguments we presented in Chapter 3 about the poor prospects currently provided by stocks even for an immortal investor. The further ahead you look, the lower are your chances that stocks will either outperform indexed bonds or match their own historic returns.

TABLE 15.4

Probabilities of Stocks Outperforming Indexed Bonds, as of Year End 1998

Horizon	Probability
1 year	29.7%
2 years	22.7%
5 years	12.5%
10 years	6.1%
20 years	2.9%
30 years	2.3%

THE BAD NEWS ABOUT STOCKS AS AN INVESTMENT FOR THE LONG RUN

The message should by now be pretty clear. At the end of the twentieth century the odds were probably more heavily stacked against the investor in stocks than they had been at any other point in the past 100 years. Because returns are unpredictable, returns for the next year or so may still turn out to be acceptable. But, just as in roulette, the longer the investor sits at the table, the lower the chances that this will happen.

The implication is also clear: The long-term investor should get out of stocks. In Part Five we shall look at what you should do with your money instead. But first we need to do two things.

- First, in Chapter 16, we need to look behind the probabilities of q falling, to understand why q will fall.
- Second, in Chapter 17, we want to remind you of the good news about q. We shall show that q helps explain why stocks have been such a good long-term investment in the past. At some point, we hope in the not too distant future, after the collapse of the greatest stock market bubble of the twentieth century, stocks will again be an excellent long-term investment. q will again play a crucial role, by providing reassurance that stocks can and do offer fair value.

CHAPTER 16

Why *q* Has Risen, and Why *q* Will Fall

THE IMPORTANCE OF KNOWING WHY

The previous chapter showed you that the stock market has a high probability of falling, and hence a very low probability of offering decent returns. We should not, however, be satisfied with an explanation based solely on statistical evidence. We must also understand why. To an economist, statistical evidence and understanding are vitally connected. Without understanding, statistical evidence runs the risk of being a "black box." By the same token, without statistical evidence, mere reasoning on the basis of economic logic never gets a reality check. We have had the reality check in the previous chapter. We now turn to the economic logic.

INCENTIVES MATTER

When we looked at *q* in Chapter 12, we pointed to a central idea in economics, that, through the forces of competition, prices are brought down to the costs of production. In Chapter 9, we had also introduced you to the idea of arbitrage. The two concepts of arbitrage and competition are very closely linked. Both are driven by an incentive that arises out of the possibility of making a profit, when prices are too high; both, in action, bring about a reduction in price disparities. The only real difference is that we normally associate the idea of competition with firms that actually produce goods, whereas arbitrage is normally thought of as simply buying in the cheap market, and selling in the dear market.[9]

The very crucial point to note is that the same incentive drives both processes. This is central to our assertion that *q* will fall. In an uncertain world, we cannot say precisely how *q* will fall. We certainly cannot say exactly when *q* will fall. We can speculate on both of these themes; but in the end all that we can offer is informed speculation. But we can say that *q* *will* fall, because incentives matter.

In Chapter 12 we showed that *q* is really just telling you how far the price you have to pay for companies in the stock market deviates from the underlying cost of producing those companies. *q* is therefore telling us that there is a massive incentive to exploit this discrepancy. There is a clear incentive to engage in *some* form of arbitrage, using the word in its most general sense. It is our confidence in the idea that incentives matter that gives us the confidence to assert that *q* must fall.

We do not wish to belabor the point too much, but we should stress what an important difference there is between economists saying something will happen and their saying how or when it will happen. If economists had to survive on their ability to forecast events with any precision, they would probably have about the same status as astrologers or fortune tellers. But economists have done much better than this, because time and time again they have shown that, given the right incentives, people can be relied upon to do the rest.

A classic example is the history of oil prices since the early 1970s. When OPEC managed to quadruple the real oil price over the course of 1973 and 1974, general panic set in. It was widely assumed that the Western economies were going to be permanently at the mercy of a few Arab states and that shortage of fuel would be the dominant economic force for the foreseeable future. Of course, those who were convinced that the world was already

---

[9]The difference is in fact more apparent than real. For goods and services are nothing more than the combination of different goods and services which went into their production. So a firm that produces something at a profit is really engaging in arbitrage too: The "cheap" market it is buying in is the market for inputs to production, and the "dear" market is just the market for the goods the firm sells.

on the brink of running out of everything from oil to copper saw the oil price rise as just the first of what was to be a spiraling rise in the price of everything that mattered.

In the midst of all this, Milton Friedman took a rather different view, based on the simple premise that incentives matter. He noted that the rise in the real price of oil had absolutely nothing to do with an increase in the real cost of producing oil. Nor was there any real evidence that supplies were on the brink of running out. So, Friedman concluded, the price of oil would not stay high. He was, of course, entirely right. In 1998 the price of oil was lower, in real terms, than it was in the early 1970s, before the first major oil price hike.

Writing in 1973, the precise mechanism of how or when the oil price would fall was not clear, but this did not matter. It was easy to see that there was now an enormous incentive for oil producers outside OPEC to increase their output, and to go out looking for new supplies. There was a strong incentive for members of OPEC itself to break ranks and cheat on the quotas that had been set in order to push oil output down, and thereby raise prices. There was a strong incentive for consumers of oil to find ways to cut back on their oil consumption, and thereby lower demand. It was impossible to tell which of these forces would be most important in breaking OPEC's power over oil prices. Nor was it possible to tell when these things would happen, or whether other mechanisms would arise that would bring prices back down. But it was possible to say with complete certainty that *something* would happen, because the incentive was so strong.

Exactly the same applies with *q*. The fact that *q* is 2.5 times its average value means that you currently have to pay roughly 2.5 times more than you would normally pay for a share in the U.S. corporate sector. The higher *q* gets, the stronger the incentive grows for a response. The precise nature of the response must be unclear, but it will happen.

This assertion clearly begs two questions:

- If the incentive is so strong, why has there not already been a response to the high value of *q*?
- And how did *q* get to be so high?

The answers to both are revealing. We shall deal with them in turn.

CHART 16.1

U.S. Household Savings and the Stock Market

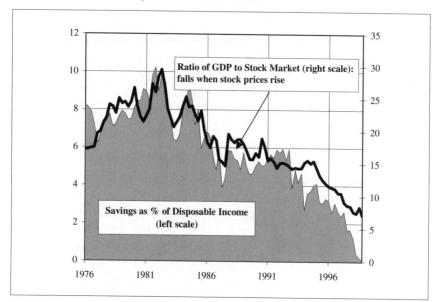

THE RESPONSE SO FAR

The answer to the first question is straightforward. There already *has* been a very significant response to the high level of *q*. The response can be seen in different contexts.

Chart 16.1 shows one pretty clear response. *q* has had an important effect on savings. The main reason that people save is to be able to live comfortably when they retire. The amount that people need to save to have enough money to retire depends therefore on what they can earn on their savings. The higher the return that people expect therefore, the less they save.

Chart 16.1 shows the powerful effect on savings of a high stock market. As the stock market has become increasingly overvalued, the savings of the average American have fallen to nothing. This doesn't of course mean that no one is saving, but it means that the people who are living off their savings, or increasingly getting into debt, are having as important an effect on the economy as those who are saving.

When *q* is high, it really has two effects on saving. First, it raises the value of the savings that have already been accumulated. Second, it raises people's expectations of the returns that they are likely to get on their savings in the future. As we pointed out in Chapter 2, it would actually be a lot more rational to expect low returns in the future after a long period in which the stock market has given a high return, but all the evidence points to the opposite happening.

At the same time as q has lowered saving, it has increased investment. The reason is obvious, and relates directly to Tobin's original idea of how q would work. Firms can buy capital far more cheaply by investing in it directly than by purchasing it through the stock market. Since on average, through competition, they must earn the same profits either way, returns from buying real assets are far higher than those from buying stocks. So firms are responding to the incentive too. Chart 16.2 shows that investment has also clearly tracked the upward path of q.

CHART 16.2

Investment and q

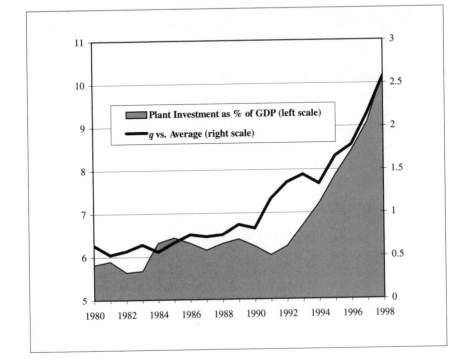

The effect of a high q has thus clearly been to encourage investment and discourage saving. If the USA were the only country in the world, and stocks were the only way that companies could raise finance, the effects would be clear-cut. There would be a reduced demand for stocks, as consumers chose to save less and liquidated existing stock holdings in order to consume more. There would simultaneously be an increased supply of stocks, as firms issued new equities in order to fund higher investment. The only way that the two tendencies could be reconciled would be by a reduction in stock prices. Once stock prices had fallen by enough to bring q back down to its normal level, incentives would have done their work, as usual.

But stocks are not the only way that companies can raise capital. If companies use debt rather than equity financing, then the fall in stock prices can be delayed. But this would still leave investment tending to run ahead of savings. As a result, demand will tend to rise faster than supply, leading ultimately to inflation. In today's conditions, inflation can be held at bay, provided the excess demand is satisfied by rising imports. This is possible because the USA is of course not the only country in the world. A country that is investing more than it is saving can do so if other countries are prepared to lend it the money. This is precisely what has been happening; and the counterpart has been a rising trade deficit.

The fact that stocks are not the only way that companies can raise capital is an essential condition for allowing q to remain high. The fact that the USA is not the only country in the world is also a key point, because meeting excess demand through imports can slow the impact of inflation. This illustrates an important point, however: A high q is basically inflationary, because it means that the cost of capital is being temporarily kept below its equilibrium level.

These two factors explain why the responses to q have not yet brought down stock prices. But they leave open the question of why companies have preferred to borrow by issuing debt, rather than equity. As we shall see shortly, however, this apparent perversity is a rational response to recent changes in management incentives.

HOW DID q GET SO HIGH?

If the country as a whole is saving less and investing more, we would normally expect prices on all financial assets, including stocks, to fall. But this need not happen if there is a simultaneous tendency for participants in the stock market collectively to switch into stocks. The very fact that q has risen so much makes it clear that this must have been happening.

But the word "collectively" is very important, for what matters is the net pressure of demand from buyers and sellers in the stock market.[10] Chart 16.3 shows who has been buying and selling stocks in recent years. It is highly revealing.

What the chart shows is that the arbitrage that will ultimately bring q down is already taking place. Contrary to popular

CHART 16.3

Net Buyers and Sellers on Wall Street

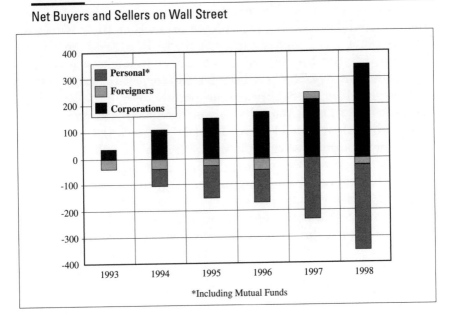

*Including Mutual Funds

---

[10]After the event the number of buyers must, of course, equal the number of sellers. But if, at a given price, the number of buyers exceeds the number of sellers, the price must rise. Reasoning backward, a rise in the price must imply net buying pressure. We deal with this issue in more detail in Chapter 28.

myth, which holds that a "wall of money" is piling into the stock markets from the personal sector, whether directly or via mutual funds, quite the reverse is the case. In fact, in net terms, U.S. households are doing the sensible thing, and selling the stock market. So, in all but one of the six years shown, are overseas investors.

Of course, we should stress that these figures are in net terms. Plenty of individual American investors are still buying into the stock market; but their purchases are being more than offset by the sales of other American investors, and it is net purchases or sales that matter.

The chart also shows to whom they are selling stocks, and the answer is, at first sight, astonishing. Almost the only buyer of the U.S. corporate sector in recent years has been the U.S. corporate sector itself! Since stock prices have been rising, we can see that what would otherwise be downward pressure on prices from households selling Wall Street has been more than offset by ever rising demand from U.S. corporations to buy back their own stock.

We should perhaps remind you of why this is so surprising. *q* tells us it is not because corporations' own stocks are cheap—quite the contrary. Nor is it because the corporate sector is flush with cash. Although profits are reasonably high, largely for cyclical reasons, we have seen that firms are also investing more, for which they clearly need cash. Chart 16.4 shows the result: U.S. firms' net operational cash flow, which is what is left over from profits after paying out dividends, and after making new investments, has moved from being modestly positive a few years ago to being modestly negative.

In principle, firms might finance this deficit by making new issues of equity; but in fact, as the previous chart showed, they have done the reverse: Buying back their own stock in effect means that new issues have been substantially negative. The overall result—which, as Chart 16.4 shows, has been influenced far more by firms' stock market activities than by their regular activities—has been to produce a massive negative cash flow overall, which firms have had to finance by other forms of borrowing. So, in effect, U.S. firms are progressively switching from financing via equity issues to financing via debt.

Is this because debt issues are cheaper than equity issues? Quite the contrary. The fact that stocks are expensive means that

CHART 16.4

U.S. Nonfinancial Corporations' Cash Flow

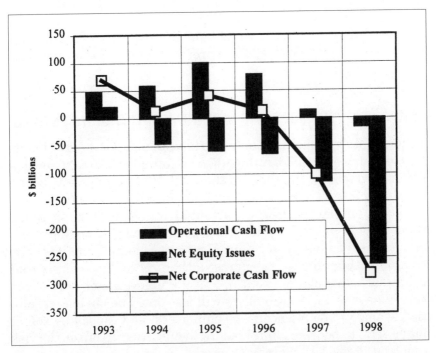

returns on them are low. But low returns to the investor mean low costs of borrowing to the borrower, so issuing new equity is currently a very *cheap* way to raise finance. On the other hand, although interest rates in nominal terms are pretty low, they are far from low in real terms. On top of this, the premia that corporations have to pay over government bonds have increased of late.[11] So debt is *not* currently a cheap way for firms to raise capital.

In summary, therefore, we can see how stock prices, and hence *q*, have risen, despite the fact that household and overseas investors have increasingly, and sensibly, been net sellers of stocks. The explanation is that corporations have simultaneously switched to being net buyers, despite the fact that, in order to do so, they have had to raise additional, and far from cheap, financing.

---

[11]We shall revert to both of these issues, from the point of view of the investor, in Chapter 18.

If this seems more than slightly crazy, it is. But, as we noted before, incentives are crucial; and it turns out that this development is quite easily explicable in terms of a massive conflict of incentives. The fact that it has been allowed to happen may well appear, after the greatest bubble of the twentieth century has broken, to have been one of the greatest follies of the twentieth century.

CORPORATE STOCK OPTIONS AND THE CONFLICT OF INCENTIVES

Unfortunately, economists may also have to take some of the blame for this particular folly, although, as so often happens, it seemed like a good idea at the time. In the early 1980s economists began to be very interested in the idea of providing better motivation to corporate employees. Initially attention tended to focus on giving them a share in profits. This was seen as providing not only benefits to the firm, but also potential macroeconomic benefits.[12] The trouble with giving away shares in the profits, however, is that profits are a return on capital, and if employees get part of the return on capital, shareholders will lose out. The obvious resolution seemed to be to encourage employees, and especially senior managers, to become shareholders themselves. To offset the risk involved, however, companies increasingly offered shares indirectly, in the form of options. Doing it this way gave managers a one-way bet. They gained if stock prices rose, in which case they exercised their options; but if stock prices fell, they could not actually lose.

This scheme was, in fact, a tremendous gain for managers in more ways than one. Not only did they gain extra income but, under current accounting procedures, they could do so without appearing to eat into profits.[13] At the same time, the arrange-

---

[12]The idea was that if a recession hit, and employees' incomes fell back with profits, there would be less incentive for firms to lay them off, compared with the situation where workers had to be paid a fixed wage.

[13]We shall resist the temptation to get diverted into a long discourse on this issue. However, for those who are curious to know more, an article was published in *Forbes* on May 18, 1998 ("Stock Options Are Not a Free Lunch," by Gretchen Morgensen) summarizing work done by Andrew Smithers, colleague Daniel Murray, and John Emerson of Robson Rhodes, which suggested that profits were being overstated by as much as 20%. See the Virtual Appendix for more details.

ment introduced a clear distortion to incentives. If managers' incomes were effectively being linked to what was happening to stock prices, managers had a very strong incentive to ensure that stock prices rose, rather than fell. This was bound to bias their financing decisions, and, as Charts 16.3 and 16.4 show, it has.

At first sight, this was a game in which no one appeared to be losing. Managers were happy, because their incomes were being boosted significantly. Investors were happy, because stock prices were rising. But in fact, as always, there must in reality be a loser; in this case, despite the apparent evidence, it was individual shareholders. They are losing, rather than gaining, because the real underlying value of stocks is reduced by the transfer of wealth to employees.

It is quite easy to show why. P/E multiples are currently around 40. We shall discuss in Chapters 22 and 23 the link between P/Es, earnings yields, and underlying returns. For now, we simply note that the linkage implies an underlying return on stocks of around 2½%. The real cost of corporate debt, which firms need to issue in order to continue buying their own stocks (which, on average yield them a return of 2½%) is somewhere around 3% to 3½%, depending on the creditworthiness of the firm.[14] Firms are therefore borrowing money at a higher cost than the return they are getting on the assets they are buying. This is always a road to perdition. It is also clearly contrary to the interests of shareholders, since in the end it can be paid for only by eating into profits.

It may not, of course, *appear* to be contrary to the interest of shareholders, since stock prices are rising. But you will probably remember a succession of scandals—that normally occur in Latin America or Eastern Europe—in which investors are lured into depositing money into schemes that, for a while, pay handsome returns but in fact prove unsustainable because these returns are simply being paid for out of the inflows of funds from yet further investors. These are normally referred to as "Ponzi schemes"

---

[14]This is the cost of borrowing after tax, to make it comparable to the return on stocks, also after tax. Interest costs of 3% to 3½% are equivalent to around 5% to 6% before tax. We shall see in later chapters that the "safe" rate of interest is currently around 4% in real terms; but corporate borrowers have to pay a premium over this rate.

after the Bostonian financier Charles Ponzi who dreamed up a particularly celebrated swindle along these lines. The process we have been describing is a near relative of the Ponzi scheme. Such schemes always collapse in the end, and they do so reliably, because ultimately, investors realize that the returns are unsustainable, and at that stage they sell out, or cease to buy. The same will happen to this one, which is why we can say, with complete confidence, that q must fall.

CHAPTER 17

The Good News About Stocks as Investments for the Long Run

q CAN EXPLAIN THE SUCCESS OF BUY AND HOLD...

It may seem surprising, in light of the doom and gloom we have been purveying in the last two chapters, that we have anything cheerful to say. But we think we do. Indeed, the good-news part of our message is of a more enduring nature than the bad news. Even though we hope we have convinced you that buy and hold is not the best investment strategy, we believe that stocks should normally be the main investment for the long-term investor.

We have shown in earlier chapters that, despite giving a pretty bumpy ride on occasions, the buy-and-hold strategy has *on average* worked pretty well for the long-term investor. Oddly enough, this would not have been the case if *q* did not work. The fact that *q* pulls the stock market back to its underlying value means that it is less risky than it otherwise would be.

We shall show in this chapter that the historic success of buy and hold is inconsistent with its own internal logic. The logic of buy and hold would only hold up if long-term returns on the stock market had been much more risky than they have in fact been. If they had been this risky, however, the strategy would never have become so popular. Investors would be at greater risk than they have actually been, and only those able to hold shares for much more than 30 years would be assured of not losing money. The

buy and hold strategy cannot therefore explain its own success.
We shall show that *q* can.

...BUT THE *q*-INVESTOR CAN DO BETTER THAN BUY AND HOLD

It is because *q* works that buying stocks is normally not too risky
for investors. But there are a number of other points.

- For investors who can only follow the buy-and-hold
  strategy, we saw in Part Two that stocks should not be
  their sole, or even predominant, investment if they are
  approaching or past retirement.
- We also know that holding stocks when *q* is high, as it
  was at the end of 1998, is far too risky to be sensible,
  whatever your investment horizon.
- But investors who do understand and use *q* can afford to
  be fully invested in stocks, right up to retirement and
  even a bit beyond, provided that *q* shows that the stock
  market is not too overvalued.

TWO REMARKABLE FEATURES OF STOCK RETURNS

There are two remarkable features of stock market returns in the
past. The first is that the average real return on stocks has been
surprisingly stable, at around 6¾% before costs. Since this finding
is attributable to Wharton economist Jeremy Siegel, we feel he
deserves to have this number named after him. We shall therefore
refer to it as "Siegel's constant," or sometimes just *s*. We think that
it is also worth emphasizing that since constants are rare in economics, *s* deserves more attention than it has yet received. The
second remarkable feature is that, although stock returns have
been risky, as we have emphasized in this book, they have actually
not been as risky over long horizons as might have been expected.
If we did not know what the long-term risks have been, but just had
some short-term data, we would assume that the long-term risks
would be greater than experience has shown them to be. It is this
feature, as much as the first, that has helped to give stocks their
desirable properties for the long-run investor.

In this chapter we shall look at both of these features. Our
primary focus will however be on the second issue. We shall see
that *q* helps provide an explanation for the surprisingly low risks

experienced by stock market investors over long horizons. Indeed, we know of no alternative theory, other than q, that provides a satisfactory explanation of the relative lack of risk involved in investing in stocks over the long term, given their shorter-term characteristics.

When stocks are as overvalued as they were at the end of 1998, it may not seem the right time to remind investors of the lack of risk associated with holding them. But the essence of our message is twofold. When q is high, get out of stocks. But once q indicates that stocks are fair value, get back in. This is of course what investors do if they follow the trading rules we looked at in Chapter 14. The message of this chapter is that there will be a time to get back into stocks, when the dust has settled after the last great bubble of the twentieth century has burst. At that point, knowing that q is indicating fair value will make it much safer for investors to buy stocks than it would be without q to provide guidance. Since investors are likely to have taken a terrible drubbing at that point, and stocks will as a consequence probably be a deeply unpopular investment, the ability to assess the risks will be much more valuable than most people will readily realize today.

SIEGEL'S CONSTANT, "s": A RARE SIGN OF STABILITY

So far we have restricted ourselves to looking back to the start of the twentieth century, since we cannot go further back than this with data on q. Thanks to Professor Siegel, however, we have data on the returns on stocks for almost another 100 years before then, starting in 1802.

Chart 17.1 looks again at the variability of stock returns, as in Chart 7.1, but this version shows the real returns that investors in stocks have received each year since 1802. It may seem strange to be talking about stability in something that has varied so much. As before, the chart also shows a range of values, between which the stock return has fallen 90% of the time. Since the range varies from a positive return of 30% down to a negative return of 22%, the chart is a reminder of just how variable returns have been in the short term.[15]

---

[15]For presentational clarity, we again have used log returns, multiplied by 100, rather than the usual percentage return to get around the problem that normal percentage rises and falls are not symmetric in their impact. See footnote 16 in Chapter 7.

CHART 17.1

The Variability of the Real Return on Stocks

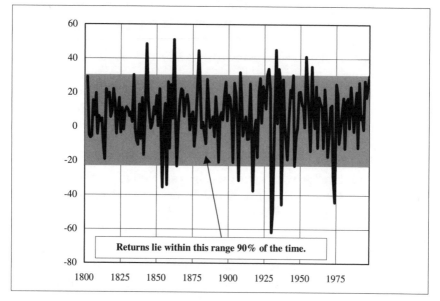

Returns lie within this range 90% of the time.

CHART 17.2

The Stability of the Real Return on Stocks

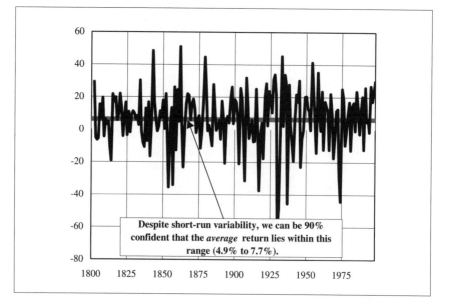

Despite short-run variability, we can be 90% confident that the *average* return lies within this range (4.9% to 7.7%).

However, although the one-year returns vary a great deal, the ups and downs will even out over time so that we can identify the average return with considerably greater precision, especially given that we have nearly two centuries' worth of data. Chart 17.2 shows returns again, but with the range of uncertainty about the average return, which is very much narrower: We can be 90% certain that the average return lies somewhere between 4.9% and 7.7% (with our best estimate of the actual average being 6¾%).[16]

It is this average return that we refer to as Siegel's Constant, or s, and that has proved to be such an important benchmark in earlier chapters. Even after nearly two centuries, we cannot know with certainty what the true value of s actually is, but we can know that it cannot lie too far from our best estimate of 6¾%.

We shall show that q can explain one thing about stock returns, which is why returns get pulled back toward s more rapidly than might be expected, but q cannot explain the stability of s itself. The question as to why s is, or appears to be, so stable is an important challenge that needs to be resolved before we can have a complete understanding of how capital markets work. We wish we could say that we have arrived at such a complete understanding, but we have not. In our own defense, this is a question that the rest of the economics profession does not yet seem to have got around to asking, let alone resolving.

THE BUY-AND-HOLD STRATEGY AND THE RANDOM WALK MODEL

There is a second puzzle about stock returns over longer horizons, one that q can, however, resolve. Although the puzzle is not a puzzle once q is taken into account, it is a very important puzzle for the buy-and-hold strategy; indeed, it reveals a crucial internal contradiction. As we shall show, it also presents an identical puzzle for the random walk model, which has been a popular spinoff of the Efficient Market Hypothesis.

---

[16]In the Virtual Appendix we explain how we derive this range, and compare it with alternative approaches. We show that it is not a completely straightforward exercise, if we are properly to take account of the surprising lack of risk in returns, which we discuss later in the chapter; but different approaches do not produce all that much difference in our estimate of the range of uncertainty around the true average return.

It may not be immediately obvious, but the buy-and-hold strategy and random walk model have a lot in common.[17] Both reject the idea that *q* can be used to value markets in any useful way.

The random walk model arises out of the notion of an efficient market, in which price always reflects all available information and in which, as a result, price is equal to value at all times. It therefore rejects the idea that *q* can indicate whether a market is over- or undervalued.

The buy-and-hold strategy also rejects the idea of using *q* to value markets. Buying and holding stocks implies that now is always a good time to be in stocks. If it were not, if it were after all possible to spot a good time to get out of stocks, then you would not buy and hold; you would buy and sometimes hold but sometimes sell. (We have already shown that this is the essence of the *q*-investor's strategy, but we have to admit that this title would not help much in marketing!)

The random walk model maintains that in an efficient market, stock returns should be random. If they were not, and were predictable, a perfectly efficient market should exploit such predictability to make profits, and thereby eliminate it.[18]

---

[17]The differences between the two are also revealing about their origins. The random walk model, which was invented by economists, has a clear and straightforward internal logic; but, as we shall show (and many others have shown before us), it does not quite work when confronted with the data. As a result, economists have gone back to reexamine their logic. The buy-and-hold strategy, which was invented by stockbrokers, has a deep internal inconsistency in its logic, but strangely enough does, in average circumstances, more or less work for the purpose it was intended. As we shall show, the data reveal the internal inconsistency in the logic of buy and hold, but, as we have already noted, stockbrokers do not worry about data.

[18]A more precise title for the random walk model, as used here, would really be the random returns model. Random returns would imply that the cumulative total return to stocks would be a random walk, rather than stock prices, as early versions of the random walk model assumed. But the contrast between the random walk theory as applied to stock prices and the assumption that returns are random is not in practice very great. Under the less restrictive random returns theory, since the dividend component in returns is fairly predictable over the short run, there must be an offsetting predictability in stock prices, such that total returns are random. In practice this would make the stock price very close to being a random walk.

The logic of the buy-and-hold strategy also holds only if returns are random. If there were any predictability in returns, this could be used to spot the bad times to buy stocks, thereby undermining the whole basis of the strategy.

Understanding the intimate connection between the logic of the buy-and-hold strategy and that of the random walk model is very helpful. One of the great attractions of the random walk model is that it makes very clear predictions about the way returns will behave, predictions that can be tested against real-world data. Any such test is therefore also implicitly a test of the logic of buy and hold. But both ideas have to face a puzzle, which is that, according to their own logic, stocks have in practice been "too safe" an investment.[19]

THE PUZZLE: HAVE STOCKS BEEN "TOO SAFE"?

Proponents of the buy-and-hold strategy do not deny the short-run volatility of stock returns; they merely argue that the impact of such volatility is diminished by the averaging-out process of returns over long horizons. This assumption has a clear basis in probability. For example, Chart 17.1 showed that there is a 10% chance of the return in any one year being better than 30% or worse than minus 22%. If returns were random, the chances of the average return over two years being in that range would be only 1%. This is simply because the chance of a 1 in 10 chance repeating itself two years running is 1 in 100 (i.e., 10×10).[20] The result is that the risks to investors would diminish over time, even if returns were random.

In practice, however, the reduction in risks that would occur if returns were random would not happen fast enough to justify

---

[19]We should stress again that we make no claims to be the first to have pointed out the failures of the random walk model when confronted with the data. The fact that it nearly, but not quite, works is now generally accepted. Indeed, two eminent financial economists, Andrew Lo and Archie MacKinlay, recently published a collection of papers with the title *A Non-Random Walk on Wall Street* (Princeton, NJ, Princeton University Press, 1999).

[20]This can be seen in actual operation in games of chance. If you bet on a horse to win at 10 to 1 against and commit your winnings in advance to a bet on another horse to win at 10 to 1 against, the odds against you winning on the total bet are 100 to 1 against.

the buy-and-hold strategy. Not because it would not happen, but crucially, because it would not happen fast enough. Chart 17.3 illustrates why. It shows the difference in risks between investing in stocks in the real world and investing in them if returns were random, as the buy-and-hold strategy must imply. Rather than looking at the average return, we look at the variability in the lump sums that investors would have received. Looking at things in this way helps bring out the scale of the differences, since small differences in returns amount to a lot of money over 20 or more years.

For those who invested $1 in every single year over the past two centuries, the inner band in Chart 17.3 shows the range of amounts they would have been able to realize in real terms depending on how long they chose to hold the investments. The chart

CHART 17.3

Buy and Hold Has Been Safer Than Its Own Logic Would Predict

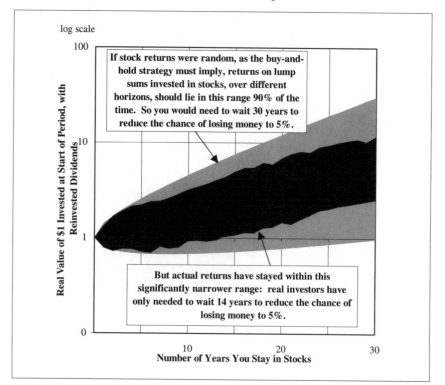

log scale

If stock returns were random, as the buy-and-hold strategy must imply, returns on lump sums invested in stocks, over different horizons, should lie in this range 90% of the time. So you would need to wait 30 years to reduce the chance of losing money to 5%.

But actual returns have stayed within this significantly narrower range: real investors have only needed to wait 14 years to reduce the chance of losing money to 5%.

Real Value of $1 Invested at Start of Period, with Reinvested Dividends

Number of Years You Stay in Stocks

shows that, 90% of the time, the lump-sum returns to investors would have been somewhere in this range. Only 5% of the time would investors have ended up with a higher lump sum, and only 5% of the time with a lower one. Ending up with a lump sum less than 1 implies that investors lost money in real terms: The chart shows that at a 14-year horizon, this happened only 5% of the time. Investors therefore had a 95% probability of getting at least some sort of positive return if they waited this long. (We saw in Chapter 11 that over a 20-year horizon this has been the case in practice all the time.)

The outer band on the chart shows the range of variation that would occur if the logic of the buy-and-hold strategy were sound. The difference is very marked indeed. Had returns been entirely random, investors would have needed to wait more than 30 years to have a 95% probability of getting at least some positive return.[21]

This says something extremely important about the buy-and-hold strategy. If the logic of the strategy were correct, stocks would simply be far too risky, even for the very long-run investor. The success of buy and hold therefore undermines its own logic. The buy-and-hold strategy cannot explain its own success.

THE GOOD NEWS ABOUT q

The good news about q is that it can provide an explanation of the success of the buy-and-hold strategy and, in so doing, offer the q-investor something better.

The explanation depends on the elastic that keeps the stock market linked to its fundamental value. When q gets very high, or very low, mechanisms are set in motion that pull it back, as outlined in the previous chapter. Because the fundamental value of the stock market, which is the net worth of the corporate sector, is relatively stable, this means that, however unpredictable the stock market may be in the short term, it is in the end tied down to something far less unpredictable. It is this stability that

---

[21]The Virtual Appendix explains how these lines were generated. The procedure is technically complicated, but uses quite standard statistical assumptions. The calculations take into account the fact that Siegel's constant, s, is not known with certainty. Over long horizons this makes quite a big difference.

reduces in such a marked way the risks to investors over long horizons.

In the Virtual Appendix we show statistical evidence of two crucial points:

- This kind of adjustment process does take place.
- It can reduce uncertainty about long-run returns in a way that matches up very well with the evidence of Chart 17.3.

Some of this evidence is of necessity quite technical, which is why we put it in the Appendix. But one part of the evidence is absolutely crucial, and also quite straightforward: The mechanism by which *q* works must mean that returns are nearly, but *not quite* random. They have to be nearly random; otherwise, the power of *q* would be a money machine. But they have to be not quite random; otherwise stocks would not have been as safe as they have been.

A crucial feature of something that is truly random is that it has no memory. This is one feature of probability that human intuition normally finds so hard to grasp. When you are in a game of pure chance, the past does not matter. Suppose you bet on the result of spinning a coin, so that you receive $1 every time it comes up heads and lose $1 every time it comes up tails. If heads have just come up ten times in a row, the chance of another head is still 50%. So you are just as likely to be able to hang on to your $10 as to have to pay it back. The stock market, however, doesn't behave in the same way. If the coin spinning occurred on stock market lines, then you would be more likely to have to give the $10 back than to keep it. In short, you would be wise after such a run of luck to quit while you were ahead.[22] In the stock market *q* simply tells you when it is time to quit.

---

[22]The only trouble with gambling analogies is that gambling is not a rational activity, while investing in the stock market can be. Thus, even with a purely random gamble, you would be wise to quit while you are ahead, assuming that you are risk-averse, which most human beings appear to be. The difference in a purely random gamble is that, although there is still a risk of losing your $10, your central estimate of how much money you will have after another ten tosses of the coin is still $10, whereas if the gamble were like the stock market your central estimate would be much closer to zero.

THE POWER OF q IS THE POWER OF KNOWING WHEN TO QUIT

We have seen that q can explain the charms of the buy-and-hold strategy in a way that the strategy itself cannot. But for the q-investor, q can do even more. Although buy and hold has been safer than its own logic would predict, it has, as we have seen, been too dangerous for investors at or near retirement, who cannot invest for long enough to be sure that the power of compound interest can get to work. q allows you to continue holding stocks later in life, provided that you sell them when they become so overvalued that your wealth is put at risk. We showed in Chapter 14 that quite simple strategies based on q give higher returns than buy and hold, but, more crucially, much *safer* returns. In Chart 17.4, we show the range of outcomes that the q-investor

CHART 17.4

...But the q-Investor Could Have Done Much Better

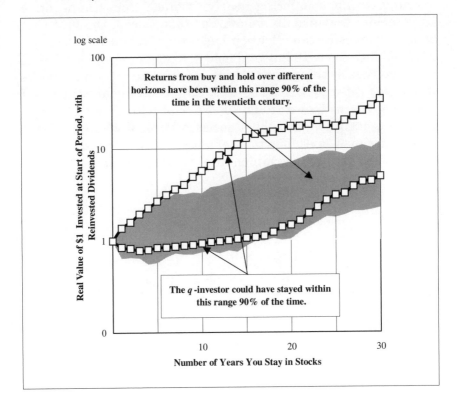

would have achieved in the twentieth century, compared with the buy-and-hold investor, on the same basis as in Chart 17.3.[23]

The chart shows that even the *q*-investor cannot rule out the possibility of losing some money over the short to medium term. There are two reasons for this. First, the stock market can and has fallen when it has been fairly valued. Second, it has not always been possible to prevent real losses occurring even when holding cash. In some periods in the past, inflation has been higher than nominal interest rates. So there have been times when not only stocks but also the alternatives to stocks have offered negative real returns. But being a *q*-investor provides you with two crucial bonuses to limit the risks of being invested in stocks. It limits your losses, and it shortens the time that you have to wait before you are back into positive territory.

Chart 17.4 shows that *q* also has important effects on the upside. Because *q* allows you to get out when the market gets overblown, you benefit from the strength of stock returns in an upswing, without suffering nearly so much from the negative adjustments that usually follow. For this reason, the best that being a *q*-investor can offer you has been very much *better* than the best outcome with buy and hold.

The crucial thing about being a *q*-investor is to sell stocks when they get expensive. The most difficult thing about using *q* is having the willpower to do so. We deal with this problem in Part Five, together with the associated issue of where to invest when the time comes to get out of stocks. It should now be clear that the start of the new millennium[24] is just one of those times.

---

[23]Except that we have to restrict ourselves to looking at the first 77 years of the twentieth century, since this is the longest period over which we can reasonably compare the two. For this reason, the range for buy and hold looks somewhat, but not very different from the range shown in Chart 17.3, which was derived from the full two centuries' worth of data. The *q*-based strategy used is the Double Threshold Rule, described in Chapter 14.

[24]We should emphasize that the link with the new millennium is purely coincidental, and not because we are in any sense attracted to the magical qualities of numbers.

FIVE

SURVIVING THE BEAR MARKET

We saw in the final chapter of Part Three that using q can make stocks a far safer investment than they would otherwise be, since q can warn you of times to get out of stocks. We have also seen that, at the start of the new millennium, q is giving the clearest warning signal that it has given for 100 years. We anticipate a massive bear market. It may come quickly, or it may come slowly, but it will come.

The two chapters that make up Part Five provide some guidelines for survival. This is the appropriate word. In a bear market it is preserving wealth that matters, not trying to increase it. For this reason, the overwhelmingly important message of the two chapters is the same: Get out of stocks.

In Chapter 18 we examine the useful alternatives. Safe investments cannot offer good long-term returns; only risky assets can do this. Fortunately, bear markets are temporary phenomena, so you will not have to hold safe assets for the long term. It is, however, important to have the best investments during the bear market, so we weigh the pros and cons of the major alternatives.

In Chapter 19 we turn our attention to what you should *not* do with your money. We focus in particular on investment products that appear to offer the upside of investing in stocks, without the downside. As you might expect, we show that you would always be better off simply holding safe assets.

CHAPTER 18

What to Do with Your Money

SELL STOCKS, BUY ANYTHING?

One of us recently shared a conference platform with Paul Krugman of MIT. Professor Krugman was asked by a member of the audience if he felt that Asian stock markets might outperform the U.S. market over the next few years. His answer was straightforward: At current market valuations, he said, canned goods stored in a basement would offer better returns than the U.S. stock market.

We assume that Professor Krugman was not implying that the best strategy for investors would actually be to buy a house with a large basement and go shopping at Wal-Mart with a large truck. The serious part of his message was essentially the same as ours: The U.S. stock market at the end of the twentieth century was so overvalued that it was actually quite hard to think of any asset you could hold that might be expected to do *worse* than U.S. stocks.

So the crucial message of this chapter is this: Sell stocks. By far the most important thing you can do with your money is get it out of stocks. What you do with it then is a second-order problem. We think you can do better than canned goods, but canned goods would indeed be a very much better bet than the U.S. stock market.

TWO PROBLEMS WITH GETTING OUT OF STOCKS

Getting out of stocks sounds straightforward, but of course it is not. There are two major problems with selling that make it harder in practice than in principle. One problem is essentially psychological; the other is more practical. But investors must face up to both. The psychological problem is the one Mr. and Mrs. Giust had to face: the impossibility of knowing exactly the right time to sell. The practical problem is that when you realize stock market gains, you also have to face the prospect of an immediate tax bill.

Since no one can tell when a stock market will peak, the decision to sell stocks must be based on fundamental value considerations and will always appear risky in the short term. As we saw in the last chapter, if investors sell into a rising market, they are likely to find that they would have done better by waiting. On the other hand, if they try to sell once the stock market has turned, they will be constantly reminding themselves that they could have done better if only they had *not* waited.

In the major bear markets of the past, as we saw in Chapter 2, stock markets have fallen to less than half their previous highs; and many individual shares have performed very much worse, including a number of companies that have gone bankrupt. This means that once share prices start to fall—after, say, the first 20%—they still have another 40% or more to fall. It still pays to sell, but investors hate to realize losses. So long as shares are not sold, there is always the comforting thought that, as long as you do not realize the loss, it is "only on paper."

The truth is that paper losses are very real. In the modern world virtually all tokens of wealth are in paper form, if indeed they are not simply held on a computer somewhere. But whether the numbers are written in printer's ink or by laser on a computer's hard drive, they have the same meaning: The lower the number, the lower your real spending power.

Quite apart from these psychological problems, you will face difficulties of a financial kind, if you sell when prices are still high, because of the tax you have to pay on your capital gains.

There are, of course, ways to reduce the amount of tax you pay, and you need to consider them from your specific point of view. This is a book on stock market investment strategy; it is not a manual on how to pay less tax (there are already plenty of these).

All we wish to emphasize is that you should consider the tax consequences only after you have decided whether to buy or sell. Tax considerations always push investors toward making the wrong decisions. This is because shares are cheapest when they have fallen and when there is usually no tax disincentive to selling, and they are most expensive when the tax disincentive is greatest.

It may seem hard to have to share with the government the gains you have made by investing in stocks. Taxing capital gains is indeed arguably one of the government's more ill-advised and iniquitous activities. There are strong policy reasons why such taxes should be abolished.[1] But it is worth remembering that, as an investor, you face the problem only if you actually have some gains to share with the government. The purpose of investing in stocks is, after all, to realize the maximum possible gain and therefore the maximum possible liability to tax—even if the purpose of accountants and tax advisers is then to reduce the liability to a minimum.

If you wait long enough, however, you may well be able to reduce the government's share of your capital gain to zero, since zero times zero is zero. But, unless you really have it in for the government, this is unlikely to be much of a consolation. Less than 100% of something is always better than 100% of nothing.

BUY AND SELL, NOT BUY AND HOLD

Hard as it may be to summon up the courage to make the decision to sell, and to live with the tax implications of doing so, it is important to remind yourself that this is, after all, why you were holding the stocks in the first place. Real investors do not buy stocks in order to hold them; they buy stocks in order to sell them.

The key point is that shares are not held forever. Only the most altruistic people save and invest solely for the sake of their children or their pet charities. This is even more true to today

---

[1]One reason is the very process we have just described. Taxing capital gains tends to make stock market bubbles even more extreme than they otherwise would be, because it becomes so expensive to sell shares in bull markets. This in turn is very bad for the economy, which has always suffered badly in the past in the aftermath of stock market bubbles (an issue we focus on in Chapter 31).

than it used to be, with dividend yields at such low levels. Holding a portfolio of shares for the dividend income alone might once have been a reasonable strategy. Today it has become virtually pointless. Investors who hold shares rather than, for example, holding their money on deposit, sacrifice 70% of their income. Almost all the return you are going to get from the stock market will come from capital gains, and, by definition, you can realize these returns only by selling stocks.

The whole concept of buy and hold is therefore just a bull market myth. Since shares are bought in order to be sold, it is vital that they be sold at the right time, which is of course exactly what being a q-investor is about. As we have pointed out, there have been several 20-year bear markets and lots of 10-year ones. If you need money at any time over the next 10 years, you are likely to be better off by selling now than by waiting.

GOOD TIMES AND BAD TIMES TO SELL STOCKS

Although the problems investors face in getting out of overvalued markets may make it seem that there is never a good time to sell stocks, this is simply not so. In Chapter 11 we saw that there have very definitely been good and bad times to buy the stock market. Exactly the same applies when you come to sell stocks. Indeed, as we saw in the last chapter, deciding when to sell stocks is *the* crucial decision for a q-investor. Now may not seem like a good time to sell stocks, but if you decide to wait, you may find yourself selling at a very much worse time.

This is not only for the reason we outlined in Chapter 15—the very high probability that, on any day over the next ten years, stock prices will be lower, in real terms, than they are today. Nor is it just because, as we noted in Chapter 2, the high rates of return you have earned over the past ten years mean that the end of the twentieth century was almost certainly the very best time in the entire century to sell stocks. It is also because there is a great risk for many investors that the time when they most need money may well be not just a bad time to sell, but the very worst of times.

We have mentioned already the economic difficulties that accompany bad stock markets. We shall deal with these in more detail in Chapter 31, but we have already examined one very important aspect, when we looked at the ten best and worst years to buy stocks. Stock market weakness has almost always been associated with periods when the economy was in extremely poor shape. These are just the sorts of times when many people find themselves in need of ready cash. The unluckiest may find themselves out of a job, as businesses retrench. Even those who keep their jobs are likely to see pressure on their cash flow, as overtime payments and performance bonuses disappear. Small businesses may run into financial difficulties, and find banks unwilling to advance money. All these circumstances are likely to force many people, however unwillingly, into selling stocks.

It is very rare for stock markets to move from being overvalued to being fairly valued. Normally they move from being very expensive to being very cheap. We saw in Chapter 15 that such times have been the best times to *buy* stocks, since the very cheapness of the market has offered high prospective returns for the future. But, almost by definition, good times to buy stocks are always terrible times to sell them.[2]

Even if you are fortunate enough not to be forced into selling at the worst possible time, sitting on losses for the next ten years is bound to give a lot of heartache, with little compensation from dividend income, now that shares yield so little. Even if the stock market drops by 50%, the return on your much reduced wealth from that point onwards will be far less than you can get today from putting your money on deposit in the bank. Moving into cash deposits instead would have the great added benefit of avoiding the pain of seeing your wealth cut in half.

Under current conditions, when stocks are not only expensive but more so than ever before, there is no sensible alternative to selling. Stocks are simply going to be a bad investment for many, many years ahead. Of course, once q indicates that the market is again fairly valued, it will be time to reconsider investing in stocks.

---

[2]It is no coincidence that markets tend to be cheap just when many investors want to go liquid. It should not be too hard to see that this in turn must help drive prices down. We show in Chapter 30 that, after the collapse of the Tokyo market, Japanese investors have shifted overwhelmingly from stocks into liquid assets, thus helping drive the market yet further down.

But this is most unlikely to happen until the market has first fallen to half, or less than half, its current level.

Our recommendation that you simply get out of stocks may sound harsh, since it must surely be true that some shares will go up over the next few years. But the consolation this might appear to offer is illusory. We saw in Chapter 10 that stock picking is far less important, for the average investor, than what is happening to the stock market as a whole. This is probably all the more true in bear markets. If you look back at Chart 10.1, you will see that, four years after the peak in 1973, not a single individual stock of the ten we examined had yielded a positive real return; and a full ten years later half were still showing losses. Of course, it is possible that a lucky few shares may swim hard enough against the tide of the next bear market to offer passable returns, but the experience of the past suggests that there is unlikely to be more than a handful of these. Needless to say, it is even more improbable that anyone could predict now which ones they will be.

WHAT SHOULD YOU BUY INSTEAD?

If you sell stocks, what should you hold instead? We have already pointed out that this question must be less crucial than the decision to sell stocks. We saw in earlier chapters that, in normal circumstances, the long-term investor needs to hold stocks most of the time in order to get decent long-run returns.[3] At times like the present, however, when stocks offer such poor prospective returns, the primary aim is to preserve, rather than add to, the not inconsiderable gains earned in the good years of the bull market. But moving out of stocks means moving into less risky assets, which must offer lower long-run returns.

Nonetheless, it is worth looking briefly at the available options once you have sold stocks. You can do better, if not necessarily very much better, than buy the canned goods that Paul Krugman recommended. There are really two options open to you if you want to preserve your wealth, and earn a reasonable re-

---

[3]Other assets, such as property, which can give comparable long-term returns to stocks with, of course, comparable risks, usually require a greater degree of specialist expertise than is needed for stock market investors.

turn. You can hold alternative financial assets, such as bonds or bank deposits; or you can invest in real assets, which for most people in practice means real estate.

BONDS OR BANK DEPOSITS?

If you opt for bonds or bank deposits, you can expect relatively safe but relatively low returns over the next few years, simply because there is always a trade-off between risk and return. Chart 18.1 shows how investors holding bonds or cash have fared since 1926.[4]

This chart is informative, but needs careful interpretation. The most obvious feature is that cash on deposit normally, as now,

CHART 18.1

Yields on Bonds and Cash Since 1926

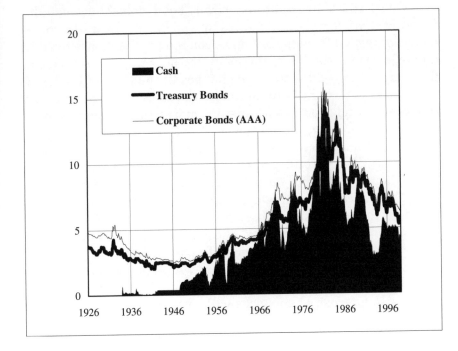

---

[4]We proxy this, as before, by the return on Treasury bills.

offers lower yields than government bonds, and that these in turn offer lower yields than corporate bonds. Of course, since these are at least reasonably efficient financial markets, you are getting what you pay for. The lower yields reflect lower risk. These risks are of two types, both of which are potentially significant for the investor who has sold stocks and is looking for a reasonably safe haven. They are:

- Volatility risk
- Default risk

Bonds share volatility risk with stocks, but to a lesser degree. As with stocks, the return on bonds is partly from income and partly from capital gains or losses. But the return on bonds is much less risky for two reasons. The first is that the income element is so much more important relative to changes in capital values. The second is that bonds are usually repayable at par, so that investors know in advance how much they will receive when the bond is repaid on maturity.

Chart 18.1 shows that historically bond yields[5] have usually followed short-term interest rates up and down, albeit in a somewhat dampened fashion. But since coupon payments are fixed in dollar terms for the life of the bond, the only way the return can differ from the yield is through changes in the price of the bond. The longer before the bond matures, the more its price will tend to move around. Bonds with distant maturities, known as long-term bonds, are thus more volatile than those with short maturities. They therefore tend to have higher yields, but are of course more risky. The volatility of the bond return is distinctly lower than that of stocks, but nonetheless can be quite significant.

The choice between bonds and cash requires you, as usual, to weigh the merits of risk and return. One important consideration is whether there is a risk, of the type referred to above, that you may need to liquidate some of your wealth in a cash flow crisis. Another, of course, is that you will at some point need to have funds readily available to reinvest in stocks. It is no more possible to forecast when stocks will bottom than it is to forecast

---

[5]Defined, roughly, as the interest or "coupon" payments you receive in dollar terms, as a percentage of the dollar price of the bond.

when they will peak. Investors who are temporarily out of the market should therefore remember that they are not long-term bond investors. The natural home for the money of investors who are out of the stock market is thus cash, since this provides the flexibility to get back into stocks at any time.

There is, of course, an element of uncertainty about the real value of bonds and cash during periods of inflation. These days, however, even this uncertainty can be avoided by investing in indexed bonds, which guarantee an upgrade in both coupon and capital in line with the Consumer Price Index. We shall come back to the important issue of inflation soon.

To compensate for their short-run volatility, bonds typically pay a higher yield than cash deposits, which face no such risk. Indeed, when government bonds are compared with short-term cash instruments that are similarly free of default risk, this is the *only* reason why returns differ. However, in many instances there is another element in yields, which is effectively compensation for the risk of default.

Chart 18.1 shows that even corporate bonds rated AAA, to which only the very biggest and safest corporations can aspire, have historically given a yield of around ¾% per annum more than government bonds. The difference in return is clearly related to the degree of perceived risk. Thus BAA-rated bonds have typically yielded an additional 1% per annum compared with AAA-rated bonds, and so forth, with yields rising steadily right up to the junkiest of junk bonds. In the reasonably transparent corporate bond market, as usual you get what you pay for. The higher yield reflects additional risk.[6]

There is a related point worth bearing in mind when you look at other places to put your money. Banks can fail. They are especially prone to fail in the aftermath of major stock market collapses. If you put your money into a bank that is part of the federal deposit insurance system, then up to $100,000 of each deposit is guaranteed; so as long as you stay within this limit, you will suffer only minor inconvenience if your bank does fail.

---

[6]Although we characterize this as default risk, it is quite probable that a significant part of the premium of corporate over government bonds also reflects liquidity risk, since there is a lot less trade in a given corporate bond than in government bonds of comparable maturity.

But beware of banks or money market accounts that offer higher rates of interest, apparently without any strings attached. The law of risk and return works pretty well in reverse. If a financial instrument offers a high return, it is at least a reasonable working hypothesis that this is a riskier place to put your money. So read the small print carefully.

HOW MUCH (OR HOW LITTLE) TO EXPECT

Chart 18.1 is informative in terms of the comparison *between* cash on deposit and bonds. It is a lot less informative in terms of real returns, since it ignores inflation. Chart 18.2 rectifies this, by looking at real yields on government bonds and bank deposits over the same time period.

We have noted in previous chapters that, taken as a whole, the twentieth century was not particularly good for either bonds or cash on deposit. Chart 18.2 makes it clear that this poor performance was due in large part to the decades following World War II, when nominal interest rates barely kept pace with inflation, so that real yields were close to or, for some periods, well below zero.

The chart also makes it clear that by the close of the century, both bonds and bank deposits were offering yields that, in real terms, were really quite respectable compared with most of the postwar era. In this respect, therefore, the aftermath of the bubble of the 1990s is almost certainly going to be distinctly better, for those who are standing on the sidelines, than the last major bear market in the 1970s. Then, both bonds and cash did better than stocks, but did not do well. There were some periods when, with real yields negative, it was simply impossible to avoid losing money. The only consolation, and a very important one, for investors holding cash was that even though they were losing money in real terms, they were certainly not losing it in the spectacular manner of those who were holding stocks.

Things are very unlikely to be so bad this time around, for two reasons.

The first reason is that, even if inflation does revive in the coming years, there is now quite a lot of evidence that the Federal Reserve, like most central banks, seems to have learned the

CHART 18.2

Real Yields* on Bonds and Cash Since 1926

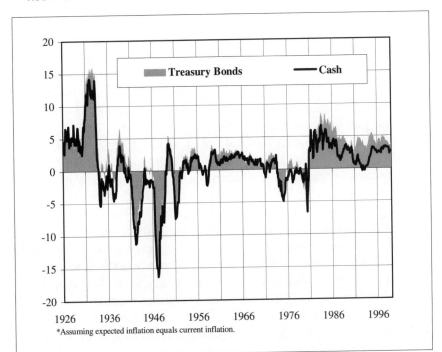

*Assuming expected inflation equals current inflation.

lessons of the 1970s, when, effectively, most of them fell asleep at the wheel. They forgot that the way to keep inflation from escalating is not just to push interest rates up when inflation goes up but, crucially, to raise rates by *more* than inflation rises. The key is to ensure that real as well as nominal interest rates rise. In the end, this policy is good for the whole economy, since it results in more stable inflation. We hope that central banks have learned this lesson well. If they have, it is clearly good news for the investor holding bonds or cash on deposit.

The prime example is the experience of Germany in the 1970s. The oil price shocks that hit the United States then hit Germany in just the same way, but German inflation, unlike that in the United States , never even rose to double figures. The reason was that the Bundesbank raised rates aggressively as soon as inflation picked up. The increase was good for German inflation; but it was also good for German savers, since for them real interest rates never once went negative.

The Bundesbank is now the ghost of its former self, as the European Central Bank takes over its central role in Europe, but its example lives on. Over the past couple of decades, the Federal Reserve, like central banks the world over, has increasingly responded to inflation in the way the Bundesbank always used to. As a result, real interest rates have almost invariably been positive. The only times they have moved close to zero have been when inflation has been low, not high.

Indeed, a case can be made that a major risk at present is not of inflation, but of *falling* prices. This is almost certainly bad news for the economy, but presents a second reason why the experience of standing on the sidelines of the stock market may not be too painful an experience. If price inflation does turn to price *de*flation, it may be much more like the experience of the 1930s than that of the 1970s. The 1930s was a pretty gruesome decade for most Americans, but not for all. Those who owned government bonds, or had cash in those banks that did not fail, did pretty well. Even when, as Chart 18.1 shows, short-term interest rates fell to zero, it was still a good time for this group of investors, since with falling prices, even a zero nominal rate of interest was a positive rate in real terms.

Charts 18.3 and 18.4 show the contrast between the two bear markets. Both show what would have happened to the real value of a notional $1 investment in stocks, cash, or bonds at the peak of the market (1929 in Chart 18.3 and 1968 in Chart 18.4).

Both periods show that it took returns on stocks around 20 years to catch up with returns on cash on deposit. But there were also important differences between the two periods. In the inflationary 1970s investors in cash on deposit or in bonds barely held on to the real value of their wealth, and indeed saw their wealth fall toward the end of the decade. In the deflationary 1930s, they would have prospered. Bond investors doubled the real value of their wealth over the course of the Great Depression.

Because there is a significant risk of deflation in the next recession, the coming bear market might resemble that of the 1930s more than the 1970s. Of course, there is no guarantee of this. Inflation may neither pick up nor become significantly nega-

CHART 18.3

Total Real Returns in the 1930s Bear Market...

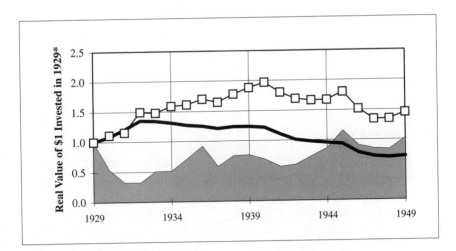

CHART 18.4

...And the 1970s Bear Market

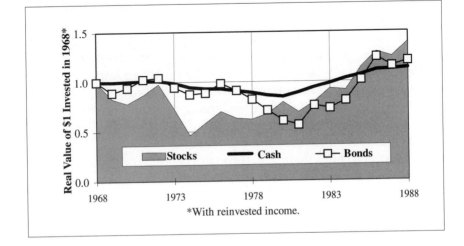

*With reinvested income.

tive, but simply remain subdued. In these circumstances, it is likely that the Federal Reserve, just like the Bank of Japan in recent years, would push short-term rates down very close to zero. If inflation were also zero, you would be at little risk of actually losing money if you held cash on deposit, but neither would you be making any. If you are worried about this latter possibility, and do not expect to be cashing in your investments in a hurry, then locking into bonds at current yields may make sense.

REAL ASSETS

For investors who are prepared to reassess their portfolios from a longer-term view, q provides a different perspective. The fact that q is so high at present means that stock prices are at a ridiculous level, compared with the underlying assets that firms own. Looking at this from the other way round, the implication is that these physical assets are, at least in relative terms, cheap compared with the stock market.

Unfortunately, most individual investors cannot go out and arbitrage this difference by buying the sort of capital assets that large corporations use. But they can choose to put a larger share of their wealth into real estate, in the form of either housing or real estate investment trusts (REITs).

The downside of this option is that, when stock markets fall, they tend to pull other asset prices, including real estate, with them. This phenomenon has been particularly marked in the recent past in Japan, where land prices and stock prices have fallen in tandem over the past decade. Any adjustment in the United States is unlikely to be anywhere near as sharp, since, in most parts of the USA, real estate prices do not nearly approach the ludicrously inflated level seen in Japan at the height of the Tokyo bubble. Nonetheless, the possibility of losses on real estate investments cannot be ignored.

The moral here is simple. If you are currently hesitating about buying a larger or a smaller property, and cashing in stock market investments would enable you to buy the larger one, this might seem like a pretty good idea. But buy a house that you actually want to live in. Unlike stocks, which, as we have noted, no sane investor would hold for the income alone, real estate offers tangible returns. There may not be pecuniary returns in terms of a capital gain on your investment, but you still get a very real "income" from the services the house provides.

ONE FINAL THING YOU COULD DO WITH YOUR MONEY

We have one other suggestion on what to do with your money that comes straight out of any introductory textbook on economics. As we have already noted, the ultimate reason to hold any investment is to sell it, and spend the proceeds. Low returns today mean that there is a lower reward to holding onto your money and spending it tomorrow. Indeed, if you are really unlucky, and real returns on cash on deposit go even mildly negative, you will be penalized, rather than rewarded, for saving.

Economics textbooks propose that, when saving is not well rewarded, the natural response is to save less, and simply spend more. That is, after all, what you've been saving for all these years. As an added incentive, those who have wealth to spend are going to get very good bargains, since the economy is likely to be on the rocks. You may even be doing the economy a favor as well.

19

What Not to Do with Your Money

DON'T BUY STOCKS

We started the last chapter by saying that by far the most important thing to do was to sell stocks, and that the question of what you do with your money instead is a second-order problem. At the risk of being repetitive, we start this chapter with an equally simply message: Do *not* put your money into stocks.

This may look like just the same message, and in large part it is, although it is such an important message that we offer no apology for repeating it. But there is also a new element in this message, which is more subtle: Do not take your money out of the stock market only to put it back in again. We shall see that this is actually easier to do than you might think. Unfortunately, explaining why may on occasion take us into areas of investing that are slightly more technical than most of what we have covered so far. We shall, however, try to keep the discussion as simple as possible.

But before we do so, we need to issue a very important warning.

DON'T TRUST THE PROFESSIONALS

Trust your own judgment. On the question of whether to hold stocks, it is unwise to put any trust in the advice of stockbrokers and investment managers. We should stress that we do not give this advice to be unkind to people in the investment business. We are just pointing out that they have a massive conflict of interest that gets in the way of acting in their clients' best interest. Indeed, if there were not such a strong conflict of interest, the stock market would not be where it is today, since most fund managers would have switched the funds they handle out of the stock market a long time ago.

The conflict of interest exists between the interests of the fund management businesses and the interests of their clients. As we have pointed out earlier in this book, even at today's exceptionally overvalued level, the chances of the market falling over the next year are only around two in three, although the odds are much higher over the next five to ten years. The whole purpose of this book is to point out that, given such a balance of probabilities, any sensible investor would switch out of stocks. If investment managers were acting in the best interests of their clients, this is what they would being doing too.

From the viewpoint of fund managers, however, things look very different. Their businesses are highly valued by the stock market. They are valued in terms of the amount of money they manage rather than the capital invested in the business. Goodwill is a huge factor for fund managers, and any manager who reduces that goodwill is likely to lose his or her job very quickly.

For fund managers, therefore, the risks of going liquid are simply too high. If they sell and the stock market goes up, they will appear to have a bad performance record, since other fund managers will outperform them. Investors will not give them money to manage and they may well lose their jobs. Remember that a probability of roughly two thirds that the market will fall over the next 12 months implies a probability of one third that it will continue to rise. This is too big a risk for most fund managers to take. If, on the other hand, they stay in stocks and the market does go down, the chances are that they will perform no worse than their competitors. So they stay in stocks, against the better interest of their clients.

The overvaluation of the stock market is not a secret. The reason fund managers do not sell is not because they believe that the market is reasonably valued, but because they can't take the risks involved. This is not their fault.[7] If it is anyone's fault, it is the fault of the average investor, who judges the performance of fund managers over too short a period of time. The behavior of the average investor means that a sensible individual investor cannot delegate the key investment decision to fund managers. The decision whether to stay in stocks cannot be taken on investors' behalf by fund managers. Their interests are too deeply in conflict with investors' interests, and investors need to recognize this fact.

Of course, lots of people, particularly stockbrokers, deny that shares are expensive. Stockbrokers are, however, paid for selling shares, not for the objectivity of their advice. As usual, people get what they pay for. Stock markets tend to dry up when they are falling, so that even though any broker who did predict the bear market might get a better share of the business when it arrives, there would not be much business to get. Since no one can predict market timing with any precision, and there is much more business in bull markets than in bear markets, there is little percentage for brokers in ever being bearish. The fact that, nonetheless, some stockbrokers are at least sometimes bearish is cheering, and we like to think that it reflects credit on them.

Because of these conflicts of interest, the advice of stockbrokers and fund managers is always biased against getting out of stocks. Ultimately you yourself have to make the fundamental decision on whether to hold stocks. To make good decisions you need good information, which is what this book is about.

Of course, you are bound to read other arguments that the stock market is fundamentally attractive. If you do come across such claims, we suggest that you ask yourself two key questions:

- How does the bullish view deal with the case we present in this book? The most common procedure is simply to ignore the sorts of arguments we offer.

---

[7]Which may not prevent people from thinking it is. We suspect that one of the consequences of the coming bear market is that a lot of investors are going to be blaming other people for their misfortunes. Only the lawyers will benefit from the rash of lawsuits, which we can safely predict will be a major growth industry in the bear market.

- Can you really expect the person providing the advice to do so in an unbiased way? If their motivation is suspect, their arguments are likely to be suspect too.

So our key message is that you have to rely on your own common sense. It is pretty much certain that, until the market begins to fall in earnest, most other investors will not do so. For the informed investor, this is good news. It is obviously impossible for investors in general to sell stocks, since there would be no buyers to buy from them. Only a small minority of the lucky and thoughtful, who think for themselves, will get out of stocks before the coming massive bear market. They should be thankful that there are others less thoughtful than themselves who are prepared to take the stocks off their hands.

Since you are going to find it hard to come across anyone who will give you informed and unbiased advice, the rest of this chapter is devoted to a few health warnings on what not to do if, as we hope, you finally make the decision to get out of stocks.

STOCKS WITHOUT RISK?

Here is a short moral tale. It may seem like a digression, but it is not.

In the early 1980s, just as the current bull market was beginning to build steam, the finance industry, which is full of exceptionally clever people, produced a wonderful new idea. Investors could hold stocks, with barely any risk of losing money. The idea was that, through automated buy-and-sell programs, pension fund portfolios could become virtually one-way bets. Thus was "portfolio insurance" invented.

Portfolio insurance was a prime example of that rare but interesting combination: an exceptionally clever idea that is at the same time an exceptionally stupid idea. The consensus view is that portfolio insurance died on October 19, 1987, when very large numbers of computer sell orders encountered the minor obstacle alluded to above: that it is hard for everybody to be selling stocks at the same time. Someone has to be buying them. If no one or nearly no one wants to buy stocks, the market falls off a cliff, and that is exactly what happened.

The computer programs that implemented portfolio insurance were not ready for this. The fundamental flaw in portfolio insurance was that prices had to be "continuous" in order for it to work. Here is how portfolio insurance was supposed to operate. Fund managers decided the maximum loss (say, 10%) that they were prepared to accept. If the market started to fall, the computer programs were supposed to "rebalance" the portfolio away from stocks, toward cash, to an ever increasing extent, as the loss on the portfolio increased toward the notional maximum loss.

In so doing, the portfolio insurance programs were of course selling stocks into a falling market. Whether this response added to the severity of the fall is still a subject of earnest debate among economists. But what is certain is that the programs simply did not fulfill their intended purpose. The market fell too fast for even automated trades to keep up. The wonderful idea had failed dismally, and as a result the words "portfolio" and "insurance" are rarely mentioned in the same breath around Wall Street these days.

Why are we telling you this story? Because, while the consensus view is that portfolio insurance is dead, in reality it is alive and well and living in the options market. Already there are signs that the wonders of portfolio insurance via the options market are being offered to ordinary investors. As perceptions of overvaluation grow, you are likely to come across increasing numbers of such offers.

PORTFOLIO INSURANCE VIA OPTIONS?

From the point of view of the individual investor, buying portfolio insurance via the options market does have some significant advantages over automated buy-and-sell programs, but it is still fundamentally the same thing. Realizing this is key to understanding the problem to which options give rise. Options might seem like a useful alternative to simply getting out of stocks, but in reality they are not. The significant advantage of options is that you, the investor, pass on all the risk associated with portfolio insurance to an options dealer. The downside is the price you have to pay for doing so.

Let's look at how portfolio insurance via the options market might work. Suppose, contrary to our advice, you do not sell your stocks. But you are worried about the prognosis for the market we have presented, so you want to protect yourself against the sorts of losses we are talking about. The options market can offer you this kind of protection, albeit at a price.

The options business is awash with highly complex products, with highly complex properties, often labeled with Greek letters like σ, Δ, Γ, and μ. We have already mentioned that there are exceptionally clever people working in the finance industry. Do not worry, however. You do not need to understand continuous time stochastic calculus to grasp our arguments. A simple example will do.

If you wanted to insure yourself pretty much completely against any losses on your portfolio, you could, for example, buy an "at the money put" option on the S&P 500, with a face value equal to the current value of your portfolio. A put option gives you the notional right to sell the portfolio represented by the S&P 500 at a particular price, the "exercise price." If your option is, as in our example, "at the money," then the exercise price is simply whatever level the S&P 500 is on the day you buy the put.

Assuming your portfolio tracks the S&P 500 reasonably well, if you decide to sell your stocks after the market has fallen by, say, 30%, then by a combination of selling your actual stocks and cashing in your put, you can get back, in total, pretty much exactly what your portfolio was worth on the day you bought the put.[8] You do indeed have a one-way bet.

But only at a price, of course. Put options do not come for free. The reason why we told you the story about portfolio insurance is that it is important to understand that if you buy options, you are paying an options dealer to carry out your portfolio insurance for you. There are two important implications of this fact.

First, the options dealer has to carry the risk involved, and make a profit on top, so you are going to pay through the nose for the insurance. At the end of the 1990s, an at-the-money put of this type, with a maturity of one year, would have cost you around

---

[8]Actually, if you sell before your option expires, you will get slightly more, since someone else can continue to use the protection your option provides. Note also that in principle you could hedge your actual portfolio more precisely, since put options are also available on most major individual stocks. But, as we saw in Chapter 10, most reasonably well-diversified portfolios end up looking pretty similar to a much broader basket of stocks, so this degree of precise protection would be nearly redundant.

$7\frac{1}{2}\%$ of the value of your portfolio. This means that to give your-self this kind of coverage, you would have to make a return of that amount per annum from your portfolio simply to break even, and a return of roughly 12% simply to match what you would get from holding cash on deposit. We have already shown that the historic average return on a stock portfolio is only around $6\frac{1}{2}\%$ in real terms, before costs. Thus, even in average circumstances, by far the most likely outcome is that, having paid for your option, you would not make enough of a return to outperform cash. In the current, far-from-average circumstances, you are most likely to underperform cash by a wide margin, and the chances of doing even marginally better than cash are exceedingly slim.

Of course, you *have* limited your losses. If your put is "at the money," as in our example, you cannot be any worse off than the amount you paid for the put in the first place: Your losses cannot therefore be more than around $7\frac{1}{2}\%$ per annum. But, for the sake of this limited peace of mind, you have paid a high price and are, in effect, taking a bet that the market will continue to rise very sharply, by enough to make you better off than cash. So you have certainly not removed all the risk involved in stocks; you have merely contained it.

Because such a strategy is so expensive, it is more common to buy puts that are "out of the money," meaning that they do not give you any protection against losses unless the market falls by a given amount—say, 10% or 20%. But the same principles apply. As usual, of course, you get what you pay for. You may pay a lower price, but you get a lower level of protection.

A second reason to remember the lessons of portfolio insur-ance is this. While options dealers are apparently offering you a cast-iron guarantee, they are doing so by using exactly the same techniques of portfolio insurance as were used so widely before 1987. These safeguards broke down then, and may well break down again. We therefore expect that, in a major bear market, there is likely to be a spate of bankruptcies in the options indus-try that may well make the experiences of Barings, Long Term Credit Management, and others look like a church picnic.[9] The

---

[9]We first produced evidence on this issue in a report to Smithers & Co. clients ("Stock Options: An Example of Catastrophe Myopia"), the main points of which were summarized in *Barron's* on November 24, 1998 ("Courting Catastrophe" by Kathryn M. Welling).

moral here is that, if you absolutely must buy puts, at least make sure you buy them from a firm that is "too big to fail."

We hope, however, that by now we have convinced you that you can avoid this problem by simply not buying options at all, and protecting your portfolio in the simplest possible way: by selling stocks.

DON'T PUT YOUR MONEY BACK INTO STOCKS: INVISIBLE OPTIONS

We warned you at the outset of this chapter against taking your money out of stocks, only to put it back in again. One way you might be tempted to do this is by putting your money into a fund that makes you promises of protection along the same lines as we have described above. If you are offered a product that claims to invest in stocks, but are told that the value of your investment "can only go up," or one that offers to limit your downside losses, you are in effect being offered a pretty standard stock portfolio, together with an "invisible option."

The option may be invisible, but you are still paying for it. The only way such a fund can genuinely offer such protection is by buying put options on your behalf. They are going to have to pay all the costs we described above, and on top of that you are going to have to pay a further slice of any return you get for the dubious privilege of having your investments managed. The only way that such an offer is going to add up, therefore, is if the fund produces dismal returns, and probably charges you as many hidden fees as it can on top. So, as usual, read the small print very, very carefully. Then throw the fund brochure in the wastebasket, and keep your money in a genuinely safe place.

DON'T PUT YOUR MONEY BACK INTO STOCKS: "MARKET-NEUTRAL" FUNDS

Another apparent alternative to the straightforward stock portfolio is a "market-neutral" fund. Such a fund still invests in stocks, and makes no claim to avoid risk. The only claim is that the fund is uncorrelated with the market as a whole. In other words, although, as we have noted, most reasonably diversified portfolios pretty much follow the market indices up and down, such funds do not. They are still risky portfolios, but they do not share the "systemic" risk of the market. Such a fund might appear to be offering a more credible alternative, since it does at least meet the commonsense condition that you cannot get a reasonable return without risk. But again, unfortunately, this advantage will in most cases be more apparent than real.

How do such funds work? Does the existence of market-neutral funds offer evidence against our claim that any well-diversified portfolio looks pretty much like the market as a whole, and hence shares the same "systemic" risk? No it does not, but unfortunately explaining why is a little tricky. Market-neutral funds get around the problem by in effect being made up of two different funds: one "long," the other "short."

"Long" simply means you hold something as an *asset*, as in any standard portfolio. "Short" however, means you hold it as a *liability*. Most people can be "short" only in two ways: Either they can owe cash to the bank as an overdraft or they can owe it via a mortgage, which is in effect a bond, only it is "issued" by an individual who normally puts up a house as security. But those in the finance industry can in principle be "short" of any kind of asset, including stocks.

If a fund were invested in short and long portfolios of approximately equal size, then it would indeed be market-neutral. When the market fell, for example, its long portfolio (the stocks it actually owned) would fall in value, but so would its short portfolio (the stocks it *owed*), leaving the overall value of the fund (equal to the long *minus* the short portfolio) unchanged. The same process would apply if the market rose.

Of course, if a fund actually had long and short portfolios of equal size, it would also have net assets of zero, so you could not actually invest in it.[10] For this reason, the long portfolio has to be larger, so that the fund has positive net assets. Such a fund can still be market-neutral, however, in one of two possible ways. It can hold cash equal to its net asset value, or it can buy stocks for its long portfolio that have a less-than-average degree of sensitivity to market changes, in contrast to the stocks in its short

---

[10]A fund with zero net assets would in any case not be allowed by regulators to engage in borrowing, and hence to have a short portfolio at all.

portfolio, which are picked for their greater-than-average sensitivity.[11]

Of course, as usual, there has to be a catch. The catch in this case is pretty obvious when you think about it. Unless market-neutral fund managers do better on average than other investors, they will on average earn the same returns, before costs, as cash on deposit, and after costs they will actually do worse.

To see why, for simplicity, think about the case where the short and long portfolios are of identical size, and net assets are invested in cash. If market-neutral fund managers are averagely good at picking stocks for the long and short portfolios, then both portfolios should yield something close to the return on the market as a whole. The net return on the two portfolios would therefore be roughly zero, and the return on the fund as a whole would be simply the cash return on the fund's net assets.[12] After deducting the fund's not inconsiderable costs, you would therefore be considerably better off simply putting your money on deposit.

So the only way a market-neutral fund can possibly expect to offer you reasonable returns is if the people who manage it are better than average at picking the stocks that go into their portfolios. But then we are back in Lake Wobegon, where all the children are above average. Some market-neutral funds may offer reasonable returns, either by skill or (more likely) by good luck. But the usual problem arises: You are not going to be able to tell the bad from the good until it is too late. Since the average market-neutral fund is likely to offer very poor, or even negative returns, after costs, the moral is simple: Do not take your money out of stocks, only to put it back in via market-neutral funds.

---

[11]Finding stocks in these two categories is not especially hard: There are well-established techniques, which do not rely at all on any skill at stock picking. In the standard terminology, the stocks in the long portfolio should have a low beta, and those in the short portfolio should have a high beta.

[12]The same will apply even when the long portfolio is larger than the short portfolio, since the stocks it holds will be less sensitive to the market, and will therefore on average pay lower returns, than those in the short portfolio.

DON'T PUT YOUR MONEY BACK INTO STOCKS: OVERSEAS MARKETS

If you cannot bear the idea of putting your money only in safe assets, is there a chance of getting good returns by looking beyond the U.S. market? The answer to this question is only slightly more equivocal. It is not really a sensible strategy; but if you simply cannot bring yourself to get out of stocks, investing in overseas markets is probably the least bad alternative. The major reason it is not a good alternative is that there is a very real danger that switching your investments into overseas markets is, again, just like putting money back into the U.S. market.

It is probably the case that few major markets at the end of the 1990s were as overvalued as Wall Street; but equally very few, if any, were offering fair value. This situation is unlikely to change for a while. Furthermore, it is a pretty well-established fact that, when the U.S. market moves sharply, either up or down, it tends to pull other major markets with it, so that even those markets that might be offering somewhat better value are unlikely to be good prospects. Indeed, in modern integrated markets, you can think of any given country's stock market as behaving pretty much like a single share in the U.S. market. In the short term, movements in most markets are likely to be dominated by what happens on Wall Street.

You should also bear in mind that when you invest in overseas markets you face an additional source of risk from movements in exchange rates; and if there is anything more volatile than the stock market, it is the foreign exchange market.

Of course, as with individual stocks, there are bound to be some exceptions: markets that manage to resist the downward pull of Wall Street and, if you are really lucky, that even offer you a bonus via exchange rate movements. The problem is, again, that it is extremely hard to know which markets are worthwhile, and which will prove disastrous.

Nonetheless, the reason why investing in overseas stock markets is probably the least bad alternative is this: If you can invest in a bunch of markets that are, on average, less overvalued than Wall Street, your long-run return should at least be nearer to the sort of return that stocks have yielded historically in the United States. The problem is that, in general, the more divorced a market is from Wall Street, the less reliable are any valuation criteria you can get on that market. In particular, q can be calculated only for a very few overseas markets (all of which are currently overvalued). If you really intend to take a value-based approach to investing in overseas markets, you should read very carefully the material on alternative indicators of value (see Part Six) and be aware that the problems with using such indicators are likely to be the more extreme, the more obscure is the market you are dealing with.

Although we continue to stress that we do not recommend overseas investment, if you simply must do so, it is worth bearing in mind the main lesson of the good years to buy stocks in the twentieth century, which we learned in Chapter 11. Specifically, good years to buy stocks all appeared to be terrible at the time. Hence it *may* make sense, as a long-run investment, to go for markets that pretty much everyone agrees look like basket cases.[13] We should stress, however, that such investments must also, almost by definition, be significantly riskier, sometimes by several orders of magnitude, than investing in major markets.

Of course, as a final reminder, since it is perfectly possible that *all* overseas markets are to some extent overvalued, we would much prefer you to put all your wealth, not just a substantial fraction, into safe assets.

SURVIVING THE BEAR MARKET, AND BEYOND

By now our message should be very clear. What you should do is sell stocks. What you should not do is buy stocks. In following this policy you will not get dramatic returns, but you will avoid dramatic losses. Investments that appear to offer you the chance of the former, without the risk of the latter, are a logical impossibility. You get what you pay for.

Of course, as the title of this part of the book makes clear, this is a just a strategy for surviving during the bear market. It is

---

[13]We shall resist the temptation to name names, since one week's basket case is the following week's favorite investment opportunity—and by then the moment to get into that particular market is past.

clearly not a viable longer-term strategy. In the end, if you are a long-term investor, wanting reasonable returns, you are going to move back into stocks. Ideally you will do so in what will still *appear* to be a bear market. Stocks will probably appear to be a dreadful prospect, and will be deeply unfashionable. But if you are a value-based investor, you will be in a position to know that this is exactly the time to buy stocks again. The next part of the book is designed to make clear why, if you are a value investor, this must mean that you are a q-investor.

SIX

HOW TO VALUE THE STOCK MARKET

We hope that by now you are convinced of the case for q, which we have presented as the only valid way to value the stock market. This approach has two advantages. It has served to keep the arguments compact, and it is also fundamentally correct. However, we have not yet provided a full case in support of this latter point. We shall now seek to do so in a more thorough way, and also to show why other approaches fail to provide valid measures of value.

We start with a chapter that addresses the key issues of principle. It sets out the four key tests that any measure of value must satisfy. We then assess how the various claimants to being measures of value stand up to these tests. We show why they all fail, and how q works.

In two final chapters, we draw together the various threads. We first show that if adjustments could be made to eliminate the flaws in the more sensible alternatives, they would end up looking just like q. They become "q-equivalent." We then look at q in the context of the much used, but, alas, also much *mis*used Dividend Discount Model.

CHAPTER 20

How to Value the Stock Market: Four Key Tests for Any Indicator of Value

THE FUNDAMENTAL PRINCIPLES

We saw in Chapter 17 that both the buy-and-hold strategy and the random walk model of stock prices have a common flaw. Neither makes sense if it is possible to value stock markets. We also showed that markets are less risky than the random walk model implies, and that this lowered risk provides a strong case that stock markets can be valued. Risks are reduced because prices are pulled back toward their value when they get out of line. This of course could not happen without value and price often being very different.

Investors need to be able to measure value as well as know that it exists, or their knowledge will have little practical use. They must therefore be able to judge the merits of different indicators. In this chapter we shall examine the four key properties that are needed for a given indicator to be a valid measure of value. In subsequent chapters we show that q passes these tests, where other indicators fail.

This may come as a surprise, since q is much less commonly quoted by stockbrokers or the financial press than other indicators of value, which we shall show to be inadequate. The preference for faulty criteria over a sound one is, however, readily understandable: q has two characteristics that render it unsuitable for use by stockbrokers.

The first is that q is virtually useless as a guide to the short-term market movements that stockbrokers are asked to forecast. As we have already mentioned, this is in fact a virtue of q, not a defect. Indeed, this feature is a necessary condition for any useful indicator of value. There can be no logical short-term guides to market movements. If there were, the market would preempt them. Any criterion designed to make such predictions must therefore be nonsense and q is not such a criterion.

The second is that q can show that markets are overpriced for prolonged periods of time. This, we have seen, is good news for investors, since it can help them preserve their wealth. But it can seriously damage the incomes of stockbrokers, since investors don't buy shares if they think they will lose money. It is therefore not surprising that stockbrokers sedulously ignore q and much of the other information about value provided in this book.[1]

THE NEED FOR AN OBJECTIVE STANDARD

If someone says, "I think the market is overvalued by 50%," this could simply be an expression of opinion, like saying that red will come up rather than black at the next spin of a roulette wheel. Neither statement, however, is very interesting and it is certainly no use to anyone else. If a statement about value is to be useful, it must be objective. This means that it must not be just the view of the person who holds it, but the view that any sensible person would hold who understands what value means and has the necessary information. If one person says that the stock market is overvalued, and another says it is undervalued, this is not just a matter of opinion: One of them is wrong.

We are making this sort of claim. We are not expressing an opinion about the stock market; we are saying that if our argument is correct, any sensible person who understands it and looks at the data will arrive at the same conclusion. We cannot sustain this claim unless we can show that our argument stands up to

---

[1]Stockbrokers do not always ignore q. In Chapter 30 we shall deal with some of the ways in which arguments for q are either misunderstood or misrepresented (and frequently both at the same time).

some pretty rigorous tests. In order to test something you need to know both what it is you are testing and what the relevant tests are. We need therefore to identify the crucial features that any criterion of value must have and the tests that it must pass.

There are a number of alternative approaches to identifying fundamental value. Judging among them becomes a question of finding the right tests and then seeing if the different claimants for the title of fundamental value stand up to testing. Selecting the tests is really a matter of common sense. As we shall see, however, there are many frequently used indicators that do not pass even the most basic tests of common sense.

Test No. 1: An Indicator of Value Must Be Measurable

Our first test may seem so basic that it would hardly be worth mentioning, if it were not so important. Value must be measurable. To claim that the market is wrongly priced can make sense only if the market would be correctly priced at some other level. When the market is correctly, or "fairly," valued, price and fundamental value will be the same. When they are not, the ratio between the two will show by how much the market is overvalued or undervalued. Clearly, in order to arrive at this ratio, the fundamental value must be measurable.[2]

Some aspects of this issue are merely superficial. Confusion can, for example, sometimes arise because different approaches to value express the relevant ratio in a different way. Thus, whereas q and the price-earnings multiple both put price on the top of the ratio, with the fundamental at the bottom, the dividend yield puts price on the bottom of the ratio. When the market is overvalued, q will therefore be high, but the dividend yield will normally be low. The degree of implied overvaluation can, however, be compared by turning the dividend yield upside down.

There are also much deeper problems of measurability, which apply to all indicators. Profits, for example, which are a key element in some valuation criteria, can include significant distortions. We shall see that the problem of measurability can be quite severe for those indicators that, like the price-earnings multiple, depend on the measurement of profits. But even q depends on the

---

[2]We saw that very similar issues arose in our discussion of everyday value in Chapter 9.

measurement of corporate net worth. We noted in Chapter 15 that we could not precisely identify the extent of the U.S. stock market's overvaluation in 1998, even using q. This was because we can neither measure corporate net worth perfectly nor can we be certain of the precise value to which q mean-reverts.

The measurement problem is probably the only intellectually coherent objection to q, and we shall therefore deal with it more thoroughly in Chapter 25. At this stage we shall merely state that we do not think such objections can be reasonably maintained, but that they will naturally be overemphasized by those who stand to lose when q becomes more widely understood.

Test No. 2: The Ratio of Price to Fundamental Value Must Mean-Revert

We mentioned in Chapter 2 a feature visible in q that is crucial to any indicator of value. This feature is normally referred to as mean reversion. The ratio between the stock price and the fundamental value of the market is something that should be pulled back to its average like a piece of elastic; it must therefore have a tendency to "revert" to its "mean."[3]

It's worth considering this aspect of value a little more thoroughly, since it is so crucial to our arguments. The best approach is to use concrete examples. Charts 20.1 and 20.2 show the difference between two valuation indicators—one of which definitely mean-reverts, and one of which definitely does not—over a cen-

---

[3]Statisticians also refer frequently to a closely related property, known as "stationarity." This is almost but not quite the same thing as mean reversion. Stationarity implies, roughly, that the unpredictability of something reaches a limit, as you look further and further into the future. We saw in Chapter 17 that stationarity does not, for example, apply to stock prices—uncertainty gets greater and greater as you look further ahead. Hence stock prices are *non*stationary. But this need not necessarily be the case for the ratio of stock prices to something else. Mean reversion of a ratio necessarily implies stationarity of that ratio. In principle, the reverse need not apply. Something can be stationary without being mean-reverting; but we shall not be interested in this possibility, examples of which are rather rarefied. (As a physical example, gas particles in a glass jar are stationary, but not mean-reverting: They can be guaranteed not to get outside the jar. Hence uncertainty about where a given particle will be in the future is strictly limited; at the same time, it will have no tendency to be pulled back toward a fixed point in the jar. The equivalents of glass jars in economics are, however, rare.)

CHART 20.1

A Century of Artificial Stock Prices: A Valuation Indicator That
Mean-Reverts...

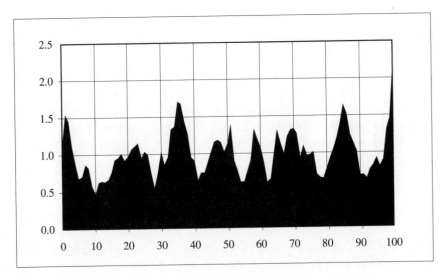

CHART 20.2

...And a Valuation Indicator That Does *Not* Mean-Revert

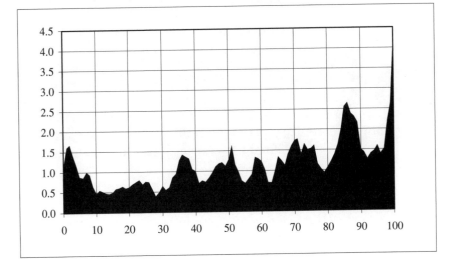

tury of data. We know the properties of these two indicators with an unusual degree of confidence, because we made up the numbers ourselves, with a little help from a "random number generator."

You could think of both as being indicators of over- or undervaluation of the same stock price, relative to two alternative measures of the "fundamental." It should be clear from the charts that both measures are being hit by the same shocks to the stock price, since both tend to rise and fall at the same time.[4] Both series are at all-time highs in the final year of our artificial century, and hence both might be taken to imply overvaluation. But the difference between the properties of the two indicators should be very evident.

The first regularly gets pulled back from extreme values—whether high or low—toward its mean. In terms of the language made fashionable by chaos theory, its average value is an "attractor." This means that the final value really is "high," implying that there is a high probability that it will fall back. The second indicator, in contrast, has no such tendency. Whether it is low or high, there is an equal probability that it will fall or rise—history simply does not matter.[5] Like any indicator that does not mean-revert, it cannot tell you anything about its own future, let alone about stock market value.

The mean-reverting ratio is different. The fact that it mean-reverts implies that the stock price cannot deviate too far from its fundamental without the elastic beginning to tug. Such an indicator therefore has information about our artificial stock market's future.

A crucial feature of mean reversion is, however, the element of uncertainty. We know the properties of the mean-reverting indicator in Chart 20.1, because we constructed it ourselves. Nonetheless, we cannot know exactly what would happen in the first year of our next century of artificial data. The precise outcome would depend on the element of "noise" injected by our random

---

[4]This is, of course, no coincidence. The "noise" we fed into the two series was identical.

[5]Think back to our analogy in Chapter 17, of being paid or losing $1 on the basis of a coin toss. Whether you currently have $10 or $1000, or owe your opponent $10 or $1000, your chances of losing $1 on the next toss of the coin are identical. This series has exactly the same property.

number generator. Although the indicator is at an all-time high, we cannot rule out that this element of "noise" might push it even higher. All we can say is that there is a rather low probability that this will actually happen.

When we come to look at real as opposed to artificial stock markets, this element of uncertainty is both a necessity and a nuisance.[6]

It is a necessity, because without uncertainty it would be too easy to make money by exploiting indicators of value. We shall see that uncertainty about mean reversion is a necessary condition for any valid indicator of value. We shall also see that it is *not* a sufficient condition; but we shall postpone discussion of this issue for now.

Uncertainty is also a nuisance. Since we constructed the data for the two charts ourselves, we have no difficulty in knowing which of the two indicators genuinely mean-reverts. This is not always so easy when you are dealing with real stock markets. In the Virtual Appendix we give statistical evidence to show whether possible indicators of value exhibit this crucial property. In the main text, we shall restrict ourselves to charts. As it happens, the two approaches are mutually supportive, but statistical tests help guard against what is perhaps an innate human tendency to spot patterns that are not really there. Rigorous testing injects a greater element of objectivity.

Unfortunately, data analysis in isolation cannot tell you everything. A major problem in economics, as in any science that cannot run controlled experiments, is that if you go out looking for statistical evidence in favor of your own views, and are prepared to look both hard enough and selectively enough, you may well find some data, somewhere, to bolster your case. If you do this, you run a severe risk of what economists call "data mining." The analogy should be quite clear. If you were a mineral prospector who used all the tricks of your trade to track down and mine a seam of gold, you would not conclude from this that gold is everywhere beneath your feet. The very activity of mining shows that the thing being mined is rare. The same applies to economic evidence. The harder you have to search to find it, the less useful it is as evidence.

---

[6]We discuss the role of "noise" in the actual stock market further in Chapter 28.

Investors should always be on their guard against evidence that is merely the result of data mining. There are two very important ways to guard against it.

The first is to use all available data, without being selective. We have 99 years of data on q, and we use it all. If we had more we would use that as well. At least an equivalent amount of data exists for all commonly used alternative indicators of value; indeed, most can be constructed for considerably longer periods. Nonetheless, it is very rare to see such large amounts of data used. To be charitable, this may well be due to ignorance or laziness. Or perhaps we should say to be relatively charitable, since the alternative to ignorance and laziness is a willful intent to deceive. But when we come to look at other indicators of value, in particular yield ratios and yield differences, we shall see that the only empirical support for them depends on selective use of data and hence on data mining. If all available data are used, the appearance of statistical evidence dissolves like the phantom that it is.

There is a second very crucial way to guard against data mining; but it is much more than just this. It is so important that it is our next key test of any indicator of value.

Test No. 3: An Indicator of Value Must Make Economic Sense

Value must have a firm basis in economics. That is, how it works must be understandable. This is not only because the search for understanding is the basic drive behind economics or any other science, though that is important. All theories need to stand up to argument, because this is an important way in which they are tested. If they are robust they are confirmed by debate, but if a better theory comes along then they are discarded. Testing and prediction are important parts of this process, but they are not the only ways in which one theory is preferred to another. The ability to enlighten is crucial.

An understandable theoretical basis provides a key protection against data mining and the human tendency to see patterns that do not exist. If we start from a theory and then test it, there is always a chance that the data will fail to reject that theory merely by accident, though if we had had more data our theory would have failed the tests. But when we find that the data do not reject a theory that illuminates our understanding, we have far less risk of data mining by accident. The more data we have, the more confidence we can have in the theory. But all data are limited, and a theory that is designed to explain an apparent pattern is far more likely to prove illusory than a theory which is first propounded because it enlarges our understanding and is then successfully tested against the evidence.

Since understanding the economic basis of any indicator of value is so important, we devote Chapter 27 to looking at value indicators in relation to the Dividend Discount Model. This is the basis of most approaches to valuing the stocks of individual companies and is so constructed that it must be true. If properly applied, the Dividend Discount Model can be used for whole stock markets, as well as individual stocks. Properly applied, it is also consistent with q. If improperly used, however, as is frequently the case, it leads to fallacious criteria such as those based on an assumed, but nonexistent, relationship between the P/Es or dividend yields on stocks and the yields on bonds.

Test No. 4: An Indicator of Value Must Tell You Something (But Not Too Much) About Future Stock Returns

This feature is perhaps not so obvious as the other three, but is absolutely crucial, both in principle and in practice.

Our first two properties required that any indicator of value must represent a ratio between price and some measurable fundamental. Furthermore this ratio must be mean-reverting. We noted, however, in our discussion of q in Chapters 2 and 15, that mean reversion can occur if either the price or the fundamental changes. Economic theory may predict that the ratio will mean-revert, but be uncertain as to how this will occur. A high value of the ratio might, for example, tell us only that there is a high probability that the fundamental is going to rise, rather than that the price is going to fall. If this were the case, we would be able to use q to predict changes in the fundamental, but not changes in the stock market. To be useful, an indicator of value must be able to tell us something about the future of stock prices. Mean reversion is therefore a necessary but not sufficient condition for a useful indicator of value. In addition, a key feature of the indicator must be that it is a "leading indicator" of changes in the level of the stock market. A high value of the ratio of price to fundamental should indicate not just that the ratio is likely to fall, but that this will come about via stock price changes.

We need data to be able to assess whether a given indicator of value passes this test. When we look at individual indicators, we shall submit them to statistical tests, as we do to see if a ratio is mean-reverting. As with those tests, however, we shall give the statistical evidence in the Appendix. We shall also explain how price acts as a leading indicator. This is important. As we have emphasized, being understandable in terms of economic theory is a necessary condition for any satisfactory criterion of value.

The more stable the fundamental, the more useful its ratio to price will be as a criterion of value. If the fundamental moves only slowly and predictably, most of the adjustment has to come via prices. A highly volatile fundamental would render the ratio of price to fundamental almost useless, since the ratio would be continually jumping around as a result of changes in the fundamental, rather than in price. Stability of the fundamental has the added advantage, in terms of commonsense intuition, that in general the stock market will get more expensive when the stock price rises, and cheaper when it falls.

As soon as we start to talk about the possibility of saying something about the future of stock prices, it should become obvious why the role of uncertainty, which we mentioned earlier, is so crucial. A valid indicator of value must say something about the future of stock prices, but not too much.

The necessity for not saying too much is perhaps disappointing, but it provides an important reality check. If movements in stock prices, especially over the short term, could be predicted, it would be too easy to make money by exploiting indicators of value. As we have shown before, we cannot expect people not to make money if they are offered the opportunity to do so without risk. There must therefore be sufficient risk to deter them from making money through arbitrage. When price and fundamental value diverge, market participants should be capable of knowing that they have diverged—and indeed of measuring by how much—at least to within some margin of error. But investors cannot profit from this knowledge without some form of risk. This is why we have emphasized that q is primarily a tool to avoid losing money rather than providing a route to untold wealth.

It is this uncertainty that has given rise to most of the misunderstandings that surround any discussion of stock market value. We are simply innocent economists trying to understand things. We don't expect to be able to make much money from the understanding we hope to achieve from our efforts, except to the extent that people are prepared to pay the price of this book in order to share in that understanding. This makes us sharply different from most other people who look at value. They are usually practical people, who wish to make money, either by buying and selling shares or by persuading others to do so. For the most part, we see nothing wrong in such attempts. We are not taking a moral stance. Our skepticism regarding attempts to time stock markets is simply that, innocent as we are, we are not perhaps innocent enough, and we consider such attempts to be naïve. The naïveté consists in expecting to be able to forecast the timing with which stock markets will move, at least with sufficient accuracy to make money out of it. This is the same as expecting people not to pick up $100 bills.

This inability to predict when things will happen, but not what will happen, can be illustrated by our example of roulette. The chances at roulette are not quite even, owing to the existence of zero. The result is that the "house" always wins in the end, and the players always lose. But this does not mean that any individual is bound to lose during the course of an evening's play. If it did, then roulette would be unlikely to draw the crowds it does. You should know that you are bound to lose at roulette if you play for long enough, but you cannot predict when this will happen. What you do know is that the chances of losing rise, the longer the game is played.

A valid criterion of fundamental value will put the investor in a similar position to the house at roulette. The stock market is as competitive as it gets, and we can thus be sure that even though any valid criterion of value must mean-revert, there must be considerable uncertainty about when this will happen. The uncertainty about timing must be large. The profits from correctly judging market fluctuations are huge. The risks over timing must be equally great, or the returns from arbitraging the market would not balance the risks of doing so.

VALUE: THE FOUR KEY PROPERTIES

Our list is now complete. As a reminder, fundamental value must have the following qualities:

1. It must be measurable.
2. The ratio of price to fundamental must mean-revert.
3. It must make economic sense.
4. It must say something, but not too much, about future stock returns.

With the necessary qualities identified, the various candidates can be considered in turn and tested. In Chapters 21 to 25 we shall consider individually the principal indicators that we have encountered, even where the lack of qualifications is glaringly obvious.

CHAPTER 21

The Dividend Yield

BASICS

The valuation criterion with the longest history is the dividend yield. It is the percentage return, calculated by dividing the annual dividend on a share by its current price. The dividend yield for a stock market index like the Dow Jones Industrials, or the S&P 500, is an average of the dividend yields on the individual stocks in the index.

The dividend yield can be very informative, whether or not it can be used as a guide to value. We have already noted that the current dividend yield of around 1% provides two key items of information. One is that income alone cannot justify an investment in stocks, since cash on deposit gives a better income. The second, which follows, is that at present it is rational to hold stocks only if sufficient capital gains are expected in the future to bring the total return up to a reasonable level.

Although these two items are useful bits of information, neither is about value. We noted in Chapter 7 that capital appreciation has been a common feature for the past 50 years and can reasonably be expected to continue at some point in the future. The question is whether it will be sufficient to provide a satisfactory return. The dividend yield in isolation cannot tell us this.

It is also clear that the dividend yield provides very little guide to value in terms of individual shares. Many companies, particularly smaller ones, pay no dividends, and this does not make them valueless, provided that there is a reasonable expectation that they will start to pay dividends at some point in the future.

It is only when the average dividend yield on the whole stock market is being considered that the possibility of using it as a guide to value can be reasonably considered. The dividend yield is not unique in this respect. The difference between trying to value individual shares and valuing the stock market as a whole is something that is common to all valuation criteria. It is common, unfortunately, to find that this important distinction is often poorly understood, even by those who write about stock markets. We shall come back to this issue when we look at the Dividend Discount Model in Chapter 27.

Test No. 1: Does the Dividend Yield Provide a Measurable Indicator of Value?

At first glance, the answer to this question must obviously be yes. One of the great advantages of the dividend yield is that both of its components—price and dividends per share—are measured very precisely, and the data are readily available. If you are so inclined, you can keep tabs on the dividend yield on individual stocks, and on market indices, on an almost minute-by-minute basis.

Reliability of the underlying data is one of the great pluses of the dividend yield. But being 100% confident of the top and bottom of the ratio between dividends per share and the share price is not the same thing as saying that the ratio provides a measurable indicator of value. We saw in the previous chapter that a measurable indicator must be able to tell us by how much the market is over- or undervalued at any time. The dividend yield does not do this. Its use involves the implicit assumption that there is some level of the dividend yield that corresponds to "fair" value. Measurability is therefore a problem. It is not a problem of measuring the actual yield, but of measuring what the yield should be for the market to be at fair value.[7]

---

[7]This issue needs to be solved for all indicators of value, but, as we shall see, some are more vulnerable than others on this score.

The most common assumption is that the appropriate value to use is the historic average, which is roughly 5½%. Since the yield is currently around 1%, this would imply that the U.S. stock market is some 5½ times overvalued.[8] Even to us this figure seems a bit over the top. It is thus clear that although there are no problems with the underlying data for the dividend yield, there are significant problems about knowing the correct average with which it should be compared.

Test No. 2: Does the Dividend Yield Mean-Revert?

Chart 21.1 shows the dividend yield as far back as we have data, alongside its average value. It suggest that the yield does not wander off indefinitely, but stays within bounds. By definition, the dividend yield cannot fall below zero and it has rarely approached double figures.[9] But it is doubtful if it reverts to a mean. We show that this doubt is justified by statistical tests set out in the Virtual Appendix, but the evidence is visible to the naked eye.

One simple check is to see how often the dividend yield crosses the line of its average value. A mean-reverting series should do this more often than the dividend yield does. Another commonsense test is to see whether it indicates that the stock market spends roughly as much time being overvalued as being undervalued and that this pattern is reasonably consistent over different periods. The dividend yield clearly doesn't do this. It suggests that the market was nearly always undervalued in the nineteenth century and nearly always overvalued in the past 50 years. This simply contradicts common sense.

---

[8]It should be noted that when the dividend yield is high it is an indication of cheapness, whereas with other indicators it is usually indicates overvaluation. This is because the dividend yield is expressed as a ratio of dividends per share to share price, with price on the bottom, whereas the P/E multiple, for example, is a ratio in which price is on the top. Any ratio can be expressed in either form, and it is only by convention that we use one form rather than the other.

[9]At first sight this seems to imply that the dividend yield may be stationary as defined in note 2 in Chapter 20. This, however, is something of an illusion. Although the yield cannot fall below zero (as long as firms continue to pay dividends), there is no limit to the extent to which stock prices can rise. For example, if the yield fell from 1% to ½%, the market could still double and it could double again if the yield then fell to ¼% and so on literally ad infinitum. The yield will never fall below zero however many times the price is doubled.

CHART 21.1

The Dividend Yield, 1802–1998

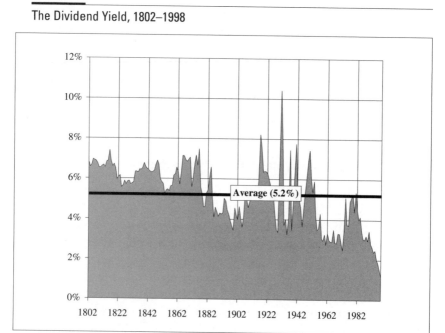

The observation that the dividend yield is currently around 1% means that it cannot fall by more than 1 percentage point, but this is little use for indicating the degree of overvaluation. In particular, there is no reason to believe that the dividend yield is going to be "attracted" back to its historic average of over 5%.

To avoid this problem it is common to find comparisons being made, not with the historic average derived from all the available data, but with only more recent information. Sometimes comparisons are made with the average over the twentieth century, which is lower than the average over both centuries; sometimes only the last 50 years are used, which makes the average lower still. Another approach is to fit a trend, so that the "fair" yield falls over time. These techniques simply cloud the issue, since there is no logical justification for any of them. They underline why mean reversion is such an essential property.

Chart 21.1 clearly shows the tendency for the dividend yield to fall over time. The crucial question is whether we could have predicted this in advance. Since the answer is clearly no, it is equally clear that we cannot know the "fair" yield with which we should compare today's yield. Whether we simply change the period to calculate our average or use sophisticated techniques to fit a trend, the same answer applies. Since we could not predict the changes, we cannot justify a preference for one average over another.

These techniques offer endless opportunities for data mining. If analysts wish to show that the market is overvalued, they can simply compare today's dividend yield with the long-term average and claim that the market is roughly 5½ times overpriced. If they want to show that the market is cheap, they can usually find another period and point out that the current yield is above its three-year or three-month average. In current conditions, however, things are getting pretty tough for those wishing to make a bullish case with the dividend yield, since the three-minute or three-second average is about all that they can use. The usual result is that people simply turn to other criteria of value. The crucial point is that without evidence of mean reversion, it is impossible to say that any claim based on the dividend yield is incorrect.

We must therefore conclude that since the dividend yield fails the test of mean reversion, it fails altogether.

Test No. 3: Does the Dividend Yield Make Economic Sense as an Indicator of Value?

The answer to this question is a pretty unambiguous no. Investors can in principle still get decent returns with a low dividend yield, as long as they get higher capital appreciation. Taking the historic average value of the dividend yield as indicating "fair" value is entirely arbitrary. The fundamental problem is that *any* level of the dividend yield can in principle be consistent with fair value.[10]

---

[10]An important caveat to this statement is that, although the same return can be achieved with any combination of the dividend yield and capital appreciation, achieving the same degree of volatility of returns is more complicated, since the dividend component is generally more predictable. Hence if capital appreciation becomes more important, as it has over the past 50 years, to achieve the same degree of volatility of the total return, the capital appreciation element, taken in isolation, has to become less volatile. This does appear to have happened, and is often confused with a fall in the volatility of the total return, for which there is much less evidence, as Chart 17.2 shows.

This is not just a theoretical possibility, but a very real one. We noted in Chapter 17 the remarkably historical stability of the real return on stocks, which we have dubbed "Siegel's constant." This rate of return has remained stable, over time, despite the historic tendency for the dividend yield to fall, because the lower income has been balanced by greater capital appreciation.

There is some evidence that lower dividend yields could be sustainable, though nowhere near as low as current levels. Chart 21.2 shows that in the latter half of the twentieth century firms paid out lower dividends in relation to their profits than they did before.[11] Undistributed profits, which are those not paid out in dividends, increase companies' net worth, and this increases their ability to pay additional dividends in the future. The more earnings companies retain, the lower their current dividends, but the faster they can grow dividends in the future. Because value is made up of both current dividends and their ability to grow in the future, we cannot say that low dividend yields are necessarily a sign of an overvalued stock market, let alone use them to say by how much the market is overvalued.

Whether payout ratios have or have not changed, and whether they have changed *enough*, are thus crucial questions that need to be considered before the dividend yield can be used to measure value. Neither point, however, is at all easy to establish. The problem is that we are concerned with the long-term payout ratio, rather than with short-term fluctuations. This raises a number of issues that relate not to dividends, but to earnings. If we could answer these questions in any satisfactory way, they would point to using the P/E multiple, rather than the dividend yield, as an indicator. But we shall see, in Chapter 26, that, if we could in turn remedy the faults of the P/E multiple, we would end up back where we started, with q.

It is not unreasonable to consider that the extremely low dividend yield indicates that the market is very expensive. This would hold even if the payout ratio had changed massively. We are not, however, looking for subjective, albeit reasonable beliefs; we are looking for objective and measurable criteria of value. The

---

[11]Note that the time scale for Chart 20.2 is shorter than that for Chart 20.1, since we have earnings figures only from 1871 onward.

CHART 21.2

The Payout Ratio, 1871–1998

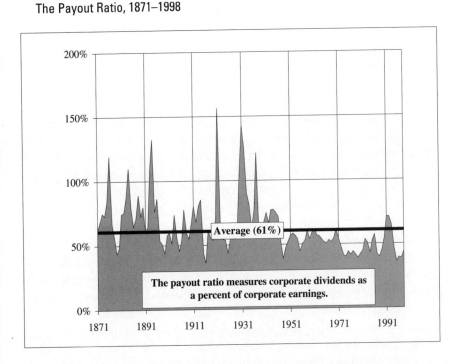

The payout ratio measures corporate dividends as a percent of corporate earnings.

fact that the payout ratio may change greatly over time is a valid objection to using the dividend yield as an objective measure of value.

In principle we could stop considering the dividend yield at this point. It fails to pass two of our tests, and a valid criterion of value must qualify on all counts. However, for completeness, we consider the last test as well.

Test No. 4: Does the Dividend Yield Tell You Anything About Future Stock Returns?

In Chapters 11 and 13 we introduced the idea of Hindsight Value, which measures value in any year in terms of the returns that were subsequently realized. Hindsight Value is useless for today's stock prices, since we cannot apply hindsight to the future. But it is a very useful way to look at history, since we can compare it with the indicators that could have been measured at the time. We saw in Chapter 13 that q and hindsight value tracked each other closely, implying that q gave a good indication of future returns.[12]

We also showed, in Chart 13.3, the performance of what we called "dividend value," which is just the dividend yield turned upside down. If you look back at Chart 13.3, you will see that the dividend yield does better on this test than in the previous two. High levels of dividend value, and hence low levels of dividend yield, have frequently been associated with high figures for hindsight value, which means that subsequent returns were below average. So the dividend yield *has* acted to some extent as a useful "leading indicator" of lower returns in the future.[13]

However, the usefulness of these signals is severely limited by the fact that the dividend yield fails the mean reversion test. The downward drift in the dividend yield means that the market nearly always seemed cheap until the 1950s and nearly always seemed expensive after that. This signal was not reflected in uniformly better returns in the earlier period, or uniformly worse returns afterward. So, although the dividend yield seems to give useful warning signals, the magnitude of the signal does not indicate the magnitude of the risk. It is like an unreliable smoke alarm that sometimes goes off in response to a major fire, or sometimes because a visitor has been imprudent enough to light a cigarette.

CONCLUSION: THE DIVIDEND YIELD AS AN INDICATOR OF STOCK MARKET VALUE

Table 21.1 summarizes the performance of the dividend yield in relation to our four tests. The table makes it clear that the dividend yield has severe defects. It can provide useful information, but as an indicator of value the dividend yield is deeply flawed.

---

[12]q also met our condition that it should not say *too* much, since hindsight value measures only an average of returns over lots of different investment horizons. We made no claim that q could have told you anything useful about *when* the bad returns would be, and no such claim could be made.

[13]This conclusion, based on our informal comparison with hindsight value, is supported both by statistical tests, which we present in the Virtual Appendix, and a very wide range of research by academic economists.

TABLE 21.1

The Dividend Yield and the Four Key Tests for Any Indicator of Value

Test	Dividend Yield
1. Is it measurable?	Data are reliable, but the average is unmeasurable.
2. Does it mean-revert?	No.
3. Does it make economic sense?	No.
4. Does it say anything about future stock returns?	Yes, but the signal is inaccurate.

CHAPTER 22

The Price-Earnings Multiple

BASICS

Along with the dividend yield, the price-earnings multiple (often referred to as the P/E multiple, P/E ratio, or simply, the PE) has historically been the most commonly used measure of value. It is very important therefore to understand its strengths and limitations. It is essential to comprehend the difference between using the P/E multiple to value individual companies and to value the stock market as a whole. Unfortunately, a failure to make this distinction is extremely common.

The P/E multiple is exactly what it sounds like. For an individual corporation, it is the ratio between the value of the firm on the stock market and its annual earnings, which are profits after depreciation, interest, and tax. Earnings are always measured at an annual rate, but may be measured either over the past year or, for some companies, over the past three months. If you divide through both top and bottom of the ratio by the number of shares, thereby leaving the ratio itself unchanged, you have the share price on top and earnings per share on the bottom—hence the name. For a market index like the Dow Jones or the S&P 500, the P/E multiple is the average of the P/Es of the individual firms that make up the index.

Today, when the PE is around 35, the average share costs the equivalent of 35 years of its share of the company's current earnings. If you turn the P/E multiple upside down, and put earnings on the top of the ratio, it can be compared with the dividend yield, and is therefore known as the earnings yield. The P/E multiple and the earnings yield are therefore one and the same thing, expressed in two different ways, as any ratio can be.

The earnings yield is almost invariably higher than the dividend yield, since firms almost invariably pay out less than 100% of their profits in dividends. This is why the earnings yield and P/E multiple are so widely used. They reflect the profits of the company, not just the actual dividends it pays out. Since underlying profitability determines not just the current dividend but also the firm's capacity to pay dividends in the future, there is a strong case for preferring the P/E over the dividend yield as an indicator of stock market value. We can go further, and state that the earnings yield must, over a long enough time period, be precisely equal to the return you will get out of the stock. Unfortunately, this very significant advantage of the P/E multiple is offset, as we shall see, by some very significant disadvantages.

Test No. 1: Does the Price-Earnings Multiple Provide a Measurable Indicator of Value?

We saw that one of the dividend yield's advantages is that the underlying data are reliably measured. This is certainly true for the top of the price-earnings multiple, which is of course simply the share price; but it is a lot less clear for the bottom, which is earnings per share. This is derived from figures that appear in company accounts. But whether you regard this feature as a good indicator of the quality of the data depends on your view of company accounts.[14]

If it were not for the fact that the P/E multiple has many other faults, we would linger on this issue. Nonetheless, there are certain aspects of accounting profits that are worth bearing in mind.

---

[14]Economists and accountants tend to have a rather ambivalent relationship, based on incomprehension at best, and downright distrust at worst, so our view on this question should perhaps not be regarded as entirely impartial.

- There are clearly identifiable biases in accounting profits as an indicator of sustainable profitability, which even accountants acknowledge. The most obvious arise from inflation. Among other things, inflation distorts the charges for interest and depreciation.
- Company accountants are endlessly innovative in their treatment of corporate profit and loss accounts, and balance sheets. They naturally seek to make profits look as high as possible. A recent innovation has been the treatment of employee stock options. In recent years most U.S. corporations have excluded this part of their payroll from normal costs. As a result, the published profits of U.S. companies have been significantly higher than their true profits.[15]
- Indirect evidence of some upward bias in accounting measures of earnings can be found by comparing the historic average earnings yield with the historic average return on stocks. We deal with this issue later, in Chapter 27.[16]

In addition to problems of measurement, the P/E multiple shares with the dividend yield a failure to give a direct indication of value. We therefore need to find a figure for "fair" value, so that we can measure over- or undervaluation by:

$$\frac{\text{Current P/E Multiple}}{\text{"Fair" P/E Multiple}}$$

or, expressing it another way,[17] by:

$$\frac{\text{"Fair" Earnings Yield}}{\text{Current Earnings Yield}}$$

There are two possible ways to estimate the "fair" P/E or earnings yield. One is simply to take a historic average. The al-

---

[15]An article in *Forbes* (May 18, 1998), previously referred to in Chapter 16, summarized the work done by Andrew Smithers on this topic, together with colleague Daniel Murray.

[16]Note that other issues, most notably a tendency to overstate inflation, cloud the picture too.

[17]These are only exact equivalents if we use geometric averages.

ternative is based on the fact that the long-term average earnings yield and the long-term return on stocks must be the same. This approach uses the apparently stable historic average real return on stocks, or Siegel's constant.

Both approaches give very similar answers about the current degree of overvaluation, and indeed answers that are similar to those obtained from q. The historic average P/E multiple is around 13, which corresponds to an earnings yield of 7.7%. This is not too different from our estimate of Siegel's constant. Under either approach, the market is currently over 2½ times overvalued.

We have already warned, however, against the temptation to assume that different valuation criteria are sensible because they support each other or give similar results to q at any particular time. The degree of agreement could be coincidental. So, having noted our caveats on the reliability of profits measures that feed into the P/E multiple, we move on to our second test.

Test No. 2: Does the P/E Multiple Mean-Revert?

Since the P/E multiple and the earnings yield are just two different ways of looking at the same ratio, and since, if a ratio mean-reverts, it does so whichever way you look at it, everything that is true of the P/E multiple must also be true of the earnings yield.

Chart 22.1 shows the P/E multiple on the U.S. stock market since 1871, along with its historic average. The chart indicates that there is a much stronger case for concluding that the P/E is mean-reverting than in the case of the dividend yield. Visual evidence is supported by formal statistical tests, which we set out in the Virtual Appendix. The actual multiple crosses its average more often, there is no apparent tendency for the P/E to drift either up or down, and it spends roughly equal proportions of time above and below its average value.[18]

This feature of the P/E multiple is very important. It suggests that, like q, the P/E multiple has a strong capacity to pre-

---

[18]Note that the apparent tendency for movements above the average to be more extreme than those below is purely because we have not used a log scale for this chart. In proportional terms there is no such asymmetry.

CHART 22.1

The P/E Multiple, 1871–1998

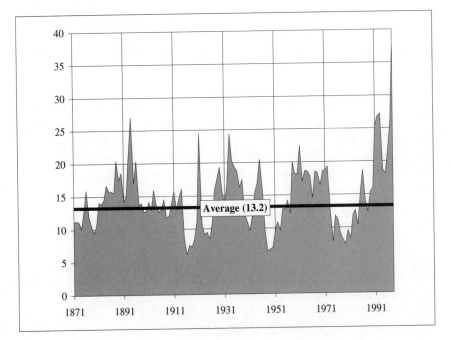

dict its own future. When it is high, or low, there is a very high probability that it will move back toward its average. Since the P/E multiple is currently at a record level, there is a record high probability that the multiple will fall back.

We should remind you, however, that mean reversion is a necessary, but *not* sufficient characteristic for a useful indicator of value. This is because mean reversion of a ratio can come from movements in either the top or the bottom of a ratio. This caveat turns out to be crucial in the case of the P/E; but before we delve further into this issue, it is helpful to look at our third test.

Test No. 3: Does the P/E Multiple Make Economic Sense as an Indicator of Value?

The answer is unfortunately neither a strong yes nor a clear no. The economic case for the P/E multiple makes more sense than that for the dividend yield, but less than that for q. It all depends on why the P/E multiple reverts to its mean. Over a sufficiently long time period, the returns that firms make and the returns that investors get must be the same.[19] The returns earned by investors have been pretty stable over time; otherwise there would be no Siegel's constant. The stability of Siegel's constant and the mean reversion of the P/E multiple are just two sides of the same coin.

So if you are happy to accept the statistical evidence that investors demand a particular return, a demand that is in effect hard-wired into them from birth, then you may be happy with the case for the P/E multiple on the grounds of economic sense. The problem with this assumption is that unless Siegel's constant is constant, the economic basis for using the P/E multiple as an indicator of value becomes suspect. If the return demanded by investors were to fall permanently, the P/E multiple would also rise permanently. As we shall see in Chapter 29, exactly this claim has been made in the recent past. Although the claim has no historic backing, it underlines the fact that using the P/E multiple as an indicator of value has no solid foundation in economic logic.

So far, despite the above caveat, things have not been looking too bad for the P/E multiple. But this is because we have, contrary to the approved practice of children's stories, left the worst, rather than the best, till last.

Test No. 4: Does the P/E Multiple Tell You Something About Future Stock Returns?

We have already shown that even though the P/E multiple has on occasion given accurate signals, it has sometimes been disastrously wrong. Chart 13.3 showed that the worst example was in the early 1930s, when the P/E indicated that value was extremely poor, at the very moment that hindsight value tells us was the best ever to buy stocks. The P/E's wrong signals are thus very different from those given by the dividend yield, which we compared to a smoke alarm that is sometimes set off by a cigarette. The P/E in 1932 told you that you that the house you were planning to buy,

---

[19]We shall go into this in more detail in Chapter 27.

at rock-bottom prices, was about to be destroyed by an earthquake. It wasn't and, if you had paid any attention to this signal, you would have missed the bargain of the century.

We explained briefly in Chapter 17 why these problems might occur, and hence why the P/E multiple fails the fourth test so badly.[20] Looking at this issue in rather more detail, we see that are two crucial features of the P/E multiple that cause it to fail.

- Earnings, which represent the fundamental for the price-earnings multiple, are highly volatile.
- The stock price may itself be a leading indicator of earnings, rather than vice versa.

The primary, but by no means the only, reason earnings are volatile is that profits are highly dependent on the state of the economy. When the economy goes into recession, employment and wages both weaken but sales usually fall much more quickly. Operating margins are squeezed. Meanwhile the charges for depreciation and interest continue. What is left over, which is firms' profits, can thus fall like the proverbial stone.

The year 1932 provides the most extreme example of the twentieth century. National accounts statistics for that year show that the corporate sector as a whole was actually incurring losses. If quoted companies' profits had moved in line, therefore, the P/E multiple should actually have gone negative! In fact, whether by dint of creative accounting or by superior performance, quoted companies managed in aggregate to show some profits. But, since earnings per share fell by more than the stock price (which was in itself some achievement, given how fast that was falling), the P/E multiple rose, rather than fell, as the stock market, in reality, got progressively cheaper.

The P/E was giving the wrong signal because current earnings in 1932 gave a highly misleading indication of the potential profitability of the U.S. corporate sector. Chart 13.2 showed that 1932, though the most extreme case, was by no means the only occasion when the P/E multiple gave misleading signals. In the next chapter we shall look at ways to deal with the problems presented by the volatility of profits. Unfortunately, the problem can-

---

[20]In the Appendix we present more formal tests that support this conclusion.

not be solved in any satisfactory way. However, in Chapter 26 we shall show that, if it could, the result would be the same as q.

The other problem with the P/E multiple is that it sometimes works the wrong way around, like a smoke alarm that goes off too late. Knowing that your alarm will go off after your house has burned down is among the most useless pieces of information that you can possess.

This order of events should really come as no surprise. It is often claimed that the stock market is a leading indicator, rising before the economy recovers from a recession and peaking before the boom ends. Such claims about the stock market's predictive power are at least sometimes correct. Hence the old joke that that the stock market has predicted twelve of the past nine recessions.

If the stock market is sometimes correct in predicting the state of the economy, it will also predict earnings, since, as we have already noted, earnings tend to rise and fall with the economy. So a high or low P/E may simply indicate that the stock market is predicting a cyclical recovery, or a cyclical collapse, in earnings. This clouds the picture and severely devalues the ability of the P/E multiple to indicate value.[21]

Finally it is worth noting a feature that is in essence just a corollary of the volatility of earnings per share. This is that the fundamental that underlies the use of the price-earnings ratio, which is simply current earnings multiplied by the fair P/E, is highly volatile. As a result, the P/E multiple does not have so obviously the convenient property we noted when we set up this fourth test—namely, that an indicator of over- or undervaluation should mainly rise or fall when the stock market rises or falls.

CONCLUSION: THE P/E MULTIPLE AS AN INDICATOR OF STOCK MARKET VALUE

Table 22.1 summarizes the performance of the P/E multiple (and hence of course of the earnings yield) in relation to our four tests.

---

[21]Note that in logic, if there is clear evidence of mean reversion of any ratio, this must always imply that *at least* one of the elements in the ratio is a leading indicator of the other. In principle, however, it can occur because both on occasion lead, even if irregularly, as with stock prices and earnings.

The table makes it clear that, while the P/E multiple remedies some of the faults of the dividend yield, it does so only by introducing other problems. In the next chapter, we shall examine two alternative ways in which attempts are often made to rectify these problems.

TABLE 22.1

The P/E Multiple and the Four Key Tests for Any Indicator of Value

Test	P/E Multiple
1. Is it measurable?	Yes, but profit figures may be suspect, and fair value for P/E is in doubt.
2. Does it mean-revert?	Yes.
3. Does it make economic sense?	Only if Siegel's constant actually *is* constant.
4. Does it say anything about future stock returns?	No. Its signals are inaccurate, and sometimes perverse.

The Adjusted Price-Earnings Multiple

The P/E multiple is so widely used for assessing value that ways around the problems we identified in the last chapter have naturally been sought. There have been two main approaches. The first has been to try to forecast future earnings, and the second has been to try to adjust earnings to allow for the cyclical swings in the economy.

THE "PROSPECTIVE P/E MULTIPLE"

The first approach, which results in an adjusted P/E multiple normally referred to as the "prospective P/E," is widely used by stockbrokers, and there is no doubt that it is admirably suited to its purpose, which is to sell shares. Since the profit forecasts are purely subjective, so are the prospective P/Es that result. The prospective P/E is thus without merit or utility for the purpose of seeking an objective criterion of value. We shall therefore not give it the full treatment that we have awarded to other competing indicators of value.

We pause only briefly to note the obvious reason that stockbrokers tend to prefer the prospective P/E to the usual measure (often, in such comparisons, referred to as the "historic" P/E, a term generally used in a somewhat disparaging manner, as if being historic—or in other words, true—were a severe disadvantage). The reason is that prospective P/Es almost invariably turn out lower, and hence can be interpreted, if you do not look too hard, as indicating better value. But there are two fairly obvious explanations of why the apparent impression of better value is entirely spurious.

The first is the natural tendency for stockbrokers to forecast the future through rose-colored glasses. This is illustrated in Chart 23.1, which we have taken, with kind permission, from a recent study by Sushil Wadhwani. The chart shows that even during recent years, when profits have not suffered any significant setback, brokers' forecasts have been on average 7.8% higher than the actual turnout, and sometimes much higher.[22] A persistent

CHART 23.1

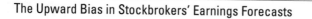

The Upward Bias in Stockbrokers' Earnings Forecasts

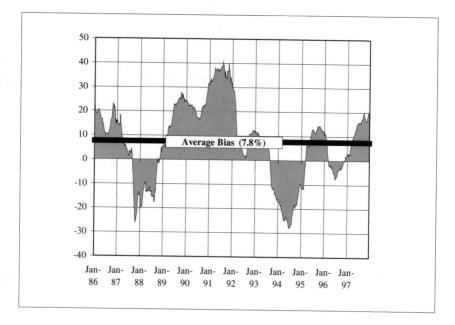

---

[22]The figures for the chart are from Figure 4 in Sushil Wadhwani, "The U.S. Stock Market and the Global Economic Crisis," *National Institute Economic Review* (January 1999). They chart shows the difference between IDES 12-month-ahead earnings forecasts and actual results.

upward bias in forecasts of earnings per share must imply a persistent downward bias in the prospective P/E multiple.

There is a second (albeit normally less important) reason why prospective P/Es are lower than historic P/Es. They would be lower even if (a big "if") stockbrokers' forecasts were usually on target. A moment's thought reveals why. If, as has been the case for the past 50 years or so, earnings per share tend to grow over time, through a combination of modest real growth and sometimes rather less modest inflation, then next year's earnings will on average always be higher than this year's. So the prospective P/E would be below the historic P/E even with unbiased forecasts of earnings.

If we take both of these factors into account, it is quite easy to pull down the prospective P/E by quite a significant amount compared with the historic P/E. Over the past 50 years, both real growth in earnings per share and inflation have averaged around 4%, giving an average annual growth of earnings per share in dollar terms of around 8%. If on top of that we build in, say, a 15% bias in brokers' forecasts (allowing for the fact that these forecasts tend to be most bullish when they need to be bullish, that is, when earnings are low or the P/E multiple is high), then forecast earnings will be on the order of 25% higher than current earnings, and the prospective P/E will be brought down accordingly. For a market that was only "modestly" overvalued, this might well be enough to appear to eliminate the overvaluation entirely.

Unfortunately for stockbrokers, even the most optimistic forecasts of growth in earnings per share cannot offset the degree of overvaluation that the P/E multiple has been pointing to in the recent past, so that the prospective P/E has fallen from favor of late. It will however no doubt resurface in due course, when the market has fallen to a more reasonable level.

THE CYCLICALLY ADJUSTED PRICE-EARNINGS MULTIPLE

The second approach involves adjusting the P/E multiple to allow for the cyclical fluctuations in profits that we discussed in the previous chapter. This approach is of much greater potential interest, and so we consider it more thoroughly.

If it were possible to adjust current earnings so as to remove the element of cyclical fluctuation and reveal, as it were, their true underlying level, then we shall see that the P/E multiple derived from these adjusted earnings might provide a valid measure of the stock market's value. In order to show why, we shall initially simply assume that such an adjustment could be made. This has the advantage of allowing us to ignore for the time being the various different ways in which it might be possible to do so. We shall therefore apply our four usual tests to the cyclically adjusted P/E, but, in this chapter, in order to simplify the argument, we shall not carry them out in the usual order, leaving the measurability test until last.

Test No. 2: Does the Cyclically Adjusted P/E Multiple Mean-Revert?

It may seem strange to answer this question when we have not dealt with the issue of how cyclical adjustment is to be carried out, but in fact we can answer it by a simple application of logic. If the unadjusted P/E mean-reverts, then the cyclically adjusted P/E must mean-revert as well. Since we have seen that there is strong historical evidence for the former, the latter follows automatically.

The reason is straightforward. If we think about the concept of cyclical adjustment, it should be fairly evident that any such adjustment, however carried out, must cancel out over the course of a full economic cycle. Thus, if earnings are depressed in a recession, the cyclical adjustment will raise adjusted earnings; but if they are boosted in a boom, the cyclical adjustment will lower them. Over a complete economic cycle, the adjustments should net out, so that the average of actual earnings over the cycle should equal the average of adjusted earnings. Only the path through the cycle should differ.

A useful analogy can be drawn with the process of seasonal adjustment carried out on most economic data by the Bureau of Economic Analysis (BEA). Actual (unadjusted) GDP is, for example, always weak in the winter months, because seasonal activities like construction and agriculture fall back to low levels.

The BEA produces data for seasonally adjusted GDP to give a more accurate picture of the underlying movements in national output. But annual figures for seasonally adjusted and unadjusted GDP must be, and are identical: Only the quarterly paths differ.

The analogy with seasonal adjustment also points, of course, to a significant difference. Everyone knows how long a year is, but identifying the length of a particular economic cycle is far, far harder. However, despite the practical difficulties (to which we shall return), the fundamental principle that cyclical adjustments should cancel out is inescapable.[23]

Anything that cancels out over time must by definition be mean-reverting (with a mean of 0 or 1, depending on whether adjustments are in dollar terms or in proportional terms). The difference between the actual P/E multiple and any cyclically adjusted P/E multiple must therefore be mean-reverting. If you add or multiply two mean-reverting series, the result is still mean-reverting. So if the unadjusted P/E mean-reverts, the cyclically adjusted P/E must too.

Test No. 3: Does the Cyclically Adjusted P/E Multiple Make Economic Sense as an Indicator of Value?

Since cyclical adjustments must cancel out over long enough periods, and the economic rationale for value can hold only in long-run terms, in general the strengths and weaknesses of the economic case for the cyclically adjusted P/E are the same as those for the unadjusted P/E. Thus, in general, the case is stronger than for the dividend yield, but weaker than for q. However, we shall see in Chapter 26 that, if the cyclical adjustment were done in an "ideal" way, the cyclically adjusted P/E would produce *exactly* the same indication of value as q. When cyclically adjusted in this way, the P/E multiple can therefore in principle be seen as "q-equivalent."

---

[23]This has not, of course, prevented many attempts to escape the canceling out. Stockbrokers frequently adjust earnings upward in a recession on cyclical grounds, but then (we assume out of absentmindedness) forget to introduce an offsetting downward adjustment in the boom. U.S. presidential aides tend to do exactly the same to GDP and tax receipts.

Test No. 4: Does the Cyclically Adjusted P/E Multiple Tell You Anything About Future Stock Returns?

Again, we can answer this question by the application of logic. If the cyclical adjustment could be done properly, the cyclically adjusted P/E multiple would have to reveal something about future stock returns. Once the adjustment had been made, the earnings for each year would move rather slowly, and would normally be a bit higher, measured in real terms, than those for the year before. This immediately overcomes one of the difficulties we identified in the last chapter when looking at actual P/E multiples, which is that earnings fluctuate too much. Since, as we have already seen, the cyclically adjusted P/E must also mean-revert, and cyclically adjusted earnings must be smooth, this would necessarily imply that the mean reversion would come about through changes in the stock price.

Notice, however, our use of the conditional tense. For, while we regard the cyclically adjusted P/E as a very useful concept, we have left until last the test that identifies its primary, and potentially fatal, weakness in practical terms. This is the problem of measurability.

Test No. 1: Does the Cyclically Adjusted P/E Multiple Provide a Measurable Indicator of Value?

We now need to address the question, which we sidestepped earlier, of how cyclical adjustment should actually be carried out. We have been assuming up until now that, however it was actually done, it was done in a way that clearly met our key conditions—that cyclical adjustment should remove the volatility in earnings resulting from recessions and booms, and, crucially, that it should do so in a way that cancels out over a full cycle. The slight problem is that, to do this job properly, you would need to be able to see into the future.

In looking at the last test, we said that cyclically adjusted profits would be expected to rise gradually over time. But this begs the question of why, and by how much. We shall postpone for now a full discussion of why, until we deal with this issue properly, in the context of "q-equivalence" in Chapter 26. But we can see even on a cursory examination that the question of how much can be answered properly only if you can see into the future.

In the simplest terms, if profits are being driven by the state of the economy, we need to know two things: first, where the economy is in relation to its long-run potential; and second, how much profits are being affected by this. When we look back at past booms and recessions, we can at least make a reasonable attempt to answer both these questions, with the benefit of hindsight. We can, for example, usually identify turning points in output after the event, and several methods can be applied to identify the average amount by which, say, profits fall, relative to their trend, when output is 1% below potential. But before the event, without the benefit of hindsight, this is very much harder. We may be able to look back at the most recent turning point, whether it be the low point of the last recession or the high point of the last boom, but we have simply no way of knowing when the next turning point will be, or at what level. Since cyclical adjustment is always essentially a process of averaging out peaks and troughs, we cannot construct the average if we have only one of its elements.

Of course, it might well be objected that, although correct in principle, our objections are too purist. It is certainly the case that cyclical adjustments can be carried out, by making reasonable projections of what to expect in the future. When we are valuing a market for which q cannot be measured, this may indeed be the best, and only, way to do so. But there is no escaping the fact that any such approach must have a strong subjective element. At any point in time, one person may decide on a large cyclical adjustment, while another may opt for a small one. The two may be able to have a reasonable argument about which approach is better, but there is no objective way of discriminating between the two approaches. The only objective test will be that of history; but by the time the case is decided it will be too late. Value requires objectivity.

We shall see in Chapter 26, however, that there is an escape route from the measurability problem. Earnings *can* be cyclically adjusted in a way that avoids the need to see into the future. But if done this way, the cyclically adjusted P/E actually ceases to depend on earnings at all, and becomes simply q.

THE DIVIDEND YIELD AS A CYCLICALLY ADJUSTED EARNINGS YIELD?

Before we close this chapter, it is perhaps worth mentioning another proposed way out of this problem. This is that the dividend yield can be viewed as, in effect, a cyclically adjusted version of the earnings yield, and hence that it implies a cyclically adjusted P/E. The rationale usually proposed here is that the best people to engage in cyclical adjustment of a firm's earnings are the people on the ground—namely, those who manage the firm.

It is a well-established fact that dividends are distinctly smoother than earnings. This approach suggests that managers smooth dividends because they wish, in effect, to cyclically adjust them. Thus, if earnings fall, firms usually maintain their dividends, on the assumption that earnings will rebound. They are in effect paying dividends, at a given payout ratio, on cyclically adjusted earnings.

This approach certainly has its attractions, but it also has a crucial flaw. The primary attraction is that, although managers cannot see into the future any more than anybody else, they may well have considerably more information about the present, and the recent past, as it relates to their particular firm. Thus, their approach to cyclical adjustment may have some advantages.[24] But the crucial flaw is that, in order to infer what managers actually are assuming about cyclically adjusted earnings, we also need to know the payout ratio they are assuming, and we do not.

If the payout ratio were clearly mean-reverting, we might be able to get away with assuming its average as the appropriate value. But, as Chart 21.2 showed, the payout ratio does not mean-revert. Indeed, since we have seen that the P/E multiple and hence the earnings yield both mean-revert, we can now see that the only explanation of why the dividend yield does *not* mean-revert is that the payout ratio does not.[25] Indeed, there is no reason in

---

[24]Although we should note that this approach, which is usually proposed by economists, is perhaps symptomatic of an excessive degree of humility, which may in turn be a reaction to the overly grandiose ideas that the profession used to have of itself. Managers may well know a lot more about what is going on in their own proximity, but they are at a disadvantage, compared with economists, when it comes to the analysis of economywide phenomena. How the advantages and disadvantages balance out is anybody's guess.

[25]Since, as we noted previously, the payout ratio can be expressed as the ratio of the dividend yield to the earnings yield.

principle why it should. So, from a different angle, we have come back to the two primary reasons we originally rejected the dividend yield as a criterion of value.

Understanding this link not only provides insight into the connection between earnings and dividends as alternative bases for valuing the stock market. We shall also see in Chapter 26, that if we *could* resolve the problem of knowing the appropriate payout ratio, then, if an ideally cyclically adjusted P/E multiple is q-equivalent, the dividend yield would be as well.

CONCLUSION: THE ADJUSTED P/E MULTIPLE AS AN INDICATOR OF STOCK MARKET VALUE

This chapter has dealt with two alternative approaches to adjusting P/E multiples: the prospective P/E, and the cyclically adjusted P/E. Only the second of these should be taken at all seriously.

We dealt with the prospective P/E, which uses forecasts of earnings, in only a cursory way, which is all that it deserves. Its use as an indicator of value is easily explicable in terms of its ability to help stockbrokers sell shares. It has no other merits.

Table 23.1 summarizes the performance of the much more serious candidate, the cyclically adjusted P/E multiple (and hence, of course, the cyclically adjusted earnings yield), in relation to our four tests. The table is a reminder of the fact that, as an analytical concept, the cyclically adjusted P/E does resolve most of the problems of the unadjusted P/E. If only we could measure it.

TABLE 23.1

The Cyclically Adjusted P/E Multiple and the Four Key Tests for Any Indicator of Value

Test	Cyclically Adjusted P/E
1. Is it measurable?	In general, no.
2. Does it mean-revert?	Yes.
3. Does it make economic sense?	In general, only if Siegel's constant actually *is* constant.
4. Does it say anything about future stock returns?	It would if you could measure it.

24

Yield Ratios and Yield Differences

SOME LIGHT RELIEF

Before we move on, in the next chapter, to the serious business of looking at how q matches up to our tests, we can pause and have some fun. This chapter is devoted to a set of valuation indicators that share a rare distinction, whichever particular version you choose, compared with those we have examined so far.[26] They all fail on all four of our key tests.

If these indicators were not so widely used, we should therefore not devote too much attention to them. But at least the process of doing so offers the prospect of some light relief.

THE STOCKBROKER'S FAVORITE VALUATION INDICATOR

In the search for a measure of value the recent fashion among stockbrokers has been to compare shares with bonds. The comparison has taken a variety of forms, but they have much in common and we will refer to them under the general, albeit incomplete, title of yield ratios. From the viewpoint of economics they are really rather bizarre, since their lack of validity can readily be

---

[26]We are extremely grateful to Daniel Murray of Smithers & Co., from whom we have shamelessly borrowed some of the material in this chapter.

shown whether they are examined from either a practical or a theoretical stance. They are, in some ways, all the more interesting for this reason. They are probably the criteria of value most widely used by stockbrokers, and financial journalists often refer to these indicators, without apparent scorn or awareness of their defects. Looking at yield ratios thus provides an outstanding and rather amusing example of the different approaches that economists and stockbrokers bring to the stock market.

As far as we can tell, the first ratio of this type that was claimed as useful for valuing shares was the ratio between bond yields and dividend yields. For example, the yield on long-term Treasury bonds was compared with the average dividend yield on the S&P Composite Index. If the ratio was less than, say, 2, shares were declared to be cheap. In recent years, however, this ratio has tended to show that the stock market was expensive, and there has been a tendency to change to the ratio between bond yields and earnings or to the difference in yields rather than to the ratio. As these indicators have, in turn, shown stocks to be expensive, the fashion has changed once again. The current tendency is to compare forecast earnings, after adding back certain expenses that are assumed to be nonrecurring.[27] The introduction of opinion in place of evidence is very useful, since the forecasts and adjustments can be changed to ensure that stock markets never appear overpriced.

This in fact underlines a particular charm of yield ratios from the viewpoint of stockbrokers—namely, that profits and interest rates tend to move in the same direction. In a strong economy, profits are strong and interest rates rise. In a weak economy, the opposite happens. Stockbrokers using yield ratios should therefore never be without some good news that they can use for selling stocks.

Although yield ratios have obvious attractions for stockbrokers, their acceptance by the financial press is bizarre in that these ratios so obviously don't work. It is intriguing to ask how and why the idea developed that yield ratios might provide a measure of fundamental value, in the face of overwhelming evidence to the contrary.

---

[27]On the issue of forecast earnings, see our discussion in the previous chapter.

The main reason bond yield ratios have become so popular is quite simply that the bull market of the 1980s and 1990s was accompanied by falling inflation, and hence falling nominal interest rates. As we show in Chart 24.1, by using only the data from this period it could be claimed that there was a relationship between falling bond yields and falling dividend and earnings yields (hence rising P/Es). It has therefore become fashionable to argue that falling inflation is good for share prices. There is even a new theory to account for this relationship. It is argued, reasonably enough, that low inflation means lower nominal interest rates. Lower nominal interest rates increase the value today of future payments in dollar terms. If you are promised $100 in a year's time, you can sell it for a larger sum when interest rates are low than when they are high. The argument then jumps to claiming that, as a result, future earnings are worth more today, when interest rates and inflation have fallen.

The supreme nonsense of this argument is best illustrated by comparing it with the exact opposite view that was held, generally with equal enthusiasm, in the previous 20-year bull market, from 1950 to 1968. As shown in Chart 24.2, in this period inflation was rising and there was an equally accidental correlation between rising bond yields and rising P/Es. It is interesting to note that from a statistical viewpoint, the evidence in this earlier period, which exactly contradicts the bond yield ratio, was actually stronger than it was in support of the theory in the later period. While the stock market, interest rates, and inflation were all rising together in the 1950s and 1960s, it was then believed that inflation was good for shares. The theory used to support the argument was that inflation would boost future earnings and that shares were worth more today because earnings in the future would be higher.

In practice, of course, neither of these mutually contradictory theories holds up. Inflation increases both future profits and interest rates, in nominal terms. The result is that the two factors knock each other out, and it makes no difference whatever to the fundamental value of stocks if the rate of inflation rises or falls.

The statistical case for valuing equities in relation to either bond yields or inflation is a prime example of selecting data to support the case you wish to make, rather than using data objec-

CHART 24.1

Do Bond and Equity Yields Move in the Same Direction? (1981–1998)

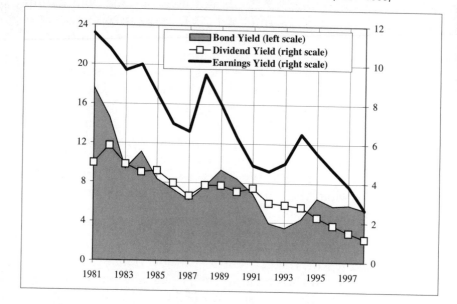

CHART 24.2

...Or Do Bond and Equity Yields Move in Opposite Directions? (1950–1968)

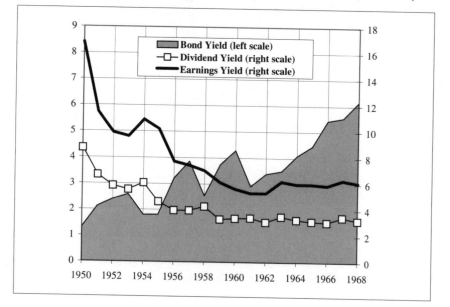

tively in an attempt to discover the truth. In other words, it is data mining, against which we issued a warning in Chapter 20. If you look ahead to Table 24.1, you will see that when all the available information is used there is essentially no correlation between bond yields and dividend yields or P/E multiples. Theoretical expectations are thus borne out in practice.

We noted at the start of the book the difference between economics and stockbroker economics. Economists, when faced with a conflict between theory and evidence, discard their theory. Stockbrokers discard the evidence. Bond yield ratios are a prime illustration.

For the sake of completeness, we now briefly examine yield ratios in relation to our four key tests.

Test No. 1: Do Yield Ratios and Related Indicators Provide a Measurable Indicator of Value?

No. It is true that the only new element that enters the picture when we consider yield ratios and related indicators is the long-term interest rate, which can be measured with some precision. However, as we discovered in the case of the dividend yield, simply having something that is well measured does not of itself imply that the associated indication of value can be so well measured, or indeed measured at all. We noted at the start of this chapter that at one time the appropriate ratio between the bond yield and the dividend yield was considered to be 2. This particular number, we also noted, has now fallen out of favor—as well it should, for there is neither a statistical nor an economic case for *any* particular number. Without that crucial number, however, it is impossible even to begin to use yield ratios to give an indication of value.[28]

Test No. 2: Do Yield Ratios and Related Indicators Mean-Revert?

No. One of the most obvious features of the history of yield ratios is that they clearly do not mean-revert. There is no ambiguity

---

[28]This is another example of the link between the two tests of measurability and mean reversion. If the yield ratio mean-reverted, there might be a case for picking the number to which it mean-reverts. But since it does not, as we shall see, there can be no such case, and accordingly there is no such number.

CHART 24.3

The Yield Ratios,* 1871–1997

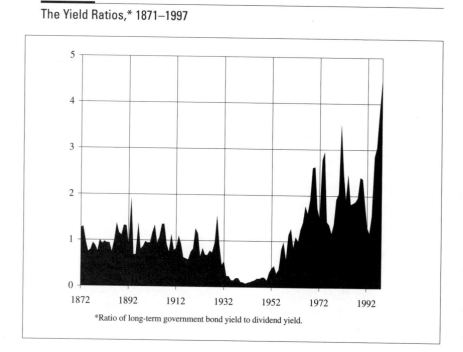

*Ratio of long-term government bond yield to dividend yield.

about this. Nor should it be at all surprising. Chart 24.3 summarizes the evidence by looking at the most common definition, the ratio of the bond yield to the dividend yield. A similar picture would emerge for all alternative measures of this type.

Table 24.1 helps explain why. It compares average bond yields, dividend yields, and earnings yields over a range of different periods. We have already pointed out that earnings yields have been mean-reverting, and that even dividend yields have shown some degree of stability. This indeed has been one of the key attractions of both as potential measures of value. Average bond yields, however, have been far from stable. They have fluctuated greatly with inflation, being much higher over the past 30 years than they had been over the previous periods. The recent tendency for stockbrokers to prefer bond yield ratios over dividend or earnings yields has therefore constituted a preference for something that most clearly doesn't work over something that may be imperfect but has a much better claim to be useful, even if subject to the objections we have raised in the preceding chapters.

TABLE 24.1

The Myth of Yield Ratios

1871–1997		Correlation Coefficient		
Bond and earnings yield		0.08		
Bond and dividend yield		–0.13		

Time Period	Average Inflation Rate	Average Dividend Yield	Average Earnings Yield	Average Bond Yield
1871–1997	2.1	4.8	8.1	4.9
1928–1948	3.1	5.2	7.6	1.6
1948–1968	1.7	4.6	8.6	3.2
1968–1997	4.7	3.9	8.2	7.9

As Chart 24.3 shows, the yield ratios that can be derived from these figures are thoroughly unstable. Average ratios were very different in the last 30 years than they were before, and the difference is associated with very different levels of inflation.

Test No. 3: Do Yield Ratios and Related Indicators Make Economic Sense as an Indicator of Value?

Again, unambiguously no. It should be said, in defense of some who have used yield ratios, that the attempt has at least sometimes been based on some idea, albeit mistaken, that the ratio might be theoretically justified. To the extent that it has any economic rationale at all, the use of yield ratios is based on the use, or more appropriately, *mis*use of the Dividend Discount Model, which we shall examine more thoroughly in Chapter 27.[29] On closer examination, however, the fact that yield ratios provide no guide to stock market value is no surprise whatever, since they have no economic basis. Indeed, it would be a grave shock if they did. This is because

---

[29]The possibility that the Dividend Discount Model might be misused in this way was in fact pointed out in a very prescient manner back in 1979 by the eminent economist Franco Modigliani and a colleague. See Modigliani and Cohn, "Inflation, Rational Valuation, and the Market," *Financial Analysts Journal* 35 (March–April 1979), pp. 22–44.

shares represent the ownership of real assets, while bonds provide an income that is fixed in nominal terms. Shares should therefore provide a protection against inflation, at least in the longer term, that bonds don't provide. Changes in inflation thus cause interest rates to rise and fall, but there is no reason to expect such fluctuations to affect dividend or earnings yields. The ratio of bond yields to earnings or dividend yields should therefore vary with inflation, being high when inflation is high and vice versa. In fact, theory correctly forecasts what has happened. As Chart 24.3 shows, the ratio between the long-term bond yield and the dividend yield was low when inflation was low, but rose steadily in the more inflationary period after World War II.

In recent years the U.S. government has issued indexed-linked bonds that guarantee both the interest and principal in real terms rather than nominal ones. The payments received by investors are tied to changes in the Consumer Price Index. Comparisons between the yields on index-linked bonds and shares do not therefore suffer from being affected by changes in inflation. Yield ratios cannot, however, be rendered usable by substituting index-linked bond yields for the traditional sort, because the failure to allow for inflation is not their only logical defect. Since yield ratios still make no sense on economic grounds, even without these additional defects, we shall not discuss them here, but we shall address this issue briefly when we come to look at the Dividend Discount Model, in Chapter 27.

Test No. 4: Do Yield Ratios and Related Indicators Tell You Anything About Future Stock Returns?

No. We can again answer this question using logic alone. We saw in Chapter 20 that mean reversion of any indicator is a necessary but not sufficient condition for its usefulness in stock market valuation. Yield ratios do not come anywhere near satisfying the necessary condition; therefore they cannot possibly satisfy the sufficient condition.

CONCLUSION: YIELD RATIOS AND RELATED MEASURES AS INDICATORS OF STOCK MARKET VALUE

Table 24.2 speaks for itself.

TABLE 24.2

Yield Ratios and Related Indicators, and the Four Key Tests for Any Indicator of Value

Test	Yield Ratios
1. Is it measurable?	No.
2. Does it mean-revert?	No.
3. Does it make economic sense?	No.
4. Does it say anything about future stock returns?	No.

CHAPTER 25

Corporate Net Worth and q

RESTATING THE CASE

Given that q is at the heart of this book, it may seem strange that this chapter will actually turn out to be shorter than some of the previous chapters on indicators that fail one or more of our tests. This is because we have already covered virtually all the ground we need to at various stages in this book. The main aim of this chapter is therefore not to repeat ourselves, but to show how what we have already said fits into the framework against which we have tested other indicators.

We shall therefore proceed, as with the alternative indicators, by seeing how q fares against our four tests. In an imperfect world, even q has its problems, about which we try to be open. But we imagine that it will be no surprise to you to discover that q does significantly better, on all four tests, than all other indicators.

If you are of a cynical turn of mind, you may suspect that this is because we have rigged the tests to produce the desired result. We have two responses to this. The first is to ask you to consider again whether the tests themselves are flawed. The second response is to note that these four tests have arisen out of our own experience of attempting to arrive at a satisfactory way of valuing stock markets. In the ten years that Smithers & Co.

has been running, we have considered dividend yields, P/E multiples, and cyclically adjusted P/E multiples as possible indicators of value. We confess that we have even looked at yield ratios. The defects of all these measures led us to look at q, and to an increasingly strong view that this was the right place to be looking. It also led us to look back at these alternative indicators and try to pin down what was wrong with them. In this process we developed the tests. We did not develop them because q satisfied them; we became satisfied with q because it passed them.

Test No. 1: Does q Provide a Measurable Indicator of Value?

As we have noted, the apparently simple property of measurability presents some surprisingly significant challenges and q is no exception. Indeed, objections to the measurement of q are probably the least unreasonable ones that can be made. These objections do not carry anywhere near enough weight to invalidate the evidence, but they merit being taken seriously. We therefore devote a major part of this chapter to them.

We have already mentioned two aspects of this problem in Chapter 15, when we considered the uncertainty surrounding precisely how overvalued the U.S. stock market was at the end of 1998. This uncertainty was of two kinds: uncertainty surrounding the precise value to which q mean-reverts, and uncertainty about the reliability of the data. In fact, the two forms of uncertainty are closely related. If we could be completely confident of the quality of the data, there could be no uncertainty about the value to which q mean-reverts. q is just the ratio of two different valuations of exactly the same thing—namely, corporate net worth. If these valuations differ, there will always be an incentive for arbitrage, and therefore they must be pushed toward equality on average. Hence q, if we could measure it properly, should have an average of 1.

In a world of imperfect statistics, q, as measured, has an average, not of 1, but of around 0.65. This may seem like quite a large discrepancy; but for a number of reasons, it is by no means as worrying as it might appear.

The first reason is that if you have ever worked with economic statistics, you will know that 0.65 is actually pretty close to 1. It is not 0.03, or 42.6. As a comparison statisticians can, for example, measure the trade deficit—the gap between imports and exports—in two different ways, the details of which we need not worry about here. The crucial point is that they routinely produce "statistical discrepancies" between the different measures, which can on occasion easily be as large as the measured deficit itself. It is important to be aware, however, that discrepancies occur despite the fact that the statisticians *know* that there can only be one true measure of the trade deficit. For this reason, if one measure proves to be higher than the other, they usually spend a lot of effort attempting to "reconcile" the two, yet nonetheless end up with discrepancies. The process of reconciliation, of course, typically involves looking for reasons to reduce the "too high" measure, and to increase the "too low" measure. Once again, this is of course data mining, but at least with good intentions, since the hypothesis that there is only one true measure of the trade deficit must be correct.

If the statisticians who produced one measure of the trade deficit were kept permanently away from the statisticians who produced the alternative measure, and were unaware of their figures, you may be sure that the discrepancies would be very much bigger. But this is in essence the way that figures for q are produced. The top element of q, the market value of nonfinancial equities, is produced by statisticians at the Federal Reserve Board. By far the most important element that feeds into the figures for corporate net worth is an estimate of the physical capital stock of the corporate sector. These figures are produced by analysts at the Bureau of Economic Analysis, who worry about the data in complete isolation. They certainly do not attempt to match the Fed's figures on average, over long periods, which is all that would be expected. In many ways, of course, this very independence is a tremendous advantage, since it means that there is absolutely no incentive for the statisticians to engage in any form of data mining. But it should therefore be no surprise that the numbers are somewhat inconsistent.

The second reason not to be too concerned by the fact that the average value of q, as measured, is not 1 is that it is very easy to see why a particularly important form of mismeasurement might lead to this result.

Of the two elements in the ratio, the top, the market value of equities, is reasonably well measured. The primary problem therefore must lie with the bottom of the ratio. If the ratio itself is on average lower than we would expect, this must imply that net worth is being systematically overstated. Probably the most likely explanation lies in the calculation of the capital stock. This is not the place to engage in a long discourse on the methodology of producing capital stock data—a subject that has long been debated among economists and statisticians. In brief, there are two main problems with attempting to measure the capital stock. The first is that you can never measure the capital stock directly; you can measure only the *change* in the capital stock. At some point (preferably as far back as possible), statisticians simply have to guess the level of the capital stock, on to which they then add the increases, which they can measure somewhat better. The second serious problem is how to measure the rate at which capital depreciates.

The first of these problems can easily lead to the capital stock being systematically mismeasured, since if the statisticians get it wrong initially, values can easily be affected for years, or even decades, afterward. But, we have to admit, this problem could just as easily lead to undermeasurement as to overmeasurement. So, while it makes mismeasurement of q more likely in general, it does not suggest any tendency to a downward bias.

The second problem, one of depreciation, is much more likely to lead to downward bias. When statisticians think about depreciation, they are essentially asking how long it takes for a given piece of capital—whether a machine, a computer, or a building—to become useless. If a given item is expected to last, say, ten years, they then normally depreciate the asset by one tenth of its initial value each year. Given their primary purpose in measuring the capital stock, which is to measure the productive capacity of the nation, this is perfectly reasonable. But there is a sounder economic approach. Normally, a capital asset is replaced, not when it physically wears out, but when it ceases to yield a profit. Economic depreciation occurs more rapidly than that measured by the statisticians. Since the whole idea of q is an economic concept, an ideal measure of q would use economic depreciation. But if capital is being depreciated too slowly, this must imply that the capital stock is being systematically overstated.

The word "systematic" is a very important one. It provides the third, and probably most important, reason that we are not too worried by the fact that the average value of *q* is not 1. If you had a wristwatch that was always ten minutes fast, you would have no problem telling the time, once you had figured out the "bias" in the signal it was giving you. The same applies to *q*. We would be much more worried about mismeasurement if there were not nearly a century's worth of evidence that *q* appears to be mismeasured on a pretty consistent basis.

The evidence for this is, of course, the performance of *q* in relation to the second test, with which we shall deal shortly. There is strong evidence, as we have already shown in earlier chapters, that *q* mean-reverts. This could not have come about if the mismeasurement were not on a reasonably regular basis. The mismeasurement complicates matters somewhat, because we need in effect to form an estimate of the average measurement error, given that "true" *q* must have an average of 1. But, as we saw in Chapter 15, given nearly 100 years' worth of data, we can form a pretty good estimate of the extent of the bias.

Since *q* is systematically underrecorded, overvaluation is indicated, not by whether *q* is greater or less than 1, but by whether it is greater or less than its average value. Of course, when the market is severely overvalued, as it has been since 1997, *q* is well above both. But a value of *q* of around 1.5 at the end of 1998 did not mean that at this time the market was "only" 50% overvalued. If the benchmark figure for comparison were 1, a glance at Chart 15.1 would suggest that the U.S. stock market was undervalued for the greater part of the twentieth century. This cannot make sense. It is, therefore, the comparison with the average value of around 0.65 that leads us to the conclusion, presented in Chapter 15, that at the end of 1998 Wall Street was around 2½ times overvalued.

This is not quite the last mention we shall make of the measurement issue. It turns out that many of the criticisms of *q* we have encountered are in effect concerns about measurement. So in Chapter 30 we shall look at some of these specific criticisms, alongside a range of other concerns often raised.

Test No. 2: Does *q* Mean-Revert?

We have already presented you with charts of q in various different guises that show how q mean-reverts, so we shall not bore you with yet another. But if you want visual evidence, look back at Chart 2.1, or Chart 15.1. Since, as we have already remarked, there appears to be an innate tendency of human beings to spot patterns when there may in reality be none, you may, if you wish, look at more objective statistical tests, which we provide in the Virtual Appendix. These do not, of course, give a completely unambiguous answer. They suggest that the probability that q does *not* mean-revert is pretty low, at around 3%, but is not zero. Such is life, when you are dealing with real data, and the degree of uncertainty which we saw in Chapter 20 is a necessary feature of any indicator of value. Indeed, we are not even entirely unhappy with this result. In general, if a statistical test rejects some hypothesis (in this case, the hypothesis that q does not mean-revert) with 100% probability, the reason, as often as not, is that the test has been carried out wrongly in some way or has even been rigged.[30]

We do not, of course, derive our confidence in q from its strong performance on the mean reversion test alone, which is only one, albeit an essential one, of our tests of value. The P/E multiple, for example, passes the mean reversion test as well as q, but falls down badly on others. This does not happen in the case of q. Possibly the most important point of all is that q is the *only* indicator of value that unambiguously passes our next test.[31]

Test No. 3: Does *q* Make Economic Sense?

Again, we have largely answered this question, both in Chapter 12, when we first discussed the idea of arbitrage which under-

---

[30]If, for example, we carry out the same tests on the mean-reverting indicator of value for our artificial stock market, which we looked at in Chapter 20, we also get low, but nonzero probabilities that this indicator does not mean-revert. Since we constructed the series ourselves, we know that the true probability is of course zero, but with "only" a century's worth of data, no test can come up with such a clear-cut answer.

[31]In Chapter 26 we shall show that the cyclically adjusted P/E multiple can also pass this test, but only because it is q-equivalent.

pins *q*, and in Chapter 16, when we showed why *q* must fall from its current levels. So we shall resist the temptation to repeat ourselves. We shall focus instead on the key issue that explains why *q* is different in the *way* that it makes economic sense.

We saw that the whole basis for using the P/E multiple to value markets rests on its mean reversion. The P/E is just the earnings yield turned upside down, and the earnings yield in turn must in the long run be equal to the return on stocks. So when we look at the P/E we are in effect asking if the stock market is offering a "fair" return, where our criterion of fairness is the historic return on stocks. This return has been remarkably stable over the past two centuries—indeed, that is why we refer to it as Siegel's constant. But the P/E works only if Siegel's constant *is* constant. Because economists have not yet figured out an explanation of why this should be so, it is perfectly possible in principle that it might *not* be constant. We could, for example, imagine a set of parallel universes, each of which had a different value of Siegel's constant. Each of these parallel universes would have a different "fair" return, and would therefore have a different P/E multiple in equilibrium. But in all these parallel universes, *q* would work just as well. Furthermore, it would mean-revert to the *same* value.[32]

There is a simple explanation for this constancy of *q* in equilibrium. The view we have presented so far is that *q* is a way of comparing prices in different markets. When *q* is high or low, this implies that the price of buying the corporate sector's assets via the stock market is high or low, compared with buying them directly. But there is also an alternative (but equivalent) way of thinking about *q*, as a comparison of rates of return. When *q* is high, this implies that rates of return on assets bought in the stock market are *low* compared with rates of return on assets bought directly.

So we can see the crucial difference between *q* and the P/E multiple. When we value the stock market using the P/E, and compare the earnings yield with Siegel's constant, we are implicitly saying that the latter is the "correct" return. When we use *q* to compare returns, there is no similar presumption that either

---

[32]Ignoring the measurement problem. We are in effect referring here to "true" *q* rather than measured *q*.

of the two returns we are comparing is correct: We are simply saying that they are *different*. Knowing this is sufficient to know that there is a clear incentive to arbitrage. So the economic case that q must mean-revert holds, whatever Siegel's constant may be or, indeed, whether or not it actually *is* constant.

Test No. 4: Does q Tell You Something About Future Stock Returns?

We have already shown, in considerable detail, that it does. In Chart 13.1, we showed that q and hindsight value had historically been very closely related, and hence that q would have given reliable danger signals of weak returns in the future. In Chapter 14 we showed that anyone who had used q to guide the decision to be in or out of stocks in the past would have earned both higher and less variable returns than investors who had simply followed the buy-and-hold strategy. We also gave another perspective with the good news about stocks as a long-run investment. Chart 17.4 showed the range of variability of returns that q-investors would have earned at different horizons, compared with buy-and-hold investors. Specifically, q-investors would have had a far lower probability of weak or negative returns, and would have had a higher probability of strong returns.

If this is not evidence enough for you, in the Appendix we also present statistical tests that confirm, on standard criteria, that q is also clearly a strong leading indicator of future returns. There is of course always a possibility that such a result could be spurious. So we also cite evidence from academic research by Stephen Wright and Donald Robertson, which investigates the likelihood that such a result could have arisen by chance if, in fact, q did not mean-revert and had no predictive power for stock prices. The probability is very low indeed, at around 3%.

RESTATING THE CASE FOR q

We have now achieved the primary aim of this part of the book. In Chapter 20 we set out our four key tests that any valid indicator of value must satisfy. Table 25.1 shows that q is the only indicator that passes all four tests. In an important sense, the very

TABLE 25.1

q and the Four Key Tests for Any Indicator of Value

Test	q
1. Is it measurable?	Yes. Modest measurement error is systematic, hence not a major concern.
2. Does it mean-revert?	Yes.
3. Does it make economic sense?	Yes.
4. Does it say anything about future stock returns?	Yes.

fact that all four tests yield positive results gives an additional significance to the individual tests. The whole is greater than the sum of its parts.

Even q is, of course, not a perfect indicator. We have seen, however, that the only significant limitation of q does not relate to q itself, but to the fact that we can measure it only imperfectly. This indeed is the limitation that prevented the use of q as an indicator of value until relatively recently, and that continues to rule out q for markets that do not have economic statistics of such a high quality as those for the United States.[33]

The remaining two chapters in Part Six are devoted to filling in details. The next chapter shows that, under certain assumptions, the signals given by both the P/E multiple and the dividend yield are equivalent to those given by q. This is reassuring, for two reasons. First, it supports our position, stated earlier, that there can only be a single true objective criterion of value. Second, it suggests an appropriate strategy when looking at stock markets for which q cannot be measured. Then, in Chapter 27, we go on to look at q in relation to the Dividend Discount Model. We show that a consistent approach to the model brings us back, yet again, to q.

---

[33]With colleagues at Smithers & Co. we have managed to construct a long run of data for q in the United Kingdom that shares many of the features of U.S. q. However, because of much greater limitations on data quality, the evidence for mean reversion is less strong. We have also constructed q over a rather short period (around 15 years) for Japan. In both countries the average value of q is reassuringly close to 1. In the case of Japan the average value is actually above 1, but this is unsurprising, since the period over which we constructed it covered the heights of the Tokyo bubble.

CHAPTER **26**

q-Equivalence

ALL INDICATORS OF VALUE LEAD TO *q*

As we seen in the last five chapters, *q* clearly outperforms all other indicators when judged by the four key tests. This might reasonably be considered all that is needed. Our approach, however, is rather different from that usually taken by those who comment on stock markets, so we will delve rather deeper into these matters in the next two chapters, in order to give greater depth to the case we are putting forward. Because we are discussing complex issues, which raise some fundamental issues of economics, we have found it necessary to introduce a few formulas in clarifying our arguments.

In Chapter 24 we made a strong claim for *q*. We said that if the defects of the dividend yield and the P/E could be rectified, we would simply arrive, by another route, at the same answer given by *q*. We call this feature "*q*-equivalence," and in this chapter we show how it works.

THE TWO CRUCIAL WEAKNESSES OF THE P/E MULTIPLE

We have shown that the P/E multiple has two crucial points of vulnerability. The first is the volatile way in which profits fluctuate. It is difficult to adjust for such fluctuations, and impossible to do so with complete accuracy, without a crystal ball, that gives us a complete view of the future. The second problem is that even if the P/E could be correctly adjusted, we would still need to know what it would be if the stock market was fairly valued. History suggests that the average P/E of around 13 represents fair value, but no economic theory has yet been produced to explain why. We do not know why the P/E should mean-revert or why, if it does, the figure to which it reverts should be around 13. If the average return to investors fell permanently, as some economists claim it has, then average P/E multiples would also rise permanently.

The idea of q-equivalence is that we can kill two birds with one stone. We can eliminate both problems associated with the P/E multiple at the same time, but in doing so, we effectively turn it into q.

VALUING THE STOCK MARKET WITH THE CYCLICALLY ADJUSTED P/E

If we could measure the cyclically adjusted P/E and knew what it should be if the market were fairly valued, we could estimate the degree to which the stock market was overvalued, by dividing the cyclically adjusted P/E by the "fair value" or "benchmark" P/E; thus:

$$\text{Overvaluation} \ = \ \frac{\text{Cyclically Adjusted P/E}}{\text{Benchmark P/E}}$$

Since the P/E is simply the earnings yield turned upside down, we can rewrite this as follows:

$$\text{Overvaluation} \ = \ \frac{\dfrac{1}{\text{Cyclically Adjusted Earnings Yield}}}{\dfrac{1}{\text{Benchmark Stock Return}}}$$

Since dividing by a fraction is equivalent to multiplying by the same fraction turned upside down, this in turn becomes:

$$\text{Overvaluation} = \frac{\text{Benchmark Stock Return}}{\text{Cyclically Adjusted Earnings Yield}}$$

Our problem, of course, is that, though we can estimate the benchmark stock return for the past, we do not know if this is the appropriate value for the future. But let's just assume that we know what the appropriate future value is. If the cyclically adjusted earnings yield equaled the benchmark stock return, then, since the ratio of any number to itself is 1, this measure of overvaluation would be equal to 1, and the market would be fairly valued. If the earnings yield were below the benchmark return (corresponding to a high P/E), then the ratio would be above 1, indicating overvaluation, and vice versa for undervaluation.

A CLOSER LOOK AT CYCLICAL ADJUSTMENT OF PROFITS

To progress from here, we need to look carefully at what cyclically adjusted earnings are, and we do this by looking at how capital is rewarded.

Profits represent the reward for investing capital. The capital that is financed by loans receives its reward from interest payments. The remainder, which is the equity capital, is entitled to all the rest of the profits, which are those that remain after deducting interest and tax. The capital that generates these profits is thus the physical capital (including machinery, building, inventory, and real estate) and the financial capital that businesses need to cover the debts that customers owe but have not yet paid. From this we can deduct the amount that each business owes to its suppliers and the amount borrowed from banks and raised through bond issues. The value of all this is the current replacement cost of the physical assets less the net financial liabilities. If this sounds familiar, then it should be. This is, of course, corporate net worth, which feeds into the bottom of our definition of *q*.

The profitability of companies' equity capital is thus their earnings, which are profits, after interest and tax, divided by their net worth:

$$\text{Return on Net Worth} \quad = \quad \frac{\text{Earnings}}{\text{Net Worth}}$$

which is the same thing as:

$$\text{Earnings} = \text{Return on Net Worth} \times \text{Net Worth}$$

In order to put this on the same basis as the P/E and earnings yield, we need to divide both sides of the equation by the number of shares, to give:

$$\text{Earnings Per Share} = \text{Return on Net Worth} \times \text{Net Worth Per Share}$$

So far we have been dealing only with unadjusted earnings. We now need to think about how we might make the correct cyclical adjustment. The right-hand side of the above equation has two parts. One of these, net worth per share, is, as we saw in the previous chapter, pretty slow-moving. Net worth is so large in relation to GDP that it cannot change rapidly. This means that any adjustment we make to cyclical earnings will be virtually the same as any adjustment we make to the return on net worth.[34]

An obvious way to get a correct adjustment for cyclical earnings per share is, therefore, to estimate what level they would be at if the return on net worth were at some fair or benchmark level:

$$\text{Cyclically Adjusted Earnings per Share}$$
$$= \text{Benchmark Return on Net Worth} \times \text{Net Worth per Share}$$

This way of adjusting earnings matches neatly the conditions we demanded of any cyclical adjustment in Chapter 23. It will produce a measure that is slow-moving and predictable, since net worth is slow-moving and predictable. The cyclical adjustment will also cancel out over long enough periods, since other-

---

[34]We shall come back to this issue later in the chapter.

wise the benchmark return on net worth, whatever it may be, would be an unreasonable return to use.

THE RETURN ON EQUITY CAPITAL MUST EQUAL THE COST OF EQUITY CAPITAL

We don't know either the benchmark return on stocks or the benchmark return on net worth. So introducing these two concepts may therefore seem to complicate matters. In practice it greatly simplifies them, because of a basic principle of economic theory. While we can't know what either is, we know that they must, in equilibrium, be the same! Just as the cost of borrowing for companies has to be the same as the return to the lenders, so the cost of equity to companies must also be the same as the return to investors. The return on capital must in equilibrium equal the cost of capital. This applies to both the debt of corporations and to their equity. So the benchmark return on net worth must be the same as the benchmark return on stocks.

All that is now needed is to use the formula for the cyclically adjusted earnings yield:

$$\text{Cyclically Adjusted Earnings Yield} = \frac{\text{Cyclically Adjusted Earnings per Share}}{\text{Share Price}}$$

and to plug this into our formula for overvaluation, to give:

$$\text{Overvaluation} = \frac{\text{Benchmark Stock Return}}{\dfrac{\text{Cyclically Adjusted Earnings per Share}}{\text{Share Price}}}$$

Finally, using our formula for cyclically adjusting earnings per share, the benchmark return on net worth equals the benchmark stock return, so we have:

$$\text{Overvaluation} = \frac{\text{Benchmark Stock Return}}{\dfrac{\text{Benchmark Stock Return} \times \text{Net Worth per Share}}{\text{Share Price}}}$$

We can simplify the formula using two handy mathematical rules. One is that the ratio of any number to itself is 1. This means that we don't need to know what the appropriate benchmark stock return actually is, since it drops out of the formula. The other is the rule that dividing by a fraction is the same as multiplying by the same fraction turned upside down. This leaves us with a greatly simplified version of the formula for overvaluation using the cyclically adjusted P/E, namely:

$$\text{Overvaluation} \ = \ \frac{\text{Share Price}}{\text{Net Worth per Share}} \ = \ q$$

So the cyclically adjusted P/E takes us right back to q! This is what we mean by q-equivalence.[35]

In demonstrating q-equivalence, we have not just performed a sequence of mathematical tricks, but illustrated the crucial point that, in the end, any indicator of value must be independent of rates of return. This can be illustrated by imagining a world where investors really did demand lower returns. P/Es would in equilibrium have to be higher, but returns on net worth would also have to fall by the exact same amount that P/Es rise. This is because P/Es represent the cost of equity capital and the cost of capital has to equal its return.

In this imaginary world of lower returns, profits would fluctuate around a lower level, in relation to net worth, than before. The rate of return earned when profits were at their average and cyclically adjusted level would thus need to be lower too. If you tried to cyclically adjust profits assuming a higher return, over the course of time your cyclical adjustment would not cancel out. Cyclically adjusted profits would be higher, on average, than actual profits, which would breach our obvious condition for any reasonable cyclical adjustment. The only cyclical adjustment that

---

[35]Note that, for the sake of simplicity, we are assuming here that what we are measuring is true q, or the measure of q that mean-reverts to 1. We saw in the last chapter that measured q mean-reverts to a number less than 1. The necessary implication is that, in the data, the measured return on net worth has on average been lower than the return on stocks. But the explanation is the same one we offered in the last chapter: If the capital stock is habitually overstated, then the return on net worth must of necessity be habitually understated.

would work would therefore be the one we propose above. If you use that one, however, rates of return drop out of the formula altogether, and all that is left is q.

IS THE DIVIDEND YIELD *q*-EQUIVALENT TOO?

We saw in Chapter 23 that one way to view the dividend yield is to see it as a cyclically adjusted earnings yield, divided by the appropriate payout ratio. The only problem with this approach is that there is no way of knowing what the appropriate payout ratio is. But if we did know what it was, we would be able to know the cyclically adjusted P/E by simply multiplying the current dividend yield by the appropriate payout ratio. Since the cyclically adjusted P/E is q-equivalent, the appropriately adjusted dividend yield must be q-equivalent too.

FUNDAMENTAL VALUE REVISITED

There is one complication that we now need to address. When we carried out the cyclical adjustment earlier, we simply changed the return on net worth, but made no change to net worth itself. We justified this by saying that net worth is slow-moving and predictable, and thus cannot respond much to short-term movements in the economy. In simplifying our analysis in this way, we used an approach that is very common in economics. We were treating net worth, which is the fundamental for q, as if it were "exogenous." Being exogenous is not the same as being constant. It simply means that net worth is unaffected by the other bits of the economy we are looking at.

This is not, however, totally correct. Net worth is not truly exogenous. Nothing in economics ever is. Looking for a fundamental that is entirely exogenous is like searching for the Holy Grail. (As an example of something truly exogenous, economists used to cite changes in the weather—but since global warming became an issue, even the weather appears to be affected by the economy.) Everything, it seems, responds to something else.

In fact, markets could never get out of line with their value if net worth was completely exogenous and thus unaffected by the economy. We saw in Chapter 20 that uncertainty about mean reversion is absolutely essential if value is ever to differ from price. If there were no element of doubt about the market's fundamental value, stocks would always be correctly priced. To see why, we need only look at what would happen if we could measure fundamental value perfectly, and predict it with perfect precision. The ratio of the share price to fundamental value must be mean-reverting, so while, at the dawn of capitalism, there could be some uncertainty about short-term stock market fluctuations, over the longer term we would have a money machine that would become 100% reliable. It would seem barely credible if, after 300 years or more of stock market trading, the profits from buying cheaply and selling dearly would not have smoothed away all divergence of price from value. Stocks would then not just be relatively safe investments, but perfectly safe ones, which must be impossible in an uncertain world.

It is therefore important to ask whether we should be worried about the fact that there can be no truly exogenous fundamental value. The answer is clearly no, and the explanation lies in the idea of arbitrage, which underpins q. We saw that, when q is high, it must fall. This can, and indeed does, take place at least in part through changes in the fundamental, as well as changes in price. We saw, indeed, that when James Tobin first invented the idea of q, it was usually thought of as adjusting primarily through changes in the capital stock (i.e., changes in the fundamental, rather than the stock price). We do not differ on the point of principle, which is that the capital stock changes in response to changes in q. There is, however, an important difference of emphasis. The evidence shows that the major adjustment comes through changes in stock prices.[36] Far from being shaken by the evidence that net worth responds to q, it is a help. Provided, as the evidence shows, that the major response comes through stock price changes, the fact that net worth responds to a small degree simply helps add the necessary element of uncertainty, without which value could not exist separately from price.

---

[36]Unfortunately, the evidence for this response is of necessity rather technical, but is presented in the paper previously cited by Stephen Wright and Donald Robertson. It shows that the response of net worth is not "statistically significant," but is in line with what Tobin's theory would suggest.

The evidence of history shows that net worth is not exogenous: It responds, as James Tobin suggested it should, to high and low values of *q*. But it does not respond anywhere near enough to explain the mean reversion of *q*. Far more of the adjustment has come through prices, which explains why *q* satisfies the leading indicator test so well.

It is easy to see why net worth cannot respond enough to make *q* mean-revert—especially from extreme values. Net worth is simply too large in relation to GDP for changes in net worth to occur other than very slowly. Anyone with a modest knowledge of the speed with which stock markets have fallen will, however, know that massive changes in stock market valuations can occur only too easily and very rapidly. On the other hand, it is virtually unimaginable to see how *q* could adjust back from such extreme values via changes in net worth alone.

Even in 1998, which was a good year for profits, it would have taken 42 years of retained profits to bring net worth up to equal the value placed by the stock market on companies. It might therefore seem that the gap could be closed, without an adjustment in stock prices, provided investors were simply prepared to wait for 42 years. But even then, the moving-target problem arises again. For if stock prices were actually unchanged in nominal terms, investors in stocks would be getting a return equal to the dividend yield, minus the inflation rate, which is certainly not what they were expecting and which certainly does not represent a decent return. We saw in Chapter 15 that stock prices would need to rise by around 2½% in real terms for investors even to match the return on a perfectly safe indexed bond. Hence net worth would need to increase by at least this amount in real terms each year, just to keep the gap constant. To close the gap, it would have to rise even faster.

We can begin to see why the historic record shows that net worth has played such a limited role in bringing about mean reversion of *q*. As we have seen, nothing is exogenous, but, because the feasible changes in net worth are so small in relation to the gap that needs to be closed, we can in practice afford to ignore them. When, therefore, we say that the stock market is roughly 2½ times overvalued, we do not need to imply that all of the adjustment need come via stock prices. We can and do imply, however, that by far the greater part will.

CONCLUSION: CYCLICALLY ADJUSTED P/Es AND DIVIDEND YIELDS ARE *q*-EQUIVALENT

We hope that we have succeeded, in this chapter, in explaining in greater detail why and how rectifying the defects in other indicators inevitably renders them just another way of reaching the same answer as q. Once you think of profits as just another kind of return, on a particular kind of capital, it follows that cyclically adjusted profits simply represent a "normal" return on that capital. In the case of equity, this capital is corporate net worth. Once q-equivalence has been understood, it follows that the correct value of equity must be net worth and this leads us straight back to q.

q and the Dividend Discount Model

The Dividend Discount Model is probably the most widely used approach to valuing stock markets. It also arguably the least well understood. For both of these reasons, it would be inappropriate for us simply to ignore it. You may indeed be surprised that we have got so far into the book without making more than a passing reference to it. You may rest assured, however, that we do not wish to throw out existing economic theories in which the Dividend Discount Model is the basis for stock market value. The Dividend Discount Model is clearly correct. It is also clearly consistent with *q*. To see this, we shall draw again on a key insight that enabled us to demonstrate, in the last chapter, the idea of *q*-equivalence. That is, the return on equity capital must equal the cost of equity capital. Ignoring this key idea results in endless misuses of the Dividend Discount Model. Taking it into account brings us back, yet again, to *q*.

HOW THE MODEL WORKS

The Dividend Discount Model is based on fundamental principles that can be used for valuing other assets as well as stocks. It is therefore important to understand the basic principles involved and how they can be applied, or misapplied, to the valuation of stock markets.

The basic principle of discounting is the same as the basic principle of compound interest. A rate of discount is like a rate of interest stood on its head. If you are offered payments in the future, they are not worth as much as if they were to take place today. How much less depends on two things: how far away the payments are in the future, and the rate at which these payments are discounted.

To remind you of the key ideas in discounting, which are crucial for our purposes in this chapter, we offer the following brief examples.

1. Suppose you are offered $100 in one year's time, with absolutely no risk of default. How much would you pay for this today? The answer should be pretty familiar. If money in the bank is also at zero risk, and pays you 10%, then you would be prepared to pay roughly $90 (or, precisely, $90.91), since if you put this amount on deposit in the bank, you would also end up with $100 in a year's time ($90.91 \times 1.1 = 100$). So the "present value" of $100 in a year's time is $90.91.

2. It should also be pretty familiar that you will pay less for $100 in two years' time. On the same assumptions, you would pay, very roughly, $80 (or, precisely, $81.16), since if you put this amount on deposit for two years, it would also end up being worth $100 ($81.16 \times 1.1 \times 1.1 = 100$). So the present value of $100 in two years' time is $81.16.

3. What if you were offered $100 per annum *forever*? There are two ways to answer: one simple, and one complicated. The complicated way is to treat each of the $100 you will receive as in the last two examples. The further away each payment is in time, the less is its present value. You could keep on adding up the present values of each of the payments, with each being worth progressively less, until either you get bored or your calculator runs out of decimal places. By the time you have done this, you may have remembered the simple way to get the same answer, which is to ask how much money you would need to put permanently on deposit in order to receive an income of $100 per annum indefinitely. If the interest rate is 10%, the answer is of course

$1000. But you would have arrived at the same answer in the end, whichever approach you had used.[37]

4. Finally, and a little harder, suppose you were offered an annual payment of just $10, but it grew every year at 9% per annum and, again, went on forever. It may not seem so obvious, but this would also be worth $1000. To see why, remember that you could get exactly the same income path by depositing $1000 in the bank, and taking only 1% of your capital in income each year, leaving the rest on deposit. In this case, your capital would increase at 9% each year, and so would the amount you could withdraw. Since you could replicate this income pattern by depositing an initial $1000 on which you were paid an interest rate of 10%, then you would pay $1000 to get the income.

The last two of these examples might seem a little rarefied, but they are actually extremely relevant to the underlying value of stocks, for three important reasons.

First, we saw in Chapter 9 that stocks and shares are, in effect, assets that last forever. The fact that human beings are not similarly immortal does not matter, as long as one mortal investor can sell off shares in a particular company to another mortal investor. The same would apply with our last two examples. So, in the fourth example, even if you wanted to hold on to the asset for only a couple of years, by then it would be worth more (since the income would have grown), and you would be able to sell it to someone else. (We are of course at present neglecting risk, but we shall get back to that issue shortly.)

Second, the two examples show that it is not the absolute level of the income you receive that matters, but the underlying rate of return that is generating that income stream. Thus, in the fourth example, any combination of an income at rate of $x\%$ and a rate of growth of that income at $y\%$ would have been worth the

---

[37]This is just like the story of Achilles and the tortoise. Despite all that your mathematics teachers may have told you, Achilles does catch the tortoise in the end, and at a very precise point in time and place. If Achilles runs ten times as fast as the tortoise, and the tortoise is one mile ahead, he catches up when the tortoise has run one ninth of one mile and when Achilles has run ten times as far—that is, ten ninths, or one and one ninth miles. The rest of the story was just invented to turn you off mathematics.

same, as long as x and y had added up to 10%. The parallel with dividends, and the growth of dividends, should be fairly clear. In the fourth example, therefore, you could think of the $10 you receive as a dividend yield of 1% (i.e., 10 ÷ 1000). But the total return the investment is generating is still 10%, which is equal to the dividend yield *plus* the growth rate of that dividend. This fundamental insight is the basis of the Dividend Discount Model.[38]

Third, there is a clear link between this model and the way of looking at total returns on stocks that we have applied so many times in this book. We have seen that the total return is equal to the dividend yield plus the capital gain or loss. Suppose you held the asset described in the fourth example for just one year, and then sold it. Someone else would be prepared to pay more for it than you did, because the initial value of the income that investor would be buying is 9% higher. Therefore, if the market was working at all efficiently, the investor would pay you 9% more than your initial investment. Your total return would therefore by your "dividend" of 1% and your capital gain of 9%. Thus, in a fairly valued market, your capital gain would precisely match the growth of dividends.[39]

All assets can be valued in this way, and the model therefore applies to both individual shares and to the stock market as a whole. The problem with using the Dividend Discount Model in practice, however, should be readily apparent. Since the value of the asset depends on discounting the future income, the investor needs to know both what the future income will be and what interest rate to use to discount that income. In our examples, both of these were assumed to be known. Since in practice neither can normally be known, the Dividend Discount Model, although clearly true, is not obviously useful. In the case of the stock market as a whole, however, it is not necessary to know either the discount rate or the future income, because the two are not independent of each other.

---

[38]Note that we are simplifying slightly, since the income you receive here is like next year's dividend, whereas the dividend yield as usually measured is calculated using the dividend received in the current year.

[39]What we have presented here is a highly simplified version of the model, which is normally referred to by economists as the Gordon Growth Model. See M.J. Gordon, *The Investment, Financing, and Valuation of the Corporation* (Homewood, IL: Irwin, 1962).

THE RIGHT DISCOUNT RATE IS THE COST OF EQUITY CAPITAL

In our examples we simplified matters by assuming away any risk, and imagining the existence of a bank that could guarantee payments ad infinitum. In an uncertain world, however, you would not apply the same discount rate to a payment to be received in, say one year's time, as to a payment to be received in two years' time. If, for example, a bond is to be correctly valued, the future income and capital payments must be discounted at the current rate of interest for bonds of the same duration and risk. Investors will wrongly value bonds if they use short-term interest rates to discount long-term bonds, or the rates applicable to government bonds, when valuing the debts of corporations.

The correct rate is always the rate of interest that it would cost the borrower to raise money by issuing that particular type of debt. Just as the cost of debt is the correct rate of discount to apply to bonds, so the cost of equity capital is the correct rate of discount to apply to dividends. What is a cost to the firm is, of course, a return to the investor who buys the firm's stocks. The cost of equity capital to the firm that issues equity is therefore, as we saw in the last chapter, simply the return that investors demand on stocks.[40]

At any particular time, of course, the cost of equity depends on the level of the stock market. When shares are expensive equity is cheap to raise, from the point of view of the firm, and vice versa. When valuing stocks, rather than observing their current price, however, we should not use the current cost of equity, but what it would cost if stocks were fairly priced. As we noted in the previous chapter, we can never be certain what this correct figure is, but we do know that in equilibrium it must equal the return on equity (in other words, the return on net worth), just as we know that the cost of bonds to the borrower is the same as the return received by the investor. It is indeed one of the most fundamental principles of economics that, in equilibrium, the cost of capital must equal its return.

---

[40]There is no escaping the potential for confusion, in terms of communication, that arises from the fact that what is a return to one individual must be a cost to another. We hope we have discussed this point sufficiently to make our meaning clear.

We saw, however, in our fourth example at the start of this chapter, that if we discount any flow of dividends by the return on capital that is producing those dividends, we always get the same answer. The result is that, whatever the return on equity capital, we know that the Dividend Discount Model, if correctly applied, will value the corporations in aggregate at their net worth. The Dividend Discount Model therefore produces the same answer as q.

There are thus three separate economic principles that are mutually supportive.

- The fundamental value of the equity capital of all companies has to be the same as their net worth.
- The fundamental value of equities of all companies has to be the discounted value of their future dividends.
- The cost of equity capital for all companies in aggregate has to be the same, over the long term, as the return on it.

Each of these three principles is true in isolation. Alternatively, once any two have been demonstrated, the third must follow. This is because they are not only true but mutually dependent. The reason that all three economic principles are mutually supportive is that they are based on the same basic assumptions about economics.

HISTORICAL EXPERIENCE

We should by now have made clear that we cannot be certain about the correct discount rate to use for the future. But we do know the correct one to use in the past. As we have already pointed out, one of the so far unsolved mysteries of economics is why the long-term real return on stocks has been so stable at around 6½%, the value we have referred to as Siegel's constant. The rule that the return on equity must equal its cost requires, therefore, that the average long-term cost of equity must also be around 6½%.

The cost of equity to companies would be the same as the dividend yield, if firms paid out all their profits in dividends. But as we saw in our examples, the proportion actually paid out does not matter for the fundamental value of any asset. What matters is the return that generates these dividends, since it also generates the growth of dividends. This is the earnings yield, which includes both the dividend and the retained profits that allow dividends to grow. The average earnings yield should therefore be 6½%, which is gratifyingly close to what it actually has been.

We saw in Chapter 22 that the (geometric) average of the P/E multiple since 1871 has been 13. This corresponds to an average earnings yield of 7.7% (1/13 = 0.077). Given the difficulties of measuring two things that are equal only in equilibrium, the figure is actually pretty close. But allowing for two types of measurement problem might easily explain even this modest difference. The first is the tendency we have noted for earnings figures to be manipulated upward (a prime example is the early 1930s, when corporations may well have been making losses, but reported positive earnings). The second is that the real return on stocks may have been somewhat understated if, as has recently been suggested by the Boskin Commission, inflation has been systematically overstated.

MISUSING THE DIVIDEND DISCOUNT MODEL

Although the Dividend Discount Model when correctly applied to the valuation of the stock market gives the same answer as *q*, it can of course be misapplied. Such misapplications are sadly common. As we have shown, the return on equity and the discount rate are not independent. Nor is the growth rate of dividends independent of the return on equity that generates that growth. The basis of all misapplications of the model is to assume that at least two of these, and often all three, are independent. Once this breach of basic economic principles has been made, the model can be readily misused to give virtually any answer desired. It then becomes ideal for those who wish to sell stocks, rather than to establish their true value. Markets can be valued at any level, by simply varying the assumptions regarding either the growth rate or the discount rate.

Take, for example, the fall in the dividend yield that took place over the 1990s. As we saw in Chapter 21, stocks at the end of that decade yielded less than 1½%, compared with an average of around 5%. As we also saw, there are two possible explanations, which are consistent with basic economic theory. The first is that companies have changed their dividend policies and are now retaining most of their profits. The second is that the stock market has become wildly overpriced.

If the first explanation is correct, then the higher retentions should enable dividends to grow more rapidly in the future. The problem is that, as Chart 21.2 showed, payout ratios have not changed enough for this to be a satisfactory explanation. From the stockbrokers' viewpoint, therefore, there is an obvious danger that the second commonsense view will become accepted and people will stop buying stocks that are so wildly overvalued.

In their anxiety to prevent the commonsense approach from becoming widely accepted, stockbrokers like to assume that the discount rate has fallen, but without having any impact on the future growth of dividends. The two most frequent examples are valuation models that use bond yields to derive discount rates and models that claim Siegel's constant is not, after all, constant, but has fallen.

Proponents of the latter group usually argue for a change in the "equity risk premium," and therefore, by implication, that Siegel's constant has changed. They argue that this justifies a much higher P/E ratio, and that this in turn justifies the current level of the stock market or an even higher one. We shall deal with this argument in more detail in Chapter 29. At this stage we shall simply point out, first, that such arguments have a chronic tendency to mutual inconsistency and, second, that such claims ignore the fact that the cost of capital must in equilibrium be equal to its return.

We have already dealt with the silliest arguments used by the former group. In Chapter 24 we showed why equities cannot be valued in relation to nominal bond yields. So at this point we shall merely point out again that those who rely on bond yields are wrongly assuming that the future growth in dividends can remain unaltered, in spite of a change in the rate of discount. If inflation falls, as it has done over the past two decades, then future streams of income become more valuable. This has of course been why bond prices have risen so strongly while inflation has fallen. What is not reasonable is to assume that profits and dividends will grow as fast in the future, when inflation is assumed to be lower, as they have in the past. Clearly profits and dividends will grow more slowly if inflation is low.

It is not, of course, necessary to fall into this particular trap. The difference between nominal and real interest rates is widely understood.[41] Now that the U.S. government issues index-linked bonds, we can also easily find out what long-term real rates of interest are, without having to make assumptions about future inflation. Therefore, it might appear to be possible to use the Dividend Discount Model to price stocks by reference to real rates of interest. Some academic economists have applied this approach; but it is a matter of interest that, as far as we know, stockbrokers have not done so. The reason, we suspect, is quite simple. We shall see that any such analysis leads to the conclusion that the stock market is wildly overvalued. Since stockbroker valuation methods are designed not to value stocks but to sell them, this approach has no attractions among stockbrokers.

It is no surprise that using real interest rates to value the stock market results in estimates of severe overvaluation. This approach implies virtually the same approach to valuation as using the P/E multiple. The real bond yield is the correct rate at which to discount real bonds, but not assets that are more risky. It is therefore necessary to add some estimate of the "equity risk premium" to the bond yield used. Given the current real bond yield of nearly 4%, a rate of well over 6% would be appropriate if the evidence of the past were used, because the long-term return on stocks has been on the order of 1% to 3% above the long-term return on bonds. As we have already shown, the correct discount rate should, in a fairly valued market, be the same as the earnings yield. Earnings yields of between 5% and 7% would be equivalent to P/E multiples of between 20 and 14. Since current P/Es are 2 to 2½ times these figures, this approach ends up giving essentially the same answer that we obtained by using the P/E multiple to value the market. Since we have already noted that

---

[41]Professor James Tobin told one of the authors a nice story, which illustrates that this understanding has not always been universal. In the 1960s, he met with a group of senior managers of a major corporation, and was discussing the present value calculations they carried out for investment projects (which must follow the same principles as those that underpin the Dividend Discount Model). He asked them if, in doing so, they used real interest rates. "Sure," came the answer. "We get them out of the *Wall Street Journal*...."

the P/E multiple has fallen from favor, it is easy to see why stockbrokers prefer to misuse the Dividend Discount Model by ignoring the existence of real bond yields and the information that can be derived from them.

But we should also note that the approach is in any case flawed in one crucial respect. Dealing with the flaw properly would make the implied figure for overvaluation not just similar but *identical* to that arrived at by using the cyclically adjusted P/E and, hence, of course, *q*.

The crucial flaw is that using current real interest rates results in an implied valuation criterion that is not independent. All this approach does is value stocks *relative* to bonds. But long-term bond yields are not "exogenous."[42] Although the short-term rate of interest is pretty much under the control of the Federal Reserve, this is very much not the case for the long-term, real rate of interest. That is ultimately set by markets, and cannot be independent of the return on stocks.

Any estimate of "fair" value measured this way can therefore, at best, be as good as the value that markets put on bonds. If stock markets can deviate from fair value, there is plenty of reason to expect (plus quite a lot of evidence) that bond markets can as well. Thus, even though the stock market *does* currently look overvalued relative to the bond market, the situation might easily have arisen by accident.

The only way to deal with the fact that the bond yield is not independent of the stock market is to use, instead of current yields, some benchmark value for the long-term real bond yield, plus some benchmark value for the equity risk premium, calculated by looking at the average gap between real returns on stocks and bonds. If historic averages are used, however, this is just the same as using Siegel's constant directly! We have ended up precisely where we would have been if we had used the P/E multiple to value the market, with all the attendant problems that we discussed in Chapter 22.[43] If we dealt with these problems by cyclically adjusting earnings, we would, of course, as the previous chapter showed, end up, yet again, with *q*.

---

[42]See our discussion of this concept in the previous chapter.
[43]The fact that the answer we arrived at using current real bond yields was so close is due to the fact that these are very close to their historic average.

CONCLUSION: *q* AND THE DIVIDEND DISCOUNT MODEL

The Dividend Discount Model must be correct, but misuses of it are extremely common, because they ignore the necessary links between the elements that feed into it. In this chapter we have shown that the Dividend Discount Model, if it is used properly, must bring us, yet again, back to *q*. If we use the correct discount rate, and take proper account of the necessary link between this, the return on capital, and the rate of growth of dividends, then the fundamental value of the stock market is simply corporate net worth. The degree of overvaluation is shown by the ratio between actual and fundamental value, which is thus the ratio between market value and net worth. This is, of course, simply *q*.

SEVEN

q AND THE ANTI-*q*s

We have to acknowledge the sad but rather obvious fact that not everyone agrees with us about *q*. If they did, Wall Street would not have reached the heights it has. In Part Seven, rather than examining the case for *q*, we shall examine the case against.

In Chapter 28 we address objections that some economists have raised, not to the idea of *q* itself, but to the idea that it can be possible to value markets in any useful way. These are serious objections, which should be dealt with seriously, but they can, as you will see, be readily answered. Indeed, our approach to *q* can reconcile several implicit inconsistencies among economists.

In Chapter 29 we address the possibility that current market valuations might be justified by a permanent rise in the P/E multiple. The case is derived from theoretical economic arguments involving the "equity risk premium." The unfortunate result has been a crude misrepresentation of a very respectable piece of economic research. We show that such claims cannot be reconciled either with the evidence or with economic logic.

Finally, in Chapter 30, we address objections by those for whom the case for *q* is unambiguously bad news. Stockbrokers argue against *q* because they have to. As a result their objections are a hodgepodge of unsubstantiated assertions, logical inconsistencies, and sheer obfuscation. Nonetheless, we list, and refute, all the objections to *q* we have come across from the stockbroking community.

CHAPTER 28

The q Debate
Among Economists

WHEN ECONOMISTS DISAGREE

Economists are an argumentative lot, but probably no more so than members of other professions that deal with intellectually challenging ideas. Noneconomists tend to get a rather distorted picture of the degree of disagreement among economists, largely because disagreement is so much more fun than consensus, and thus attracts more media attention. Contrary to this impression, however, the majority of economists in fact share a consensus view on quite a range of issues. When they disagree, they disagree within a common framework.

The ideas set out in this book, and the arguments we use to support them, are also a product of this common framework. To the extent that we disagree with other economists on the use of q to value markets, it is a disagreement on how we apply our framework, not on the framework itself. This chapter is intended to show where our conclusions fit within this shared outlook and to relate them to the different conclusions arrived at by other economists. Although we would not necessarily be able to convince all economists of our conclusions (although there is quite a lot of evidence that our views are by no means uncommon), we do feel confident that they would regard our arguments as worth taking seriously. For the same reasons, we believe that serious arguments for alternative approaches should be taken seriously.

To provide some backing for our claim that our approach is "mainstream," this chapter (and to a lesser extent, the next) will include more than the usual number of footnotes to supply points of detail together with references to key contributions by academic economists. For a nonspecialist, some of this research would make pretty heavy reading, but its existence at least provides some reassurance that we are not making unsubstantiated assertions.[1]

q AND THE EFFICIENT MARKET HYPOTHESIS

An idea central to most economic theory is that markets tend to be reasonably "efficient." From this general concept, a host of specific ideas has sprung. Two in particular are key to this book: the idea of *q*, and the Efficient Market Hypothesis. Both concepts have a common element, which is that someone will try to make a profit if prices get out line. This is commonly called arbitrage.[2] We saw in Chapter 9 that arbitrage, if not inhibited somehow, brings prices back into line; and in Chapter 16 we discussed the process in relation to *q* in particular.

It should by now be evident that we are in entire agreement with the general idea of market efficiency. To the extent that we disagree with other economists it is only about the mechanisms by which arbitrage operates. Virtually all economists accept the validity of *q* in principle; the only debate is whether it can be used to value markets. The key point at issue relates to our fourth

---

[1]To make a start, we should back up our claim that we are not the only economists to think that Wall Street is overvalued. We have already cited Paul Krugman's informal remarks. Recent examples of more formal research by eminent economists that comes to the same conclusion are John Campbell and Robert Shiller, "The Long-Run Stock Market Outlook," *Financial Analysts Journal* (Fall 1998); and Sushil Wadhwani, "The U.S. Stock Market and the Global Economic Crisis," *National Institute Economic Review* (January 1999).

[2]We should note that even among economists the term "arbitrage" is not always used consistently. In finance theory, the term is usually applied only to any opportunity to make money that is entirely riskless. More generally, however, it is used to indicate a process that may or may not be risky (indeed, there is some academic debate as to whether arbitrage can ever be truly riskless). Financial economists normally call the more general form, which is what we mean, "approximate arbitrage."

test for any indicator of value, which is whether q can say something useful about future stock returns.

Since James Tobin first proposed the principle in 1969, q has been subjected to detailed analysis, both theoretical and statistical. But most of the analysis has assumed that financial markets are efficient and that stocks are therefore always correctly priced. If this assumption is made, it has to be the capital stock and net worth of companies, not their stock prices, that adjust when q gets out of line. This process must, however, take time. Unlike financial markets, which are assumed to be instantaneously efficient, the real economy is expected to take time to adjust. Working within this framework, economists have come to two general conclusions. First, q is a pretty robust concept theoretically; second, even though q does help predict investment (changes in the capital stock), the evidence for this mechanism is rather weak.[3]

Economists tend to specialize, asking questions within their field and accepting the general consensus outside it. Thus, economists who specialize in the study of investment have tended to assume that financial markets are perfectly efficient, while those who specialized in financial markets have been busy questioning whether this assumption is valid. The financial specialists have come to two broad conclusions. The first is that perfectly efficient financial markets must be a logical impossibility. The second is that it is difficult to reject the Efficient Market Hypothesis on the basis of real-world data, because it is very close to being an untestable hypothesis.

So far, however, there have been relatively few attempts to reconcile the two sets of conclusions arrived at by economists

---

[3]On the theoretical side, for example, there has been debate about whether measured q, which is an average concept, will be a good proxy for "marginal" q, that is, whether new investment can be valued in the same way as that which has been made in the past. However, Fumio Hayashi ("Tobin's Marginal q and Average q: A Neoclassical Interpretation," *Econometrica* 50 (1), January 1982) showed that as long as standard conditions for competitive markets are reasonably close to holding, this will not be a major problem. On the statistical evidence there has been an enormous range of research, of which a recent example is a study by Gabriel Sensenbrenner ("Aggregate Investment, The Stock Market and the q Model: Robust Results for Six OECD Countries," *European Economic Review* 35 (4), May 1991). An important, but rare example of a study that allows for the possibility that financial markets may not be fully efficient is Olivier Blanchard, Chanyong Rhee, and Lawrence Summers, "The Stock Market, Profit and Investment," *Quarterly Journal of Economics* (February 1993, pp. 115–136).

working in the two different specialized areas. We show in this chapter how *q* can provide such a reconciliation, and at the same time take account of the relatively new evidence that *q* mean-reverts.

PREDICTABILITY AND THE EFFICIENT MARKET HYPOTHESIS

The idea that the Efficient Market Hypothesis is extremely hard to test, and may even be untestable, has emerged gradually as numerous attempts have been made to test it. Analysis of these efforts has led to a growing awareness of just how difficult it is to devise a genuine test of efficiency. The first approaches assumed that efficiency meant that markets must be random and unpredictable. For this reason the random walk theory, which we have already discussed in some detail, was often treated as being the same thing as the Efficient Market Hypothesis.[4]

We have already shown that the random walk model does not match the data; indeed, the success of *q* in warning of low future returns clearly contradicts it, as does the more limited success of the dividend yield in the same role. We are certainly not the first economists to point this out.[5] An initial response to the evidence that returns were not entirely unpredictable was to assume that markets could not therefore be fully efficient.

But the Efficient Market Hypothesis could not be killed off so easily. Its defenders came up with an explanation of how stock prices could be predictable, without dropping the assumption of full efficiency. They assumed that the return that investors expected changed over time. These changes could not of course be

---

[4]While it is generally known as the random walk model, it is more correct to refer to it as the random returns model. The formal statement of this idea was by Samuelson in 1965 ("Proof That Properly Anticipated Prices Fluctuate Randomly," *Industrial Management Review* 6, pp. 41–49), but the roots of the argument go back at least to the start of the century in the work of Bachelier ("Theory of Speculation," reprinted in P. Cootner, ed., *The Random Character of Stock Market Prices* (Boston: MIT Press, 1964)).

[5]Campbell, Lo, and MacKinlay's graduate textbook, *The Econometrics of Financial Markets*, provides a summary of the (enormous) literature on predictability of asset prices. It also contains a forceful statement of the difficulties in testing for efficient markets.

fully predictable, or the market would have preempted them.[6] However, by implication the predictability would tell investors only what they already knew—that they were expecting lower returns.

It is important to note that here, as in our previous discussion of valuation indicators, predictability requires *something* to mean-revert. It can be thought of as Siegel's constant not actually being constant in the short run, but as having a predictable tendency to mean-revert to some stable long-run level. If it did not do so, there would be no predictability of actual returns.[7]

This interpretation matches up to historical experience reasonably well on average.[8] Indeed it *must*, since that is what it was designed to do. This is in many respects rather unsatisfactory in intellectual terms. To cope with the evidence that conflicts with its simpler form, the Efficient Market Hypothesis has been modified to become a theory that virtually no evidence can refute.[9]

However, this interpretation stretches credibility to its limits at current levels of the stock market, as we can show by doing some rough calculations.

---

[6]If all investors expect lower returns, and everyone knows this, then stock prices should rise (thereby bringing lower returns). But if everyone also knows that returns are going to come back to some stable level in the long term, this degree of predictability of expected returns will be reflected in some degree of predictability of actual returns. Of course it will not result in perfect predictability, since there must still be a random element in returns, reflecting new information, just as in the random walk model. Note that most previous versions of the time-varying expected return model use the dividend yield to predict future returns (see Campbell *et al.*, *op. cit.*). As we saw in Chapter 21, this requires an additional assumption that the dividend yield mean-reverts, which is also highly dubious; but in this context this point is incidental.

[7]A further implication is that asset returns would also be much, much riskier over long horizons. If the asset return itself does not mean-revert, then *returns* become a random walk, or near relative thereof. This would make the uncertainty around cumulative returns, shown in Chart 17.3, explode at a phenomenal rate.

[8]"Reasonably" well being the operative term. It is not very hard to replicate the sort of degree of predictability of asset returns in this kind of framework; what is much harder is to explain *why* expected returns change. In part this relates to some rather knotty issues in economics which underlie the "Equity Premium Puzzle" discussed in the next chapter.

[9]The philosopher Karl Popper pointed out that the importance of a theory can be judged by how much it excludes. On this basis, the Efficient Market Hypothesis has almost ceased to be a theory at all.

To allow for the element of predictability in actual returns, Siegel's constant must indeed be constant in the long term and we can take 6½%, before costs, as a rough estimate. Following our arguments in the previous chapter, we can also assume this to be the average return that firms will earn on their net worth.

To conform to the Efficient Market Hypothesis, the recent rise in the stock market means that investors must be expecting lower returns on a temporary basis. Just as the price of bonds goes up when future returns fall, so lower prospective returns from stocks mean higher stock prices. Since net worth doesn't change, *q* must also rise. Defenders of the Efficient Market Hypothesis would, however, contend that the market is not overvalued, because it would still be offering the returns that investors demand. One way to assess the plausibility of the theory is therefore to see whether it is compatible with the current extreme values of *q*.

This test is made much easier by the existence of perfectly safe index-linked bonds, currently offering a real return of just under 4%. This puts limits on how far expected returns can fall. Rational investors would not hold stocks if they were expecting a return lower than 4%. Since stocks are risky, they must give some additional return in compensation. This extra return is known as the risk premium. Let us suppose, for the sake of illustration, that investors are temporarily demanding only a very modest risk premium, and will be satisfied with a return of 5% until *q* has fallen back to its average. Since companies are still able to get an average return of 6½%, the difference would, in time, allow stock market valuation and net worth to come together again. But it would take roughly 65 years to do so![10] This time frame is both extremely implausible and inconsistent with the historic evidence, which shows that *q* reverts to its mean at a far faster rate.

As we pointed out, the Efficient Market Hypothesis does not dispute the existence of high or low *q* values, but offers an alternative interpretation of their significance. For the reasons set out above, we find the efficient market interpretation, which de-

---

[10]Since *q* needs to be reduced by a factor of 2.5, and $\frac{1}{2.5} = \left(\frac{1.05}{1.065}\right)^{65}$. Bear in mind also that this assumes that there is no reaction of the underlying return to the lower return that investors are demanding. If the underlying assets yielded lower returns, it would take even longer.

pends on temporary fluctuations in the expected return on stocks, to be unconvincing. There is, however, one other theory that depends on a change in the expected return on stocks. This holds that expected returns are not just temporarily, but permanently lower.

For two reasons, we shall examine this claim separately in Chapter 29. The first reason is that, although its proponents tend to claim support from serious research carried out by serious economists, relatively few academic economists consider that such a theory could provide a serious justification for current market levels. Some elements of the debate on this issue are academic in content, but the main elements underlying the claim are not. The second reason is more practical: The claim has now become so widespread that it seems necessary to show thoroughly how and why it breaks down. We should have to produce a rather long chapter if we were to combine a demolition job on these claims with our primary purpose here, which is to show how our approach relates to that of other mainstream economists.

EFFICIENCY VERSUS "ARBITRAGE EFFICIENCY"

The Efficient Market Hypothesis has several problems.

- The evidence of predictability has demanded a modification to the original form of the hypothesis, which leaves it with rather little substance.
- The hypothesis provides an alternative explanation of the significance of a high *q*, but one that is unconvincing and that fails to fit the evidence.
- It provides no satisfactory account of the mechanism by which financial markets become efficient.

Since this last point needs to be faced by any satisfactory theory, we need to consider its significance for *q*. We shall therefore look more closely at the principle of arbitrage, which we first encountered in Chapter 9 .

The arbitrage that is assumed to underpin perfectly efficient financial markets is based on the "Lucas $100 Bill Principle." This arose out of a question originally posed by Robert Lucas of the University of Chicago: "How long does a $100 bill stay on the sidewalk?" The answer is of course: no time at all. So we never see $100 bills on the sidewalk, although we know that they must sometimes be dropped. In the same way, the Efficient Market Hypothesis says that stock prices can never get out of line because millions of investors, all equally desperate to make money, would bring them back into line. The activities of countless individuals on Wall Street, and in financial centers around the world, show that the $100 principle works well in practice as well as in theory.

For this reason, many key relationships in finance are founded on the principle of the *absence* of arbitrage. It is assumed, not that arbitrage doesn't happen, but that, for all practical purposes, it already has happened. This point is important for asset prices, and there are many instances where it can be relied upon to work in practice.

A relatively simple example is the relationship between interest rates in different currencies normally referred to as "covered interest parity." The difference between the three-month interest rates paid on yen and dollar assets, for example, has to be the same as the difference between the current yen/dollar rate and the three-month "forward" yen/dollar rate.[11] Other examples, illustrating the absence of arbitrage, can be found in futures contracts on anything from government bonds to pork bellies. There is something almost magical here. In many cases we can treat these relationships as if they always hold. Covered interest parity tells you that if you know the interest rates on yen and dollar assets and the current dollar/yen exchange rate, you do not even need to look up the three-month forward exchange rate; you can calculate it directly from the interest differential.

Yet, of course, and crucially, these relationships do *not* always hold. Think back to Lucas's $100 bill. The assumption of no arbitrage is equivalent to the assumption that there are no $100 bills on the sidewalk. We know this assumption cannot be precisely correct. You may never find a $100 bill on the sidewalk, but, as we have said, this is not because they are never dropped, but because whenever they are, they are immediately picked up.

---

[11]The rate you will be quoted if you want to commit yourself to exchange dollars for yen
    (or vice versa) in three months' time, at a rate fixed today. In so doing, you
    "cover" yourself entirely against future fluctuations in the yen/dollar rate.

The result therefore depends on the mechanism. Because someone will always pick up $100 bills on the sidewalk, we can assume that the bills are never there. The same applies with examples of pure arbitrage like covered interest parity. Because profit opportunities are so clear-cut and, crucially, riskless, we can take it as given that they will always be exploited, effectively assuming that the opportunities never existed in the first place. But we can rely on this only because a few specialist arbitrageurs are perpetually watching for instances when, even if only for a brief moment, the relationship *doesn't* hold.

Here we have something of a paradox. In order to be able to assume that an arbitrage-based relationship holds, it must in reality regularly not hold; otherwise, these specialist arbitrageurs would not make money. In cases where the arbitrage is pretty much riskless, as with covered interest parity, this paradox is interesting, but not very important. For more general cases of arbitrage, we shall see that it is both interesting and very important indeed.

As we have noted, arbitrage in this more general sense underpins the whole concept of the Efficient Market Hypothesis. No actual buying and selling need take place for assets to reflect fully all information. The Efficient Market Hypothesis is therefore simply another assumption based on the absence of arbitrage. But this leads to the paradox, which we encountered before. The Efficient Market Hypothesis can hold only if it sometimes does *not* hold. There must be an incentive to engage in the arbitrage that brings efficiency about. This insight is crucial in two ways.

First of all, what is the activity that allows someone to make money from arbitrage? It is nothing less than *valuing* assets. The activity involves picking out assets that are under- or overvalued in order to choose which ones to buy or sell. This might apply to individual stocks, but, logically, it must apply equally well to whole markets. So even though the Efficient Market Hypothesis appears to hold that markets can't be valued, it won't work unless they can.

The second point that follows from our paradox relates to the nature of the arbitrage process, the information that it exploits, and what motivates the individuals who do the buying and selling. The most reliable arbitrage conditions arise when the activity involves no risk. It is then best left to the professionals.

We would certainly not recommend that investors attempt to out-guess specialist arbitrageurs who make their living by exploiting minuscule deviations from covered interest parity. But when it is the stock market that is mispriced, the shoe is well and truly on the other foot. It is professional investors like fund managers who cannot afford the risks. As we have explained, they will reduce the risks that their clients are running if they go liquid, but in so doing they will put their own jobs at risk. Even though there is a high probability that stock returns will be negative over the next ten years, the risk of going liquid is too high for fund managers to take. q tells us that the stock market has become very inefficiently priced. This is possible only because going liquid is so risky for fund managers. When arbitrage becomes risky, it also becomes less reliable. Going liquid is not risky for investors, only for fund managers. It is reasonable to think that a key reason the stock market has become more overvalued than ever before is that fewer and fewer people manage their own money.

"NOISE," INFORMATION, AND EFFICIENCY

In the idealized world of perfectly efficient markets, the acts of trading and price formation are quite separate. Since everyone has access to the same information, everyone can work out what prices should be, *without* actually buying or selling. Indeed, in a world inhabited by identical people no trade would ever occur. In such a world, if some new information arose, everyone would immediately recalculate the new prices that should prevail in the light of this new information, and, since everyone would know what these prices were, no trade would need to occur—prices would simply jump to their new levels.

Roughly 20 years ago, one of the authors and two academic economists, Sanford Grossman and Joseph Stiglitz, independently pointed out the paradox underlying this notion of efficiency, which has two major logical flaws.[12]

---

[12]The paper most usually quoted by economists is Sanford Grossman and Joseph Stiglitz, "On the Impossibility of Informationally Efficient Markets," which was published in the *American Economic Review* (vol. 70, pp. 293–408) in 1980. Andrew Smithers's article pointing out the paradox was published in *The Investment Analyst* in September 1978.

1. Where does the information that makes markets efficient actually come from? In a world in which no one ever traded, no one would have the incentive to acquire the information. But if no one had the incentive to acquire the information, there would be no information (since information is not costless to produce). And if there were no information, the market could not be efficient.

2. A similar line of argument applies to the incentive to *process* this information. If you know that the market is efficiently processing the information that drives prices, you do not actually need the information— since everything you can learn from it is in the prices themselves. But if everyone followed this line of reasoning, no one would actually set the prices and hence, again, the market could not be efficient.

Thus, on both counts, complete efficiency is logically impossible.

The resolution of this paradox is not difficult. It simply requires that the market be just *in*efficient enough to provide an incentive to seek out and process information. In this imperfectly efficient world, prices *cannot* perfectly reflect all available information. If they did, no one would need to bother attempting to value anything, since people would automatically know the value once they knew the price. The only way that this possibility can be ruled out is if there is some additional "noise" in prices that serves to disguise the information.

Because a perfectly efficient stock market is not feasible, a feasible stock market must be imperfectly efficient. Stock prices must therefore be "noisy." Grossman and Stiglitz did not attempt to show where this noise comes from; they simply showed that the presence of some noise was a precondition for a feasible market. Once we have acknowledged the possibility that markets cannot be perfectly efficient, however, it becomes quite easy to see how this "noise" can arise. The evidence comes from the way that asset prices respond to trading volume.

In an efficient market the only thing that can move prices is information. Both in theory and in practice, this can occur with little or no trading. Market participants in an efficient market should all be equally able to process new information as it arises. If they all agree on the implications for prices, then there is no need for any trade actually to occur, since prices will simply be marked up or down.

This view of what determines prices runs counter to an alternative view, captured in the old stock market adage:

Q: Why did prices rise today?
A: More buyers than sellers.

This is both useless as an explanation and logically incorrect, since there must always be exactly as many buyers and sellers. But it does contain the seeds of an extremely important idea. Once we allow for the possibility that there may be "noise" in the system, a substantial number of trades may occur *without* any new information. If "noise" trades are, for example, predominantly by sellers, then the market will be able to match up buyers and sellers only if the price falls.

In contrast, in a fully efficient market, "noise" should not affect prices. If everyone knows that prices reflect information, there should be plenty of arbitrageurs who will be happy to sell stock at given prices, since the next day things may work in the opposite direction—and certainly the process should cancel out over a relatively short period. (Think of the analogy of a shopkeeper who does a lot of business on any particular day. He does not necessarily think his prices are wrong—he may just have hit a lucky day—or it may be the weekend.)

Since buyers must always equal sellers on any given day, it is impossible to identify "selling pressure" versus "buying pressure." We can, however, identify the number of transactions. A high level of transactions should reflect either selling pressure or buying pressure, and we can look to see whether this is, or is not, associated with changes in prices, be they positive or negative. If the market is efficient, there should be absolutely no link between the volume of trade and movements in prices. In a "noisy" world, you would expect to see more movements in prices on days when there was more trade.

A large number of studies have found that there *is* a quite strong association between trading volume and changes in prices.[13] This link is visible during the course of trading periods; prices are also much more volatile when trading is going on than when trading does not occur. This is not just because, as is often the case, there is more information coming on stream in trading periods. In commodity markets, where the most important form of information is the weather, the same phenomenon is visible, even though information about the weather comes in a steady flow, whether markets are open or not.

q, VALUE, AND A RECONCILIATION OF THE SPECIALISTS

We now need to draw the threads of our argument together. We have focused for most of this chapter on the inability of the Efficient Market Hypothesis to explain how Wall Street could have got so high, or how efficiency itself is brought about. We started, however, by pointing out that economists who look at *q* from the perspective of firms' incentive to invest are faced with puzzles if they follow the standard approach. First, their assumption that there are no frictions in financial markets looks questionable. Second, we noted that evidence for *q* driving investment is weak. But if this is the case, how does *q* mean-revert so strongly? Awareness of this puzzle is limited, because data on *q* have not been readily available; awareness should grow as the information becomes more widely disseminated.

Our approach, however, can reconcile the specialists. *q* mean-reverts because prices adjust far more quickly than net worth. This would be inconsistent with efficiency in the purest sense, but it is not inconsistent with the sort of arbitrage efficiency we have discussed in this chapter. However, since pure efficiency itself is a logical impossibility, this is an advantage, not a disadvantage, of our approach.

---

[13]Two key articles on this topic are E. Fama, "The Behavior of Stock Market Prices," *Journal of Business* 38 (January 1965), pp. 34–105, and K. French, "Stock Returns and the Weekend Effect," *Journal of Financial Economics* 8 (March 1980), pp. 55–69.

For a market can only be as efficient as the arbitrage that brings efficiency about. In some markets, where arbitrage is riskless, and divergences of price from underlying value are easy to spot, professional arbitrageurs can be relied upon to bring prices into line, sometimes almost instantaneously. But we have seen that the stock market satisfies neither of these conditions. When stock prices deviate from their fundamental value, arbitrage is risky, especially for professionals like fund managers, as we saw in Chapter 19. But it is also, self-evidently, not straightforward. If it was easy to value stock markets, there would be no need to write this book.

For both reasons, in a stock market that is only arbitrage-efficient, professionals may well face irresistible pressure to hold stocks even when they believe that stocks offer the prospect of very poor, or even negative, returns. The better the recent performance of the stock market, the harder it is for professionals to resist the pressure. Furthermore, because selling or buying pressure can move prices (rather than just information, as in a notional efficient market), even very modest changes in the balance of opinion can bring sharp movements in prices. In the recent past, as we showed in Chapter 16, both of these factors have clearly pushed prices up; but the strong evidence of history is that they will in due course work in the opposite direction. It will, paradoxically, become easier for fund managers to sell stocks once prices start falling. This will add further downward pressure on prices.

Our approach to *q* can therefore quite easily explain, in a coherent way, both the historic behavior of *q* and how it has managed to reach its current extraordinary levels. We have seen that, in contrast, the assumption that stock markets are perfectly efficient can do neither.

CHAPTER 29

The Equity Risk Premium and Stock Market Valuations

As we noted in the last chapter, it has recently been claimed, with much attendant publicity, that the expected return from stocks has fallen, not just temporarily, but permanently. This claim has then been used to try to justify current stock prices. The claim is a hybrid. It attempts to derive credibility from some genuine academic foundations, but the arguments presented to back it up typically reveal a serious misunderstanding of the underlying economic research.

The argument goes as follows:

- The equity risk premium has been too high in the past.
- It has now fallen.
- This justifies the current level of the stock market.

The case falls down at every step:

- There is no evidence to support the claim that the equity risk premium has been too high in the past.
- There is positive evidence that it has *not* fallen; indeed, in the recent past there is some evidence that it may actually have risen.
- Even if the premium had fallen, it would be extremely hard to justify any change in the underlying value of the

stock market, let alone an increase of the size that has actually been observed.

HAVE PAST RETURNS BEEN TOO HIGH? THE EQUITY RISK PREMIUM "PUZZLE"

The claim is that, for the past 200 years or more, stocks have been underpriced, and have therefore offered returns that were "too high." The recent rise in stock prices, it is asserted, has therefore been a one-off adjustment, as investors have finally woken up to the mispricing. The rationale for this assertion is usually claimed to arise from the "Equity Premium Puzzle," an academic debate initiated by two eminent economists, Rajnish Mehra and Edward Prescott, in 1985.[14] This paper raised the fascinating question of whether a relatively simple model of how people behave when faced with risky choices could be reconciled with the historic average returns on stocks and cash on deposit, and consumers' observed behavior, from the latter half of the nineteenth century onward. Mehra and Prescott found that it could not, and this result has spawned a minor industry among economists who have sought to understand, or amend the original finding.

The Equity Premium Puzzle is one of the most widely cited, and least understood, pieces of economic research ever carried out. In that respect it rather resembles probably the most celebrated piece of mathematical research carried out in the latter half of the twentieth century: the proof of Fermat's Last Theorem.

The charm of Fermat's Theorem is that it can be stated in terms that can be understood by virtually anyone who managed to stay awake in an introductory mathematics course. But although even nonmathematicians can understand the proposition that there is no number, n, greater than 2 that satisfies the equation $x^n + y^n = z^n$, for whole-number values of $x, y,$ and z, the proof of this proposition takes 100 pages of mathematics on such an elevated plane that only handfuls of mathematicians can understand it.

The Equity Premium Puzzle debate is not *that* difficult, although it *is* a debate among specialists that can be properly dis-

---

[14]R. Mehra and E. Prescott, "The Equity Premium: A Puzzle," *Journal of Monetary Economics* (March 1985), pp. 145–62.

cussed only in the terms used by economists. But the puzzle itself can be stated quite easily: The historic average gap between stock and cash returns looks "too high." Since this apparently simple statement can easily be interpreted as leading to conclusions that are congenial to the average stockbroker, the average stockbroker does not linger too long over the rest of the algebra.

As its name suggests, however, the Equity Premium Puzzle differs in one very important way from Fermat's Last Theorem. It is a puzzle, not a statement of truth. Fermat's Last Theorem had been demonstrated to hold for any value of n up to 4 million, long before Andrew Wiles provided the proof that it must hold for any number. Mehra and Prescott simply pointed out that the observed equity premium appeared *inconsistent* with other pieces of information, and an assumed model of behavior. A demonstration that a model is inconsistent with the evidence is normally taken as evidence that it is the model that needs adjusting, rather than people's behavior. This was indeed the conclusion of Mehra and Prescott themselves.[15] The assumption that people have been behaving stupidly for the past 200 years is far less likely and needs a great deal of other evidence to support it before it can be considered at all reasonable.[16]

Subsequent research has broadly come to the following conclusions:

- The estimate of the premium that was originally used was almost certainly overstated.

- It is quite easy to provide a reconciliation with the historic record by changing certain features of the model in ways that seem quite plausible.

We should stress that this does not necessarily mean that the puzzle has been resolved; it does mean that it is essentially impossible to tell, on the basis of economic reasoning alone, whether the equity premium has historically been clearly "too high" or indeed "too low." The paper could easily have been called

---

[15]"Our conclusion is that most likely some equilibrium model with a friction will be the one that successfully accounts for the large average equity premium." (Mehra and Prescott (*op. cit.*)).

[16]Indeed, to make such an assumption goes starkly against the approach of mainstream economics, which is that the usual assumption that people behave rationally can be justified by assuming that they learn from their mistakes. If it took 200 years to do so, the enforcement mechanism for rationality would be very weak indeed.

"Consumer Behavior—a Puzzle," since the issue it raised is most likely to be resolved by devising other models of such behavior that are more consistent with the historic data.[17] Mehra and Prescott must be pleased, however, that they chose a different title, since otherwise their outstanding work might not have received the attention that it has.

HAS THE EQUITY PREMIUM FALLEN?

Since it is most likely that the Equity Premium Puzzle will be resolved by a change in our understanding of consumer behavior, rather than a change in that behavior, it is unreasonable to assume that the equity risk premium has fallen, without strong supporting evidence. Not only does such evidence not exist, but there is a strong case that the equity risk premium has in fact risen, rather than fallen.

Claims that the premium has fallen are little more than a restatement of the rather obvious point that equity valuations, by any measure, have risen significantly in recent years. The standard approach to estimating the premium is to use the Dividend Discount Model. The return that investors expect from stocks must be equal to the dividend yield plus the growth of dividends. It must also be equal to the expected return on a "safe" asset plus the equity premium. So the premium itself can be estimated by subtracting the yield on indexed bonds from the dividend yield plus an estimate of dividend growth.[18]

This approach, when taken by conservative academic economists, produces a very low equity risk premium on current data.[19]

---

[17]Several resolutions of the puzzle involving different models of consumer behavior have been proposed. Recent examples are Campbell and Cochrane, "By Force of Habit: A Consumption-Based Explanation of Aggregate Stock Market Behavior," 1997; Benartzi and Thaler, "Myopic Loss Aversion and the Equity Premium Puzzle," *Quarterly Journal of Economics*, 1995; and Constanides, Donaldson, and Mehra, "Junior Can't Borrow: A New Perspective on the Equity Premium Puzzle," NBER Working Paper No. 6617, 1998.

[18]An alternative approach derives expected dividend growth from the earnings yield, for reasons we noted in Chapter 26. As a result, such measures end up looking like the earnings yield minus the real interest rate.

[19]The paper by Sushil Wadhwani cited previously, for example, uses techniques very similar to Olivier Blanchard's "Movements in the Equity Premium," *Brookings Papers on Economic Activity*, 0(2), 1993.

But this is exactly what we would expect. Because stocks have risen so much, any approach based on history will indicate a poor return for the future. The extra return that can reasonably be expected from stocks must also therefore have fallen, unless the return from safe assets has gone down as well. But this has not happened.

This is just another way of showing how poor the likely returns from equities are. It can therefore be interpreted in one of two ways. Either it is a temporary aberration, which means that stocks are extremely overpriced, or it represents a complete break with the past.[20]

There are three separate bits of evidence that can be used to decide between these two propositions.

- Surveys about investors' expectations
- Bond yields
- Returns from equally risky assets

If the equity risk premium has fallen, it means that investors have woken up to the fact that equities are less risky than they thought and that returns from equities will be lower in the future than they have been in the past. Surveys of expectations point, however, to the exact opposite. Far from expecting a fall in long-term returns, investors are expecting the recent exceptionally high returns to continue. As noted in Chapter 3, anecdotal evidence clearly shows that investors are expecting very high returns that are way out of line with historic experience. This is borne out by survey evidence[21] reporting expected returns by individual investors of anything up to 34% over a ten-year horizon.

The second source of evidence about the premium is to see if expected returns on bonds have also changed in a compatible way.

---

[20]Just how complete a break can be seen by noting the following: (a) this view can be reconciled with historical experience only if such a change has never happened before, since if it had Siegel's constant would not appear to have been constant for 200 years; (b) by implication, therefore, it is distinctly different from the story of time-varying expected returns, discussed in the previous chapter, which require that Siegel's constant be constant in the long term, if not in the short term; and (c) it can also make sense only if such a change will never happen again, for the reason noted in the last chapter, that otherwise this would imply that returns were not mean-reverting, and as a result, stocks would be much, much riskier.

[21]Cited in the article by Sushil Wadhwani to which we referred previously.

If the equity risk premium had fallen, then the premium on nonindexed bonds, which are also risky (because of the unpredictability of inflation), should also have fallen dramatically. If, therefore, past returns have been too high on stocks, they have also been too high on long-term bonds. If investors have seen the light regarding stocks, they should have seen the light regarding bonds as well. It is clearly impossible to hold any such view. We have already noted that riskless inflation-protected bonds are currently paying around 4% in real terms. Since nonindexed bonds are clearly riskier than this, no sane investors would hold them in preference to indexed bonds unless they expected a higher return. But even an expected real return of 4% would be fairly high in historical terms.

There is a third source of evidence about the premium. Stocks are not the only assets that investors can acquire that are more risky than bonds. There are alternatives, which may be considered as "stock substitutes" and which have the same characteristics as stocks in terms of risk. Clearly these assets should provide the same return as stocks. If the equity risk premium were to fall, the reduction in the expected return on stocks should be reflected in a reduction in the expected return on "stock substitutes." Evidence as to whether the equity risk premium has, or has not, fallen on a permanent basis can therefore be found by considering whether the return on these "stock substitutes" has changed in a compatible way. The answer is clearly that it hasn't. Indeed, it appears to have risen.

One way to create "stock substitutes" is through credit markets. The return that investors expect from taking the risk of investing in the stock market should be mirrored in the return that they can achieve by taking the risk of lending to corporations via the bond market. This return can be gauged from "credit spreads," which are the differences in yield between lending to companies and lending to the U.S. government. If the expected return on stocks were to have fallen, it could have done so in one of two ways: either because the P/E multiple *had* risen or because investors expected a rise in bankruptcies—which would depress expected future returns, since stocks of bankrupt companies lose all their value. But it is, to put it mildly, extremely unlikely that the optimism shown by rising P/Es should happen when investors are expecting an increase in bankruptcies. If, therefore, the high level of current P/Es is the result of a fall in the expected return on stocks, with an unchanged rise of bankruptcy there should also have been a matching fall in the expected return from investing in corporate bonds, versus less risen government bonds. In fact, credit spreads have risen sharply. Over the very long term, the average spread on AAA (i.e., triple A) bonds of long maturity has been 0.6% and, as we write, it is around 1.4%.

The evidence of credit markets therefore supports the evidence provided by investor surveys and the yield on long-term bonds. Rather than suggesting that the premium expected from stocks has fallen, it provides clear evidence that it has probably risen.[22]

THE EQUITY PREMIUM AND INFLATION (OR, YIELD RATIOS REVISITED)

A different type of argument that has been made for a fall in the premium is the claim that this is justified by a fall in the rate of inflation. It is then claimed, by leaps of faith rather than logic, that current valuations can be justified by the fall in inflation. If this argument sounds familiar, it should, for we encountered it in another guise when we looked at yield ratios. As we showed then, the argument is entirely without merit.

The case that the equity premium is related to inflation is entirely a statistical one, which, like the case for yield ratios, relies entirely on data mining, whether deliberate or inadvertent.[23]

---

[22]A report published by Smithers & Co. in January 1999, entitled "Synthetic Equity" by Daniel Murray, Andrew Smithers, and Stephen Wright, showed how investors can create "substitute stock portfolios," by combining index-linked government bonds with credit spreads. The return on such portfolios is normally the same, for the same degree of volatility and thus risk, as it is for investing in stocks. It does, however, vary and the trade-off between risk and return is currently much better than the historic trade-off. The evidence that the very long-term returns are the same is support for a modified version of the Efficient Market Hypothesis, such as that provided by q. It is not compatible with the variable return version of the hypothesis, which would require the same variations in return to be found in both equity and credit markets.

[23]Among the examples of inadvertent data mining we include, unfortunately, Professor Blanchard's otherwise fascinating study previously cited. In his defense, Blanchard merely notes a correlation between inflation and his estimated risk premium, and notes also that it is hard to explain.

As we have noted, estimates of the equity premium tend to show a sustained fall over the past 20 years, a period over which inflation has also shown a sustained fall. If, however, longer periods of data or data from other countries are examined, this relationship breaks down entirely.[24]

If the statistical basis for the link with inflation is weak, the case in logic is even weaker. If anything, a case could best be made the other way around. Inflation should have no impact over the longer term on stock returns, since stocks represent a claim on real assets, which generates real returns. It can, however, have a major effect on the returns on alternative assets like bonds or cash, on which returns are fixed in nominal terms. The main reason for rises and falls in the real returns on bonds and cash has been fluctuations in inflation. If inflation really has become permanently lower and, more important, more predictable, the real returns on nonindexed bonds and cash will be much safer, without any reduction in the risks of investing in stocks. If anything, therefore, lower inflation should *raise*, rather than lower, the equity risk premium.

IF THE EQUITY PREMIUM WERE LOWER: *q*-EQUIVALENCE REVISITED

But even if we suspend judgment for now, and suppose, despite all the evidence, that the equity premium has fallen, there are still two very important obstacles to overcome. The first is that there is no necessary correspondence between a falling risk premium and a falling return on stocks; the second is that, even if there were, we have no reason to suppose that it would justify valuations anywhere near as high as at present.

A point often forgotten is that the equity premium is only the gap between the return investors demand from stocks and the return they expect from "safe" assets. A reduction in this gap could thus, in principle, occur without any fall in expected the return from stocks if there were simply an increase in the return

---

[24]Sushil Wadhwani, a previous proponent of a related view, recants of this in the paper cited above, and provides evidence that there is no stable link.

from safe assets.[25] In many ways this is the more plausible assumption. The evidence from 200 years' worth of data, shown in Chart 29.1, is that, while the return from stocks has been relatively stable, that from bonds and cash on deposit has not. It would, therefore, be more consistent with the evidence of history to expect a rise in the return from cash and bonds than a fall in the return from stocks.

But, casting this evidence aside for now, let us make the further leap that a fall in the equity premium *would* be accompanied by a fall in the returns investors demanded of stocks. Would this provide a justification for current valuations? It is very far from clear that it would. The reason is the simple point we made in the last chapter: If stock returns were to fall permanently, then

CHART 29.1

Real Returns* on Stocks, Bonds, and Cash Since 1830

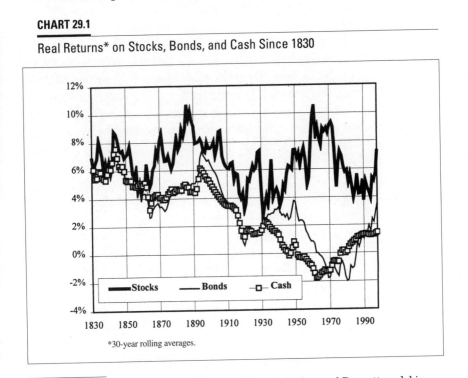

*30-year rolling averages.

---

[25]Indeed, one little-noted implication of the logic of the Mehra and Prescott model is that if the premium fell as a result of an effective reduction in the degree of risk aversion of the average investor, this would imply a *rise* in the return on stocks, at the same time as a reduction on the premium. Savers who are (by assumption) "excessively" risk-averse tend to save more, thus pushing down returns. If they become less so, returns should rise.

so, ultimately, must the returns on the underlying assets that generate them.[26]

We can demonstrate this very simply by revisiting the idea of q-equivalence, which we introduced in Chapter 26. We have not yet asked ourselves to believe the requisite number of impossible things that the White Queen in *Through the Looking Glass* thought that everyone should try to believe before breakfast.[27] So let us suppose, for the sake of argument, that the risk premium has *entirely* disappeared. Investors in stocks will therefore be happy to receive a return of only 4%, which they can currently get without risk by investing in indexed bonds. As we saw in Chapter 26, this should imply a one-off shift in the cyclically adjusted earnings yield to the same value, and hence a cyclically adjusted P/E of around 25 (100/4). In mid-1999, the actual P/E was around 35, so on this crude measure the stock market would be "only" 40% overvalued. But, as we saw in Chapter 26, if we were to look at the cyclically adjusted P/E (which we clearly should), then we could read it off by looking straight at q. Hence the market is still around 2½ times overvalued, *irrespective* of the long-run return.

The resolution is that, as we noted in Chapter 26, if returns on stocks were permanently lower, so must be the returns on the underlying assets that generate them. By implication, therefore, after the "New Era" cyclical adjustment, profits would be enormously *lower* than currently. It is thus perhaps no wonder that "New Era" enthusiasts do not pursue the logic of their assumptions to this unpalatable conclusion.

Of course, in principle, we should note that, as we saw in Chapter 26, net worth can adjust at least in part to close the gap indicated by q. But we have already seen that the extent of such

---

[26]Because the original Mehra and Prescott framework was extremely abstract, this issue did not arise. Their model assumes the capital stock to be completely "exogenous" (see our discussion of this issue in Chapter 26) so that all adjustments would have to come in terms of stock market valuations.

[27]As the following extract from Lewis Carroll's *Through the Looking Glass* (1871) shows, the White Queen missed out on a great career in stockbroking.

> Alice laughed.
> "There's no use trying," she said. "One can't believe impossible things."
> "I daresay you haven't had much practice," said the Queen. "When I was your age, I always did it for half an hour a day. Why sometimes I believed six impossible things before breakfast."

an adjustment would effectively be both impossible and, the evidence on q suggests, entirely out of line with past experience. Furthermore, even in this White-Queen-before-breakfast world, there would still be an enormous incentive to sell stocks (which by assumption would be yielding only 4%) in favor of other assets that offered higher returns for the foreseeable future. That this process of adjustment could occur without major falls in stock prices is so hard to imagine that even the White Queen might struggle to do so.

THE EQUITY PREMIUM: A NONANSWER TO A NONQUESTION

We have seen that attempts to use the Equity Premium Puzzle as a rationale for current market valuations simply do not hang together, for several reasons.

- There is no basis for assuming that the premium has been too high in the past.
- There is no evidence that it has fallen.
- There is some evidence that it may have risen.
- Even if it had fallen, this need not imply any fall in the equilibrium return on stocks, since returns on safe assets might rise.
- Indeed, the evidence of history is that the return on stocks is extremely stable.
- Even if all the above points are ignored, and we did assume, like the White Queen, that expected returns on stocks have fallen, there is still no way to avoid the logic of q, which shows that Wall Street is massively overvalued.

CHAPTER **30**

The *q* Debate
Among Stockbrokers

The objections raised to *q* by stockbrokers are very different from those raised by economists. At first glance, this seems a bit odd. If there were any merit in the stockbrokers' objections, economists might quickly have latched on to them, since questioning theories, testing hypotheses, and debating minutiae are what academic economists do for a living. In fact it is not really as odd as it may seem. The objections of stockbrokers are different from those of economists, because their purposes are different. It is not the arguments underlying *q* that stockbrokers really object to, but the conclusions these arguments lead to. We shall see this in considering the individual objections, in the fact that stockbrokers very rarely allow minor details like evidence or logic to get in the way of their arguments.

THE MYTH OF THE "LOW CAPITAL" ECONOMY

A common claim by stockbrokers is that *q* is relevant to manufacturing but not to services, since this sector requires less capital; further, because the economy is increasingly oriented to services, we should ignore *q* altogether. This claim is an admirable illustration of the nature of stockbroker economics: first, because the relevance of *q* is independent of the amount of capital employed and, second, because no evidence is produced to back the assumption that services need less capital than manufacturing.

It is a mistake to imagine either that services don't need capital or that their returns would be higher than in manufacturing if they didn't. The point that matters for both services and manufacturing is competition. If the economy is a competitive one, then the return on capital will be the same in service industries as in manufacturing. There will, of course, be variations around the average among different companies in all industries, as a result of good luck and good judgment. If, however, any one industry tends to show an above-average return, then the companies already in that industry will accelerate their investment plans and outsiders will seek a way in. By the same token, capital will not be attracted to industries with below-average returns. The result will therefore be a constant process of pulling returns toward the average.

The idea that services need less capital than manufacturing seems to be so generally accepted that it is surprising to find evidence suggesting that this belief may rest on a pretty shaky foundation—at least with regard to what we are interested in when we look at the stock market, which is the corporate sector. We realize that using evidence may make us open to the charge of being spoilsports, since we are calling upon a technique to which stockbrokers seem too proud to stoop. Nonetheless, it is interesting to note the inconsistency of the evidence with these claims. Chart 30.1 shows that the amount of capital that corporations need has not been falling in recent years, despite the fact that the importance of services has indeed been rising.

What is perhaps more surprising is that there is some evidence that service companies may use more tangible assets capital than manufacturers, per person employed. A recent UK government report showed this to be the case, at least among large companies, whether they were based in the UK or in other major countries.[28]

This evidence relates to the corporate sector, rather than to the whole economy. Many small-scale services, such as newspaper delivery, hair-cutting, and shoe shining, require little capital, but there are many larger service industries, such as hotels, cruise

---

[28] *1998 Capex Scoreboard*, published by the UK Department of Trade and Industry.

CHART 30.1

The Output–Capital Ratio

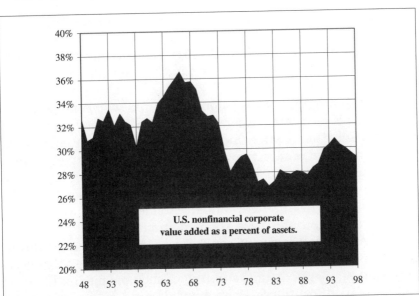

U.S. nonfinancial corporate value added as a percent of assets.

liners, and supermarkets, with very big capital requirements. It is natural for services that require a lot of capital to be backed by companies. It is almost impossible to raise capital on a large scale without incorporation.

The assumption that services need less capital than manufacturing is thus not necessarily true for companies and, even if it were true, there is no reason to expect services to have higher returns on their capital than manufacturing. It is therefore important to appreciate that *q* is every bit as relevant in a service economy as it is in a manufacturing one. The shift to services might lead to further reduction in the contribution of the corporate sector to the economy; but however large the corporate sector may be, it will need capital, since that is why it exists.

THE MYTH OF THE "NO CAPITAL" ECONOMY

The claim that firms need less capital is sometimes taken to the point of suggesting that they require almost none at all. Such claims usually make reference to the growing importance of knowledge, R&D, software, and "intangible" assets in general. These developments are not in dispute; but they make no difference at all to the case for *q*.

Arguments in support of such claims tend to be muddled; so we shall try to impose on them a degree of structure that their proponents usually ignore. To do so, we divide intangible assets into two distinct types: those that have been bought and paid for, and those that have not.

Most intangible assets belong to the first category, and thus have been paid for at the expense of profits. Since net worth, which sits on the bottom of the ratio in *q*, is simply the accumulated value of retained profits, it is an unavoidable fact that any intangibles that have been paid for affect net worth. Hence any claim that the growing importance of "paid-for" intangibles like software and R&D results in an understatement of net worth is really just a claim that profits are being understated.

Of course, all forms of capital, whether tangible or intangible, have to be paid for in the end out of profits. The only difference that may arise is in the *timing* of such payments. Physical capital is paid for progressively by deducting depreciation from profits. The only possible way that intangible assets might appear to differ from tangible assets, therefore, is that they are effectively depreciated in a single year, although the returns may continue for (somewhat) longer. But it is important to realize that this more rapid depreciation of intangibles actually confers an advantage on companies, since it makes intangibles entirely allowable against tax. In effect, therefore, there is an implicit subsidy on intangibles. Standard economics, and plenty of evidence, supports the proposition that when there is a subsidy or tax on one form of capital, but not on another, competition will ensure that the postsubsidy, or posttax, returns on either are equalized. Hence treating intangibles as in effect a current expense will simply push down the returns on intangibles, relative to other assets.

It would be easier to take such arguments seriously if either corporate output or corporate profits looked high in relation to recorded assets. But Chart 30.1 shows that there is absolutely no evidence on the former score; and as we shall shortly see, there is a similar lack of evidence on the latter.

The other major category of intangible assets consists of those that have *not* been paid for. Here we apply Milton Friedman's "no free lunch" principle. Any individual can obviously eat lunch for free on occasion, and possibly even on a sustained basis, but only if someone else is paying. In aggregate, lunch is clearly paid for. In aggregate, the only kinds of lunches that do not get paid for are those that do not get eaten. The same applies to the aggregate value of intangibles that have not been paid for. Their aggregate value must be zero. This is exactly the way such assets are treated by the statisticians who record the net worth figures that feed into *q*; and the statisticians are exactly right.

The prime example is "goodwill." Corporations often include goodwill in their balance sheets and may individually be justified in doing so, since intangibles, such as patents and trademarks, have value. Intangibles will have value, however, only if they enable the company to earn an above-average return. If the company could do just as well without owning the goodwill, then the claims made for its value cannot be justified. If the intangible asset does not help toward improving the company's business, no one would wish to buy it and the unwanted has no commercial value. Companies in general, however, cannot make above-average returns. It should be an obvious point that the return on capital of all companies must be the same as their average return. We apologize for laboring the point, but we have frequently encountered stockbroker reports in which it is implicitly assumed that this condition need not apply. In these reports company valuations often appear to be based on the assumptions of Lake Wobegon, where, as we have previously noted, all the children are above average.

The fact that companies in aggregate can make only average returns doesn't mean that all companies are making the same return at all times; it simply means that there must be as many companies making below-average returns as ones doing better. Those that are above average are justified in claiming that they have goodwill, but this must be balanced by an equal amount of "ill will." A little thought will show no surprise here. As we have already pointed out, capital once invested cannot easily be withdrawn. The scrap value of plant is much less than its cost, and staff cannot be laid off without added expense. Companies can be worth less than the value of their assets for many reasons. Demand for their products may fall off, their manufacturing techniques may become obsolete, or they may be unable to compete with foreign companies.

In competitive economies goodwill will exist, therefore, but it will apply only to individual companies that can make above-average returns. Struggling companies with below-average returns do not, understandably enough, register "ill will" in their balance sheets, but it is nonetheless as real as goodwill and must be of equal amount. When the value of companies is being considered in aggregate, therefore, there can be no goodwill. This illustrates again a point that we have made before. The usual ways in which analysts seek to value individual companies cannot be properly applied to companies in aggregate.

In practice there is often a strong connection between goodwill and good luck. The publisher of a well-regarded biography of Jane Austen may find a sudden increase in sales following the popularity of filmed versions of *Sense and Sensibility* and *Emma*. The resulting increase in profitability will be represented in improved goodwill and will be greatly welcomed by the publisher while it lasts. But the publisher who is unfortunate enough to have signed up the biographer of Louisa May Alcott will see a corresponding fall in profits. Unless the market for biographies grows, which would require more capital, the net effect will be zero.

The standard stockbroker objections to *q* involve these confusions over goodwill and the importance of capital in service industries. A number of other objections have been raised, and we have probably not encountered all of them. We have, however, encountered a list recently published by a well-known brokerage firm that we hope is fairly comprehensive. This is claimed that...

> ...*True corporate net worth includes many factors other than the replacement value of tangible assets. These include immeasurables such as management ability, franchise value, and worker training.*

The confusion between the value of individual companies and of companies in aggregate is well illustrated by this list. At any one moment some companies will be better managed than others, and the better-managed ones will be worth a premium over the others. But the variable quality of management does not raise the value of companies in aggregate, because the weaker ones will be worth a discount. Any higher returns that result from better management will be temporary and competed away as the better managers demand and obtain rewards that reflect the value of their services.

The attempt to cloud the issue further by including management and worker training shows a certain desperation, since these are personal skills owned by individuals and not by companies. They represent "human capital," which, since the abolition of slavery, cannot belong to a company. It is not possible in a competitive economy to pay either management or workers less than the value of their contribution. Any goodwill that attaches to a company because it has a temporary advantage over its competitors will be matched by the equally temporary ill will of the relatively poorly managed. It may be that management and labor have become more mobile and shareholders less ready to put up with poor results. This would not change the fact that no aggregate value is added by differences in skills among companies. It would just narrow the gap between the good and the bad.

The question of franchises is simply one example of the general issue of the crucial role of competition. This is because a franchise has value only if it confers some element of monopoly benefit to the owner. The key issue here is whether franchises provide a serious distortion to the assumption that the economy is generally competitive and, if so, whether this element has significantly increased in recent years. There seems no reason at all to assume that it has. In many industries, such as telecommunications and tobacco, anecdotal evidence favors a decline rather than a rise in franchise values. The opposite is no doubt the case elsewhere. Overall, however, the general comments from business favor an erosion rather than an increase in what is termed "pricing power," which is the ability of companies to maintain or increase their prices to offset weaker demand or rising costs.[29]

All forms of intellectual property raise the same issues as franchises. For example, patents and copyrights have real value for the owner. This can either be at the expense of others or it might add value to corporations in general. Thus, the invention

---

[29]This argument is indeed often used by stockbrokers in another context, to argue (quite mistakenly) that this might explain the apparent secular reduction in price inflation. The true impact on profitability is, of course, conveniently forgotten.

of "float glass" was a great boost to Pilkingtons, the owners of the process, but it was a threat to their competitors and lowered the value of their plant, which was rendered obsolete by the new development. Similarly a new drug will replace sales of older ones. Even if it provides a cure for a previously untreatable disease, it will effect the returns on other assets. For example, the discovery of drugs for tuberculosis caused many sanatoriums in Switzerland to close.

In sum, intellectual property either is a form of goodwill or represents an asset that might add to the aggregate value of companies. The difference lies in whether the additional return that it provides is at the expense of other companies or leads to a monopoly profit. The value of individual companies encompasses both the goodwill element, which may include an allowance for management capabilities, and any factor that gives rise to monopoly profits. From the perspective of companies in total, however, the goodwill will be equally matched by ill will and will have no aggregate value. Only if extra profits are produced from a reduction in competition is there a case for including a value for intangibles in the aggregate value of companies. The claims that *q* ignores the value of intellectual property and other intangibles do not therefore stand up. They arise from a confusion between two separate issues. It is a matter either of goodwill or of competition. Goodwill has no aggregate value. For individual companies it reflects above-average returns. These must exist, as returns vary around the average, but there can be no aggregate goodwill, as the average return cannot be different from the average. Competition is, however, a potential point of substance. If the economy has become less competitive, then companies in aggregate will be worth more, relative to their net worth, than they were before. We will consider this possibility, but should emphasize that we are not aware of any claims that a fall in competition justifies current stock prices, and clearly the degree of overvaluation shown by *q* would makes such claims ridiculous.

THE IMPORTANCE OF COMPETITION

It can be seen from this analysis of stockbroker objections that they really fall into two groups. The first are confusions that largely derive from a failure to distinguish between methods appropriate to the valuation of individual companies and methods required to value companies in general. The second are issues of intellectual property that are appropriate only if they are part of the key issue for economists, which is the issue of competition. It has been generally accepted by economists that this is unlikely to pose a serious problem, and we have commented on the anecdotal evidence to support this view. It is, however, obviously desirable to depend on statistical rather than anecdotal evidence if any can be found. The question that needs to be answered is whether any significant change has occurred in the competitive environment in recent years. The most obvious way to investigate is to see whether returns on real assets have changed. If they have not, then a change in basic level of competition seems unlikely, since it would mean that companies had imposed on themselves some self-denying ordinance, so that they had refused to benefit from the reduction in competition. As we have seen in earlier chapters, profitability fluctuates with the economic cycle, so it is necessary to compare changes over several cycles.

Chart 30.2 shows fluctuations in the return on corporate capital since the 1960s. As can be seen, this suggests that competi-

CHART 30.2

Returns on Corporate Capital

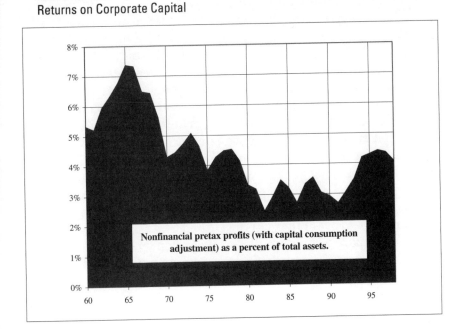

Nonfinancial pretax profits (with capital consumption adjustment) as a percent of total assets.

tion today is at least as fierce as it was in previous economic cycles—if not, in fact, more intense—with the result that it would be very hard indeed to argue that profitability looks especially high at present.

SCRAPING THE BARREL

We end this chapter by looking briefly at a mixture of arguments that normally represent the last defense of those who find the conclusions of *q* unpalatable. We deal with them in no particular order, just for the sake of completeness.

"The Wall of Money" Argument

"Yes, your logic may be correct," the argument normally runs, "but look at all the money going into mutual funds. As long as money keeps being thrown into the stock market, it can only go up." In one respect this argument is completely correct. As we saw in Chapter 28, unless the market is perfectly efficient, prices will rise if there are "more buyers than sellers." This falls under a general class of arguments that are explanations, rather than justifications, of current stock market valuations. But there are two rather important counterarguments.

The first is to remind you of the evidence we presented in Chapter 16 that, in net terms, the only buyers of the U.S. stock market are firms themselves. There may be a "wall of money" going into mutual funds, but it is more than counterbalanced by a flood of money coming out. As we saw then, the average American household barely saves. But the second, and crucial point to remember is that it is not how much is being saved, but where it is put that counts. The most enthusiastic savers in the world are in Asia, often in countries where stock markets have fallen massively from their peaks. The markets have not fallen because the countries don't have savings, but because the savers don't buy shares. Table 30.1 shows the massive contrast in the preference for liquid assets over others in the United States, the United Kingdom, and Japan. Even a small rise in caution by U.S. savers could very easily result in a wall of money coming *out* of the stock market. At that point, clearly, the argument and stock prices would go into reverse.

TABLE 30.1

Percent of Household Financial Assets Held in Bank Deposits

Country	Assets Held on Deposit
Japan	62%
United Kingdom	22%
United States	16%

"The World Is a Safer Place"...

...is another claim that is often made, usually with reference to the lack of a serious recession in the USA since the early 1980s. If the economic climate is safer, the argument usually goes, then stocks become safer. We shall see in the final part of the book that there is actually a strong argument that, largely because the current stock market bubble has been neeglected, the world is _not_ a safer place. Again, a brief glance at the problems experienced by the Asian economies provides a stark reminder that, outside the USA, the world has recently proved to be far from safe. But the crucial point about this argument is that it is irrelevant. Whatever has happened elsewhere in the economy, there is absolutely no evidence that the stock market has become any safer, nor need it do so, even if the rest of economic life were to become safer. Shares can become more volatile for reasons other than the riskiness of the economy. The key question is not whether the economy has become less risky, but whether stocks have.

The evidence that they haven't can be seen from the behavior of the options market. It is possible, from the prices of options, to know market's estimates of the "volatility" of the stock return. This is currently far from being low, as Chart 30.3 shows.[30]

In this respect, at least, the prices coming out of financial markets seem pretty sensible. For there is a very simple reason why, even if the rest of the economy _did_ get more stable, the return on stocks would be expected to remain just as volatile. The

---

[30]We noted in Chapter 17 that, with a lower dividend yield, the capital appreciation element in returns needs to get somewhat less volatile, if the volatility of the stock return as a whole is to remain unchanged. For this reason, stock price indices may look somewhat stabler in recent years; but there is no evidence for this in total returns.

CHART 30.3

Implied Volatility*

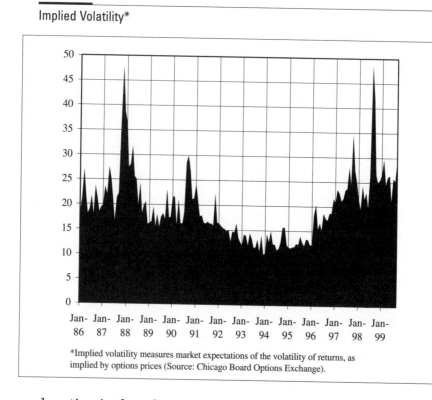

*Implied volatility measures market expectations of the volatility of returns, as implied by options prices (Source: Chicago Board Options Exchange).

explanation is that the return on net worth can easily be made more or less volatile by increases or decreases in leverage.

Indeed, the increase in overall economic stability that has been evident since World War II has, as Chart 30.4 shows, been accompanied by a steady rise in leverage. If the economy were to become even safer (which we doubt), this could and probably would be counterbalanced by yet a further increase in leverage, leaving the volatility of underlying returns unaffected.

"National Accounting Measures of Corporate Assets Are Much Less Reliable Than Company Accounting Figures"

It is improbable that this argument could be used to justify current stock prices, but it is any case unsupported by any evidence. Indeed, the contrary is the case. The fact that measures of capital

CHART 30.4

Leverage of U.S. Nonfinancial Corporations

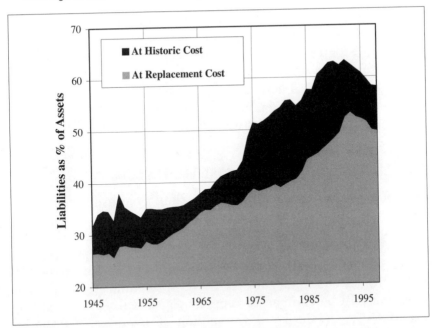

based on national accounts have to be consistent with profit figures, as well as other elements of the national accounts, is a clear mark in their favor. We have already remarked on the fact that, although there is a clear incentive for corporate accountants to invent ever more ingenious ways to raise recorded profits, there is no such incentive to reduce them. The same applies to company balance sheets. There is absolutely no check on the consistency of company balance sheets in aggregate. As a result, for example, there is no condition that "goodwill" and "ill will" balance out.

"History Does Not Matter"

The long version of this argument runs as follows: "The mere fact that stocks have produced returns of only 6¾% in the past does not mean that this figure will bear any relation to future returns; nor does the mean reversion of *q* in the past mean that it will mean-revert in the future. In recent years returns have been far higher, and *q* has shown no sign of mean-reverting."

Clearly opinions about the future can never be proved incorrect at the time they are made. It is very hard, however, to imagine a world in which we did *not* make some use of historical evidence. It is striking how often such claims are not really claims that history does not matter at all, but simply that history should be viewed through a selective filter, such that only evidence in favor of the argument being presented is used. Once we allow *some* evidence from history, we should allow all.

CONCLUSION: *q* AND STOCKBROKER ECONOMICS

We noted at the start of this chapter that the reason economists have ignored stockbroker objections to *q* is because the arguments depend on rhetoric rather than intellectual rigor. As we have pointed out at various points in this book, stockbrokers cannot be blamed for doing their job, which is to sell stocks. Their ingenuity in constantly changing the criteria used to value stocks, so that they can still be claimed to represent good value, is a striking example of necessity being the mother of invention. For the investor, however, it is both confusing and misleading. From a stockbroker's point of view, our habit of referring to evidence when examining the arguments is doubtless irritating. We hope, however, that it will have proved helpful to you, as an investor, when you next encounter such arguments, as you surely will.

EIGHT

q AND THE U.S. ECONOMY

In this, the final part of the book, we switch our attention away from the stock market, to look at the implications of q for the U.S. economy. In Chapter 31 we show the consequences of past stock market bubbles. We follow this up in Chapter 32 by considering whether the Federal Reserve under Alan Greenspan should have taken steps to avoid this potentially disastrous legacy.

Past Falls in *q* and Their Economic Impact

THE HISTORICAL BACKGROUND

In Chapter 7, when we looked at the history of the stock market, we saw that the real extremes of overvaluation, such as we have today, have occurred only five times this century. It seems to take around 20 years for people to forget the follies of past bubbles and the problems that these caused.

Chart 31.1 shows how periods of extremely high *q* have always been followed by major recessions.[1] Indeed, only the recessions of the early 1920s and late 1940s were *not* preceded by a high *q*, and these came after the two world wars. Table 31.1 shows that each of the five major bubbles, when *q* rose more than about 50% above its average, has been followed by a really serious fall in GDP. Such falls have all had their attendant miseries of high unemployment and multiple bankruptcies. They thus represent major failures in economic management.

---

[1]The official definition of a recession is two quarters of negative GDP, but quarterly data are only available since 1945. We have therefore had to define major recessions over the whole century in terms of annual data and we have defined them as any year in which GDP fell by more than 1%.

CHART 31.1

q and Major U.S. Recessions

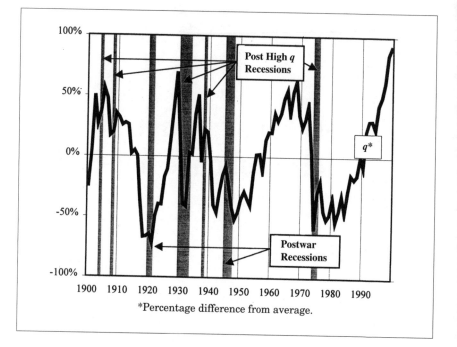

*Percentage difference from average.

TABLE 31.1

High *q*s and Subsequent Recessions

Year of Peak *q*	Level of Peak	Years of Subsequent Recession	Fall in GDP
1906	1.75	1908	−8.3%
1929	2.01	1930–33	−27.0%
1937	1.65	1938	−3.6%
1968	1.88	1974–75	−3.1%

Since it should clearly be the aim of governments and central banks to avoid a repetition of such failures, it is useful to consider why the extremes of *q* have been followed by major recessions.

q AND THE COST OF CAPITAL

q, as we have pointed out already, is basically a way of measuring the cost of equity capital. When q is high equity is cheap, and when it is low equity is expensive. Equity is not the only form of capital; clearly bonds and bank lending are also important. Equity is, however, the most fundamental. Companies and individuals can finance themselves wholly with equity, but they cannot finance themselves wholly with debt. It is therefore perhaps unfortunate that most discussions of the cost of capital follow introductory economic textbooks, and concentrate on the rate of interest rather than the cost of equity.

In the past three decades, however, economists have been much more willing than before to explore the implications of stock markets and to include them in discussions concerning the cost of capital. It seems a safe forecast that economic textbooks in the future will cease to write as if the rate of interest and the cost of capital were the same. Slow-moving as academics may appear to be, journalists tend to be even more out of date, so on past experience it will be even longer before the financial press or politicians start to consider the stock market of equal importance to interest rates in its economic impact.

At the moment, therefore, popular discussion of economics tends to assume that the impact on economies of changes in interest rates is far more important than the impact of changes in the level of the stock market. This is doubly unfortunate, because the level of the stock market not only determines the cost of equity capital but also influences the availability and thus the cost of borrowed capital. One of the unfortunate oddities of taxation is that companies and, in many circumstances, individuals are allowed to deduct interest from their profits or incomes before being assessed their tax liability.[2] This means that the tax system subsidizes the cost of debt, relative to equity finance. The ability to borrow is thus an important factor in determining the cost of capital. Even when the cost of debt is considered, it is not only the rate of interest that is important. When the stock market is strong, most banks and other lenders are inclined to treat the rise in

---

[2]It is unfortunate because it encourages the buildup of debt and thus makes economic cycles more severe.

share prices as a permanent increase in real wealth rather than a temporary fluctuation. The result is that lending expands with rising stock markets, which thus have a double impact on reducing the cost of capital. Hence, high stock markets reduce the cost of finance, even if no equity capital is raised, simply by making debt more easily available.

The problems caused by a high, or low, *q* are thus fundamentally the same as the problems that arise if the rate if interest is at the wrong level. If central banks keep interest rates too low they will ultimately generate inflation, and if they keep them too high they will cause recessions. The stock market acts in the same way. If it is too high it will ultimately cause inflation, and if too low, recession.[3]

SAVINGS AND INVESTMENT

Mispriced capital has the same impact on the economy, whether it comes from interest rates or stock markets being at the wrong level. It distorts the supply of savings and the demand for investment, though the mechanism whereby mispriced equity affects the economy is significantly different from that when interest is mispriced. This is largely due to a difference in expectations. When short-term interest rates are too high or too low, they are not usually expected to last. When equity markets are mispriced, however, the expectation must be that this mispricing will last indefinitely, since without such an expectation stock prices would change.

We have already seen, in Chapter 16, that when *q* is extremely high, the impact on savings and investment is dangerously powerful. The savings of U.S. households have fallen in recent years, and investment has increased as the stock market has risen.

There are two separate but related factors pushing down savings. The first is the direct wealth effect. As those who own

---

[3]While central banks can control short-term interest rates, they cannot directly control either bond or stock markets. There is therefore an obvious case that when determining the correct level of short-term interest rate, central banks should consider the level of the bond and stock markets. This is, however, usually denied by central bankers. We shall consider this issue in the final chapter.

stocks become wealthier, they will, until stock prices collapse, be able to afford a higher standard of living in retirement than they would before.[4] Faced with the prospect of a higher living standard in retirement, investors usually respond by saving less, so that they can enjoy the benefits of their greater wealth even before they retire.

The second factor that pushes down savings is the impact of the past rise in stock prices on investors' expectations for the future. Surveys show that investors not only expect stock prices to remain high after they have shot up, but expect such rises to continue. Investors expect to be able to retire in comfort without having to save so much. This is a sad example of thinking that you can have your cake and eat it. When expectations are rational, investors know that they cannot consume all their income, if they are to have a comfortable retirement. In stock market bubbles such ideas are considered out of date. Under the new paradigm, saving is thought to be unnecessary as well as unpleasant.

Just as a high *q* leads to low saving, we have seen that it leads to high investment. It is through this double effect of stimulating investment and depressing saving that a high *q* would ultimately lead, if unchecked, to inflation. To avoid inflation there has to be enough saving to finance all the investment. This applies, however, to the world as a whole. In recent times the United States has not been doing nearly enough saving to finance its own investment, but since there has been a recession in much of the rest of the world, foreign saving has been able to fill the gap. The rapid rise in America's current account deficit with the rest of the world has been attacked by many politicians. Without it, however, inflation would have picked up and the stock market bubble would already have burst.

HOW BUBBLES BURST

In the end, all bubbles must burst because, if unchecked, they will cause inflation, but they can burst well before that point for other reasons. Even if inflation bursts the bubble, the aftermath

---

[4] This works, of course, only if they plan to sell their stocks. If they planned to live off their income they would not be any better off, since dividends have not grown in line with stock prices.

is often a period of falling prices. The pin that bursts the bubble can be different from the pin's result. It is therefore interesting to look back at the bubbles of the past and to consider, in each case, what was the apparent cause for the bubble to burst and how the economy then reacted.

Table 31.2 shows a number of similar features in each of the bubbles that burst in the twentieth century. In each case inflation, while subdued, picked up and credit conditions tightened.[5] Inflation and rising interest rates are the most likely ways for a bubble to burst, but they are not the only ways. Because overvalued markets are built on excessive expectations, these may change without interest rates changing. As expectations rise, they produce an excessive buildup of debt, and at some point either borrowers or lenders, or both, will become nervous and wish to cut back. The pin that bursts confidence is likely to be a rise in interest rates, but it need not be.

In 1937 risk-free short-term interest rates were zero and did not change. Banks were, however, required to increase their bal-

TABLE 31.2

The Bubble, Inflation, the Pin, and the Consequence

Bubble Year	Inflation in Previous Year	Inflation in Year	The Pin	Inflation Over Next Three Years	Change in GDP During Recession
1906	0%	0%	Interest rates rose.	0%	−8.3%
1929	−1%	0%	Fed raised interest rates.	−20.2%	−27.0%
1937	2%	1%	Fed raised bank reserve ratios.	−2.3%	−3.6%
1968	3%	4%	Fed raised interest rates.	13.9%	−3.1%

---

[5]We should emphasize, however, that this has provided little indication of how to time stock market peaks. The rise in inflation had on occasion been visible for some time, but on others it was very recent. The same was even more true of credit conditions. The Fed did not raise short-term interest rates in 1937, but its action in raising reserve ratios caused banks to tighten credit.

ances with the Fed and they responded by seeking to cut back on their lending. In the fall of 1998, lenders became suddenly very nervous when the problems of Russia were followed by the near bankruptcy of the hedge fund Long Term Credit Management. The costs of issuing bonds for companies rose sharply and the commercial mortgage market dried up completely. With the help of a bailout of the hedge fund sponsored by the Fed of New York, interest rate cuts by the Fed, and buying of mortgages by Fannie Mae, the crisis was contained. Without such official and semiofficial intervention, however, a stock market collapse could well have occurred without any rise in inflation or interest rates. Nonetheless, the bubble did not burst in 1998.

High qs were beginning to have their expected impact on inflation and credit when all past bubbles burst. While they can burst for other reasons, rising inflation is the most likely trigger and it is probably a sufficient but not a necessary cause of a stock market crash. As we pointed out in Chapter 16, we cannot be sure when the pin will prick or what type of pin it will be. We can only be sure that the bubble will burst.

WHEN BUBBLES BURST

Whatever uncertainty there may be about the reasons that bubbles burst, the consequences of their doing so are clear. All the bubbles of the twentieth century have been followed by severe recessions. The high levels of investment and the low levels of saving, which have been caused by the bubble, are abruptly reversed. Falls in consumption and investment produce a major recession.

To resist such recessionary forces through policy is not straightforward. One strong lesson from past stock market crashes is that economies hit by postbubble recessions have not responded readily to interest rate reductions. There are two main explanations.

The first explanation lies in the nature of people's expectations. Earlier in this chapter we pointed out that although excessively low interest rates and high qs had the same impact on savings and investment, they operate differently, because rises in q require changes in expectations while falls in short-term interest rates do not, being purely determined by the Fed. If they were expected to last, then households would probably feel it necessary to increase their savings to compensate for the lower returns that they would expect on all their savings.[6] If the fall is expected to be temporary, however, consumers may bring forward purchases of consumer durables to benefit from the lower financing costs. In normal conditions therefore, when there are no great changes in expectations about long-term returns, falls in interest rates can encourage spending.

When expectations are changing dramatically, however, as they do when bubbles burst, falls in interest rates are much less likely to stimulate the economy. Falls in *q* mean that, even though short-term rates may be falling, the cost of equity to corporations is actually *rising*, and all the impact of a high *q* on saving and investment that we have previously discussed starts to unwind.

The second reason interest rates are likely to have weak effects once a bubble bursts also relates to the mechanisms set in motion during the bubble itself. We noted that one impact of a high *q* is that it indirectly lowers the cost of capital by increasing credit availability. When the bubble bursts, this process goes into reverse. Banks are less willing to lend to borrowers who, because of the fall in stock prices, now appear less wealthy. Banks may also wish to contract their balance sheets, owing to the fall in value of their own equity holdings. This process, which is often referred to as "debt deflation," was first noted by Irving Fisher in the aftermath of the Wall Street Crash of 1929. But it has been equally evident in the more recent experience of Japan over the past decade.

Alternative policies to stimulate the economy are also of doubtful effectiveness. Exports might in principle be stimulated by allowing the dollar to weaken; but since other stock markets and hence other economies are likely to be pulled down by Wall Street, achieving this goal may not be straightforward. The primary aim would in effect be to "export" the recession; but at such times there are few countries willing to "import" it. Higher government spending takes time to organize, and, as the recent experience of Japan has shown, appears to have only weak effects.

---

[6]If short-term interest changes are expected to last, then the returns on other assets must move in sympathy. If they are expected to be temporary, little change in other assets is needed. The yield curve simply becomes steep at the short end.

The lessons of history are therefore clear and harsh. Bubbles should be avoided. The results have invariably been bad in the past. Contrary to optimistic claims, economies do not respond in postbubble times to interest rate reductions or other attempts at stimulation.

CHAPTER **32**

The Economic Consequences of Alan Greenspan

THE POLICY QUESTION

Because of the natural tendency for strong stock markets to lead to inflation and therefore to be halted by rising interest rates, it has recently become fashionable to claim that stock market booms never die of their own accord, but are killed by the Fed. While not literally correct, since the Fed wasn't around to kill the bubble of 1906 or any of the earlier ones, it is true that since then the Fed could in principle be blamed for applying the pin that burst all the subsequent bubbles. This argument is dangerous, since it may act to inhibit the Fed from responding as early as it should to restrain both inflation and the buildup of debt. These are, as we have seen, the dangerous consequences of stock market bubbles.

The longer an overvalued stock market persists, the more likely it is that inflation will become embedded and that the debt buildup will be extensive. Both of these developments make the management of the economy difficult, and its recovery from the following recession is thereby likely to be delayed. The arguments for delaying action are thus fundamentally irresponsible. There is a much stronger case for arguing that the Fed, or other central banks, should look not just at the prices of goods and services but also at the prices of assets when deciding on the appropriate rate of interest.

THE CASE FOR WATCHING ASSET PRICES

There are three main arguments in favor of the Fed taking asset prices into consideration when fixing its interest rate policy. These are:

- The case that watching asset prices is fair only between generations.
- The case that asset bubbles are an early warning of more general inflation.
- The case that, when they burst, they are the main cause of major recessions.

The first argument rests on the point that asset values are just as important to people's welfare as the prices of goods and services. A generation of investors who benefit from a rise in stock prices do so only at the expense the next generation, which suffers from their fall. The argument does not usually carry much conviction, however, perhaps because it is only after it is too late to help the sufferers that sufficient people recognize that the rise in asset prices is not permanent.

The second and third arguments are closely related. They are basically about managing the economy, rather than trying to be fair between generations. They boil down to one question. Is it worth risking a small recession in order to avoid a big one?

THE ARGUMENTS AGAINST WATCHING ASSET PRICES

Central bankers, and the politicians who appoint them, dislike the idea of taking asset prices into consideration when they set interest rates. The tend to offer a range of arguments as to why they should not do so. But there is one very strong reason that is seldom if ever mentioned. This is that it would be politically unpopular.

If, for example, the Fed had raised interest rates in 1995, when the stock market first began to be noticeably overvalued, it might well have caused a mild recession in 1996, but it would probably have saved the economy from a really deep one early in the new millennium. If this choice were put to the vote in a referendum, the majority would probably, but not certainly, prefer to avoid the major recession at the cost of having a mild one. The first political problem, however, is that most people would prefer to believe that all recessions are unnecessary. The second problem is that the careers of those who caused the mild recession would probably suffer very badly. They would take the blame for the recession, but they would receive no praise for avoiding the depression that never happened. It is interesting to consider what would have happened if the Fed had raised interest rates early in 1995. First, it might have persuaded President Clinton not to reappoint Alan Greenspan as Governor of the Fed; second, the mild recession would probably have stopped Clinton from being reelected. It takes a great deal of leadership to accept such risks and try to persuade voters to accept the short-term pain for the longer-term reward.

Because the political case against seeking to avoid asset bubbles is so strong, but also almost unmentionable, the argument tends to be conducted on different lines.

The first line of defense is usually to claim that the overvaluation of markets can't be measured. We hope that we have convinced you that this argument is nonsense. Even if it were not, however, the case would be a poor one for those central banks, like the Fed, whose policy decisions are based on judgment. The Fed does not change interest rates automatically when inflation rises or falls; it uses its judgment. Since Alan Greenspan announced when the market was well below its current level that it was being fueled by "irrational exuberance," his judgment about its current level can hardly be in doubt.

The second line of defense is to argue that it would be inappropriate to alter interest rates because of conditions in financial markets. To do so would be to create more frequent and unnecessary recessions. The argument that recessions would be more frequent is, as we have argued, probably correct. The case that they are unnecessary is the weak point. It is probable that recessions are, sadly enough, a necessary feature of a vibrant and growing economy. What should be avoided is the trauma that results from major ones. These, as we have shown, have always followed in the aftermath of collapsing asset bubbles. We suggest that governments and central banks should concentrate much more of their efforts on avoiding this type of recession, even if it does imply the risk of milder recessions occurring more frequently.

It is sometimes claimed[7] that this objective would conflict with the primary role of central banks, which is to maintain stability of inflation. In part this reaction may reflect a (laudable) desire to avoid the mistakes of the past, when policy makers attempted to use monetary policy to achieve objectives for the real economy that were unattainable, with the inevitable result that inflation took off. But such reactions are overstated, and sometimes entirely inappropriate. Since rises in *q* must, as we have shown, ultimately be inflationary, stabilizing *q* will always over the long term be complementary with the objective of stabilizing inflation.[8]

The argument that central banks should not change interest rates because of conditions in financial markets is in any case disingenuous, because they do. But only in one direction—namely, downward. The Fed's policy in late 1998 was clearly driven by a concern that the stock market was in danger of collapsing, just as it was in the aftermath of the October 1987 crash. The result is that we have an asymmetric approach to the stock market. The Fed has made it clear that it will act to try to stop the market from collapsing, but not to stop it from booming. This of course leads to the most dangerous of conditions, in which Fed policy makes the stock market appear almost a "one-way bet." In so doing, the Fed has encouraged the conditions that prudent central bankers should most wish to avoid.

The final argument against intervening to prevent asset bubbles is that official action can, in the modern world of expert economic management, rapidly act to offset the onset of any re-

---

[7]For example, in the contribution of two academics, Ben Bernanke and Mark Gertler, to a recent Jackson Hole conference on this issue. The Chief Economist of the Bank of England, John Vickers, also made a similar claim in a recent speech to academic economists at a conference in Oxford.

[8]Even when there may be an element of conflict in the shorter term, there is plenty of evidence that central bankers do not regard inflation stability as absolutely paramount in the short term. If they did, they could almost certainly achieve far greater stability of inflation than they do, by more frequent and more aggressive changes in interest rates. That central bankers do not in fact behave this way reflects a quite reasonable (if not always acknowledged) awareness that the costs induced by such policies might be greater than the benefits in terms of more stable inflation. Since the costs of ignoring asset bubbles are, as we have seen, severe, it would seem perfectly reasonable for central bankers to take these into account also, even at the cost of somewhat less stable inflation in the short term.

cession and that the fear of recession should not therefore influence policy. Indeed, Alan Blinder, former vice chairman of the Federal Reserve, was not shy to put such faith on record, recently claiming:

> For the U.S. economy to go into a significant recession, never mind a depression, important policy makers would have to take leave of their senses.

Time will tell whether Professor Blinder's confidence proves to be admirable or foolhardy.[9] Historical evidence, both in the United States and much more recently in Japan, has shown this faith to be unfounded. We saw in the previous chapter that neither interest rates nor other policy stimuli are likely to work well, or even at all, in the conditions of a postbubble economy. We therefore doubt whether it will prove possible to act promptly and strongly enough to stop a major recession developing in the USA in the new millennium.

---

[9]We are indeed tempted to suggest that this is a case of "the Blinder leading the blind."

INDEX

Index note to the reader: The *n* with an italic number following a page reference refers to a specific footnote on that page.

Accounting, economics versus, 224–225
Aggregate stock market value, 86
Ambachtseer, Keith P., *50n*
Annual meetings, 82–83
Annuities, 52–53, 69–73
Arbitrage, 17–18, 80–82, 182, 210
  absence of, 294–295
  competition and, 143–145
  efficiency of, 293–296, 299–300
  Efficient Market Hypothesis and, 293–296
  everyday value and, 80–82
  incentives in, 17–18, 80–82, 143–145, 149–150
  mechanisms of, 288
  nature of, 295–296
  oil price, 144–145
  q and, 149–150, 258–259, 293–296
  riskless, 294–296, 300
Asian stock markets, 7–8, 169, 323 (*See also* Japan)
Asset bubbles:
  aftermath of collapsing, 341
  bursting of, 333–337
  dangers of, 8
  in Japan, 4–5, 7–8, 14, *173n*, 182, 336–337, 343
  in Southeast Asia, 7–8
  in the United Kingdom, 14
  in the United States, 4–5, 7–8, 329–330, 332–337
Asymmetric gains from *q*-based trading rules, 125–126

At the money options, 190–191
Average Rule, 118, 119–120, 122

Bachelier, Louis, *290n*
Bank deposits:
  as alternative to stocks, 175–182
  bonds versus, 176–177, 178, 179
  default risk and, 177–178
  real value during inflation, 177
  yields since 1926, 175, 176
Bank of England, *41n*
Bank of Japan, 182
Bankruptcies, 306–307, 329
Bear markets, 167–197
  following period of overvaluation, 60, 169–170
  history of, 59–60, 74
  predicting, 187–188
  stock market viewed as casino in, 4
  surviving, 196–197
Benartzi, Shlomo, *304n*
Benchmarks:
  alternative investments, 86
  cyclically adjusted price-earnings multiple and, 264–265
  equity risk premium, 282
  historical returns, 86
  nature of, 85–86
  return on equity capital, 267–268
Bernanke, Ben, *342n*
Blanchard, Olivier, *289n, 304n, 307n*
Blinder, Alan, 343
Bond yield:
  to derive discount rate, 280–282

Bond yield *(Cont.)*:
  since 1926, 175, 176
  (*See also* Yield ratios)
Bonds:
  as alternative to stocks, 175–182
  bank deposits versus, 176–177, 178, 179
  corporate, 177
  default risk of, 176, 177–178, 191, 274
  guaranteed returns from, 71
  index-linked, 26, 73, 177, 250, 271, 281, 292, 310
  real value during inflation, 177
  volatility risk of, 176–177
Boskin Commission, 279
Brown, Capability, 41
Bull markets:
  buy-and-hold strategy as myth of, 172
  free lunch claims and, 6
  of 1980s and 1990s, 62
  overvalued market and, 4–7, 9–15, 28, 34–35, 130–132, 185–188, 254, 281–282
  yield ratios in, 245, 246
Bundesbank, 179–180
Bureau of Economic Analysis (BEA), 236–237, 255
Buy-and-hold strategy:
  arguments for, 45
  breakdown of, 25–26
  buy-and-sell strategy versus, 171–172
  described, 5–6
  diversity of returns and, 96–99
  erroneous assumptions of, 40
  logic of, 155–156, 163
  q and, 24–26, 155–156, 163–166, 260
  random walk model and, 159–163, 164

Buy-and-hold strategy *(Cont.)*:
  returns from, 118–119, 161–163
  risks of, 161–163
  success of, 155–156
Buying pressure, 298
Buying stocks:
  alternatives to, 174–183
  market timing for, 99–103, 105, 173
  (*See also* Stock picking)

Campbell, John, *31n, 288n, 290n, 291n, 304n*
Capital appreciation:
  of bonds, 176
  dividend yield and, 217–219
  dividends versus, 83–85, 213
  real capital gains, 59
  taxes on, 170–171
Capital Asset Pricing Model, 109
Capital stock:
  calculation of, 256
  changes in, 270
  depreciation and, 256–257, 316
Capitalism, 270
Carroll, Lewis, 310–311
Cash flow crisis, 176–177
Central banks, 178–182, *332n*
  (*See also* Federal Reserve)
Chaos theory, 206
Clinton, Bill, 341
Cochrane, John, *304n*
Cohn, Richard, 249
Competition:
  arbitrage and, 143–145
  franchises and, 319
  importance of, 320–322
  incentives in, 107–110, 143–145
  in price determination, 107–108
  in stock market valuation, 107–110, 143–145

Compound average returns, *43n*
Compound interest, 40–45
    inflation and, 40–41, 42–43
    patience and, 41, 44–45, 123
    power of, 40–45, 52, 73–74
    regular investors and, 47–54,
        67
    weakness of arguments based
        on, 44–45
Confidence intervals, 130–131,
    132
Conflict of interest:
    of fund managers, 27–28, 186–
        187
    of stockbrokers, 33–35, 185–188
Consumer Price Index (CPI), 177,
    250
Corporate veil, 82–83
Cost of equity capital:
    credit availability and, 336
    discount rate and, 277–278
    equilibrium with return and,
        280
    historical experience of dis-
        count rate and, 278–279
    q and, 331–332
Covered interest parity, 294–296
Crash of 1929, 336
Current account deficit, 333
Current replacement cost, 265
Cyclically adjusted price-earnings
    multiple, 235–239, 264–269,
    310
    cyclical adjustment of profits
        and, 265–267
    as economic indicator of value,
        237
    future stock returns and, 238
    mean reversion and, 236–237
    as measurable indicator of
        value, 238–239
    valuing stock market with,
        264–267

Data mining, 207–208, 245–247
Debt financing, 150–152
Default risk, 176, 177–178, 191,
    274
Deflation, 180–182
Depreciation, 256–257, 316
Discount rate:
    bond yield and, 280–282
    cost of equity capital and, 277–
        278
    historical experience and, 278–
        279
Diversified portfolios, 72
Dividend Discount Model, 209,
    249, 250, 261, 273–283
    cost of equity capital and, 277–
        278
    equity risk premium and, 304
    historical experience and, 278–
        279
    misusing, 279–282
    operation of, 273–275
    underlying value of stocks and,
        275–276
Dividend yield, 35, 138, 140, 171–
    172, 213–221
    calculation of, 213
    for Dow Jones Index, 84, 213
    earnings yield and, 240–241,
        248
    as economic indicator of value,
        217–219
    Efficient Market Hypothesis
        and, 290
    fair value and, 214, 216–217
    fall in, 279–280
    future stock returns and, 219–
        220
    long-term payout ratio, 218–
        219, 240–241, 280
    mean reversion and, 215–217
    as measurable indicator of
        value, 214–215

Dividend yield *(Cont.)*:
  P/E multiple versus, 224, 228–229, 237
  q-equivalence of, 269
  (*See also* Yield ratios)
Dividends:
  capital appreciation versus, 83–85, 213
  future growth in, 280–281
  Hindsight Value and, 114–115, 219–220
  reinvestment of, 42, 89
  in total return, 59, 60–63, 83–85
Donaldson, John, *304n*
Double Threshold Rule, 121–123, 124, *166n*
Dow Jones Index:
  dividend yield for, 84, 213
  at end of 1998, *9n*
  implied levels of, 14
  P/E multiple and, 223

Earnings per share:
  calculating, 266
  cyclically adjusted, 266–267
Earnings yield, 224, 226, 240–241, 248, 279
Economics:
  accounting versus, 224–225
  disagreement among economists and, 287–288
  dividend yield and, 217–219
  Equity Premium Puzzle and, 302–304
  P/E multiple and, 224–225, 227–228, 237
  q in, 3–4, 30–31, 33–35, 109–110, 258–260, 287–300
  return on equity capital equal to cost of equity capital, 267–269

Economics *(Cont.)*:
  scientific approach in, 33–34
  statistics in, 254–257, 261
  stock market value and, 208–209
  yield ratios and, 243–251
Efficient Market Hypothesis, 15–18, 35, 109
  arbitrage and, 293–296
  described, 15
  everyday value and, 79–80, 82
  noise and, 296–299
  predictability and, 290–293
  q and, 15–18, 288–299
  random walk and, 16, 159, 290
  simplicity of, 16
Efficient portfolio, 91
Emerson, John, *152n*
Equity, return on equal to cost of, 267–269
Equity capital:
  cost of, 277–278
  profitability of, 265–266
Equity Premium Puzzle, 302–304
Equity risk premium, 280–282, 285, 301–311
  decline in, 304–307
  Equity Premium Puzzle, 302–304
  inflation and, 307–308
  past returns and, 302–304
  q-equivalence and, 308–311
European Central Bank, 180
Everyday value, 78–82
  arbitrage and, 80–82
  bargains, 78
  Efficient Market Hypothesis and, 79–80, 82
  good value, 78–82
  Hindsight Value (*see* Hindsight Value)
  imperfect substitutes and, 81–82

Exercise price, 190
Expectations, versus reality of returns, 20–23, 333, 334
Export stimulation, 336

Fair value:
  bond yield and, 280–282
  cyclically adjusted price-earnings multiple and, 264–265
  dividend yield and, 214, 216–217
  P/E multiple and, 225–226
Fama, E., *299n*
Fannie Mae, 335
Federal Reserve, 8, 176–177, 180, 182, 255, 282, 327, 339–343
Fermat's Last Theorem, 302, 303
50% Rule, 120–121, 122
Financial capital, 265
Fisher, Irving, 336
Flow of Funds Accounts of the United States, 10n
Foreign exchange market, 195–196
Franchises, competition and, 319
French, K., *299n*
Friedman, Milton, 55, *55n*, 145, 317
Fund managers:
  conflict of interest, 27–28, 186–187
  invisible options and, 192
  market-neutral funds and, 192–194
  portfolio insurance and, 188–192
  q-investors versus, 27–28
  stock picking by, 92–93
Fundamental value, 5, 10, 163, 170, 202–212, 269–271

Gates, Bill, 87
Germany, 179–180
Gertler, Mark, *342n*
Giust, Luis, 22–23, 27–28, 73, 125, 170
Good value, 78–82
Goodwill, 317–320
Gordon, M. J., *276n*
Great Depression, 114, 180
Greenspan, Alan, 8, 327, 339–343
Grossman, Sanford, 296–297

Hayashi, Fumio, *289n*
Hindsight Value, 79, 95–115
  buy-and-hold strategy and, 96–99
  dividend value and, 114–115, 219–220
  insights from hindsight, 95–96
  price-earnings (P/E) multiple and, 113–114
  of *q*, 110, 111–115, 123, 135–136
  summary indicator of, 104–106
  ten bad years to buy stocks, 99–103, 105, 173
  ten good years to buy stocks, 99–103, 105
Human capital, 319

Imperfect substitutes, 81–82
Incentives:
  in arbitrage, 17–18, 80–82, 143–145, 149–150
  in competition, 107–110, 143–145
  corporate stock options and, 152–154, 225
  importance of, 143–146
Index funds, 92–93
Indexed bonds, 26, 73, 177, 250, 271, 281, 292, 310

Inflation, 26, 166, 178–183, 225, 280–281
  adjustment of returns for, 49–52
  changes in, 250
  compound interest and, 40–41, 42–43
  equity risk premium and, 307–308
  falling, 245
  Federal Reserve and, 339
  high q values and, 333, 335
  overstatement of, 279
  protection against, 140
  real values during, 177
  slowing impact of, 148
  trends in, 180–182
  wealth overstatement and, 43
Intangible assets:
  goodwill, 317–320
  myth of "no-capital" economy and, 315–320
  patents and trademarks, 317, 319–320
Intellectual property, 317, 319–320
Interest rates:
  asset prices and, 340–343
  nominal, 179
  reduction in, 335–337
  risk-free short-term, 334–335
  (See also Compound interest)
Investment horizons:
  of long-term investors, 22–26
  of q-investors, 27
  retirement and, 22–25, 37, 165–166
Invisible options, 192

Japan:
  q in, 261n
  real estate market in, 182

Japan (Cont.):
  stock market bubble, 4–5, 7–8, 14, 173n, 182, 336–337, 343
Junk bonds, 177

Keynes, John Maynard, 24, 25, 55n
Krugman, Paul, 169, 174, 288n

Leading indicators, 210, 220
Life expectancy, following retirement, 23–24, 53, 71
Liquidity risk, 177n
Lo, Andrew, 161n, 290n
Log scales, 58–60
Long positions, 193
Long Term Credit Management, 335
Long-term investors, 7, 19–28
  buy-and-hold strategy of, 24–26
  compound interest and, 40–45
  expectations versus reality and, 20–23, 333, 334
  fund managers, 27–28
  investment horizons and, 22–26
  q-investors, 26–27
  redefining risk and return for, 19–23
  regular investors, 47–54
  stocks as investments for, 129–166
  wealth preservation by, 19, 73
Lucas, Robert, 293–294

MacKinlay, Archie, 161n, 290n
Malkiel, Burton, 88n
Manhattan Island, sale of, 40–41, 44–45, 123
Manufacturing sector:
  capital needs of, 313–315

Manufacturing sector *(Cont.)*:
  relevance of q for, 107–108
Market-neutral funds, 192–194
Market timing:
  for buying stocks, 99–103, 105,
    173
  for selling stocks, 169, 172–
    174, 187–188
  uncertainty of, 129, 211
Mean reversion:
  dividend yield and, 215–217
  P/E multiple and, 226–227,
    236–237, 259
  q and, 9, 11–15, 32, 34, 112,
    130–132, 134–140, 257, 258,
    299–300
  real return on stocks and, 39–
    40
  stock market value and, 204–
    208, 209–211
  uncertainty about, 269–271
  yield ratios and, 247–249
Mehra, Rajnish, 302–304, *304n*,
  306, *309n*, *310n*
Microsoft, 87
Modigliani, Franco, *249n*
Morgensen, Gretchen, *152n*
Moving-target problem, 271
Murray, Daniel, *152n*, *225n*,
  307n

Net worth, 10–11, 253–261, 310–
  311 *(See also q)*
New issues, 150
Noise:
  Efficient Market Hypothesis
    and, 296–299
  random number generation
    and, 206–207
Nominal interest rates, 179
Nondiversifiable risk, 91

Oil prices, 144–145, 179–180
Options *(see* Put options; Stock
  options)
Out of the money options, 191–
  192
Overseas markets, 195–196

Patents, 317, 319–320
Patience, compound interest and,
  41, 44–45, 123
Patient Native American model
  of investing, 40–41, 44–45, 123
Payout ratio, 218–219, 240–241,
  280
Pearson, F. A., *41n*
Physical capital, 265
Pilkingtons, 319–320
Ponzi, Charles, 153–154
Ponzi schemes, 153–154
Popper, Karl, *291n*
Portfolio insurance, 188–192
  development of, 188–189
  fundamental flaw in, 189
  via options, 189–190
Prescott, Edward, 302–304, 306,
  309n, *310n*
Present value, 274–275
Price-earnings (P/E) multiple,
  31–33, 35, 223–241
  average level of, 226, 279
  critical weaknesses of, 263–
    264
  current levels of, 153
  cyclically adjusted, 235–239,
    264–269, 310
  defined, 223
  dividend yield versus, 224,
    228–229, 237
  as economic indicator of value,
    224–225, 227–228, 237
  fair value and, 225–226

Price-earnings (P/E) multiple
  (Cont.):
    future stock returns and, 228–
      230
    Hindsight Value and, 113–
      114
    historic, 233–235
    mean reversion and, 226–227,
      236–237, 259
    as measurable indicator of
      value, 203–204, 224–226
    prospective, 233–235
    q-equivalence and, 263–269
    rising, 245
    Siegel's constant and, 280
Pricing power, 319
Profits:
    cyclical adjustment of, 265–
      267
    P/E multiple and, 224, 225
Put options, 36
    invisible, 192
    at the money, 190–191
    options market activity and,
      323–324
    out of the money, 191–192
    portfolio insurance via, 189–
      190

q:
    advantages of using, 7
    versus alternative measures of
      value, 29–33
    arbitrage in stock market and,
      149–150, 258–259, 293–296
    average value of, 254–257
    and buy-and-hold strategy, 24–
      25, 155–156, 163–166, 260
    as commonsense approach,
      107–108, 110
    concept of, 4
    conflict of corporate incentives
      and, 152–154

q (Cont.):
    and cost of capital, 331–332
    defined, 11, 134
    determining, 11
    Dividend Discount Model and,
      273–283
    economists and, 3–4, 30–31,
      33–35, 109–110, 258–260,
      287–300
    and Efficient Market Hypoth-
      esis, 15–18, 288–299
    future stock returns and, 12–
      15, 110, 129–130, 132–166,
      209–211, 260
    and hindsight value, 110, 111–
      115, 123, 135–136
    impact on saving, 146–148
    inflation and, 333, 335
    introducing, 9–12
    in Japan, *261n*
    mean reversion and, 9, 11–15,
      32, 34, 112, 130–132, 134–
      140, 257, 258, 299–300
    as measurable indicator of
      value, 254–257
    1900 to 1999, 9–10
    past declines in, 329–337
    in per share terms, 12
    power of, 4–5, 165–166
    reasons for rise of, 149–152
    relevance for both manufactur-
      ing and services, 107–108
    responses to high value of,
      146–148
    restating case for, 260–261
    stability of, 111–112, 342
    stockbrokers and, 313–326
    testing, 110
    as tool to avoid losing money,
      210–211
    in the United Kingdom, *261n*
    and United States economy,
      327–343

q (Cont.):
  uses of, 4
  value of stock markets and, 4–
    7, 12–15, 17, 132–141, 253–
    261
q-based trading rules, 117–126
  asymmetric gains from, 125–
    126
  Average Rule, 118, 119–120,
    122
  Double Threshold Rule, 121–
    123, 124, *166n*
  50% Rule, 120–121, 122
  quantifying gains from, 123–
    126
  usefulness of, 123
q-equivalence, 237, 238, 263–272
  cyclically adjusted P/E and,
    264–269
  demonstrating, 267–269
  dividend yield and, 269
  equity risk premium and, 308–
    311
  fundamental value and, 269–
    271
  problems with P/E multiple,
    263–264
q-investors, 26–27
  fund managers versus, 27–28
  nature of, 26–27
  qualities of, 27

Random number generator, 206–
  207
*Random Walk Down Wall Street,
  A* (Malkiel), *88n*
Random walk hypothesis:
  buy-and-hold strategy and,
    159–163, 164
  Efficient Market Hypothesis
    and, 16, 159, 290
Real assets, 182–183

Real capital gains, 59
Real estate investment trusts
  (REITs), 182
Real interest rates, 179, 281–282
Recession, 236, 323
  defined, *329n*
  delaying, 339, 341
  following periods of high *q*,
    329–330, 335
  recovery from, 230
  risk of, 4–5, 7–8, 339–343
  volatility of earnings and, 238–
    239
Regular investors/savers:
  compound interest and, 47–54,
    67
  lack of, 322
  for retirement, 48–49, 65–69,
    146
  as spenders, 183
  stock market risks and, 65–74
  stock picking by, 92–93
  10-year, 68–69
  20-year, 68
  30-year, 66, 67–69, 73–74
Relative return, 62–63
Replacement cost, 265
Retirement:
  annuities in, 52–53, 69–73
  investment horizon and, 22–
    25, 37, 165–166
  life expectancy following, 23–
    24, 53, 71
  regular saving for, 48–49, 65–
    69, 146
  rewards for investing in stocks
    during, 52–53
  spending capital in, 47
  wealth effect and, 332–333
Returns:
  average historic, 20, 21–22,
    25–26, 39–40, 70, 191, 329

Returns *(Cont.)*:
average real, 156, 157–159,
161–163
from buy-and-hold strategy,
119, 161–163
on corporate capital, 321–322
diversity of, 96–99
on equity capital, 267–269
expectations versus reality of,
20–23, 333, 334
inflation adjustment of, 49–52
link between risk and, 40, 55–
56
on lump-sum versus staggered
investments, 48–49
modest, defining, 20
recent levels of, 21–22
redefining, 19–23
of regular investors, 47–54
relative, 62–63
variability of stock, 56–57
(*See also* Total return)
Rhee, Chanyong, *289n*
Risk:
arbitrage and, 294–296, 300
default, 176, 177–178, 191, 274
link between return and, 40,
55–56
nondiversifiable, 91
of recession, 4–5, 7–8, 339–343
redefining, 19–23
of stock investments, 5, 55–74,
156–157, 161–163
systemic, 193
and wealth preservation, 19,
73
Risk-free short-term interest
rates, 334–335
Risk premium:
defined, 292
(*See also* Equity risk premium)
Robertson, Donald, *34n*, *135n*,
136n, 260, *270n*

Russia, 335

Samuelson, Paul, *290n*
Saving:
impact of mispriced capital on,
332–333
impact of q on, 146–148
Scientific approach, in economics,
33–34
Selling pressure, 298
Selling stocks, 169–174
buy-and-hold strategy versus,
171–172
market timing for, 169, 172–
174, 187–188
strategy following, 185–197
tax consequences of, 170–171
Sensenbrenner, Gabriel, *289n*
Service sector:
capital needs of, 313–315,
318
relevance of q for, 107–108
Shiller, Robert, *31n*, *288n*
Short positions, 193
Sideways market, 138
Siegel, Jeremy, 24, 42, 99, *118n*,
156, 157
Siegel's constant, 156–159, 218,
226, 228, 259–260, 278, 280,
282, 291, 292, *305n*
Smithers, Andrew, *152n*, *225n*,
307n
Smithers & Co., 35–36, 253–254,
261n
S&P Composite Index, 244
S&P 500, 213, 223
S&P Industrial Average, 135
Stationarity, *204n*
Stiglitz, Joseph, 296–297
Stock market:
asymmetric approach to, 342
average real returns, 156, 157–
159, 161–163

Stock market *(Cont.)*:
  avoiding in bear markets, 185–197
  historic average returns, 21–22, 25–26, 39–40, 70, 191, 329
  investment horizons and, 22–26
  net buyers and net sellers in, 149–150
  overseas, 195–196
  real stock prices over twentieth century, 57–60
  risks of investing in, 5, 55–74, 156–157, 161–163
  roulette versus, 129, 138, 141, 164, 211
  Siegel's constant, 156, 157–159, 218, 226, 228, 259–260, 278, 280, 282, 291, 292, *305n*
  true impact of returns on, 47–54
  (See also Bear markets; Bull markets)
Stock market value, 77–106, 199–283
  aggregate, 86
  benchmarks for, 85–86
  competition and, 107–110, 143–145
  compound interest and, 40–45
  confusion between company value and, 108–109
  corporate veil and, 82–83
  cost of equity capital and, 277–278
  current overvaluation, 4–7, 9–15, 28, 34–35, 130–132, 185–188, 254, 281–282
  Dividend Discount Model and, 209, 249, 250, 261, 273–283
  dividend yield in, 35, 213–221
  dividends versus capital appreciation in, 83–85, 213

Stock market value *(Cont.)*:
  economic basis of, 208–209
  equity risk premium and, 280–282, 285, 301–311
  everyday value, 78–82
  fundamental, 5, 10, 163, 170, 202–212, 269–271
  future stock returns and, 12–15, 110, 129–130, 132–166, 209–211
  mean reversion and, 204–208, 209–211
  measurability of, 203–204
  misunderstandings concerning, 211
  overvaluation before bear markets, 60
  price-earnings multiple in, 31–33, 35, 223–241, 263–269
  q and (*see q*)
  range of values, 136–137
  as relative concept, 81–82
  stock picking and, 87–93
  tests of, 201–212
  valuation bubbles, 4–5, 7–8, *173n*, 182, 329–330, 332–337, 341, 343
Stock options, 152–154, 225
Stock picking, 87–93
  average returns and, 88–91
  deciding whether to be in or out of stocks, 91–93
  market decision versus, 91–93
  odds in, 87–88
Stock substitutes, 306–307
Stockbrokers:
  avoiding advice of, 185–188
  conflict of interest of, 33–35, 185–188
  Equity Premium Puzzle and, 302–304
  forecasts of, 234–235

Stockbrokers *(Cont.)*:
  "history does not matter"
    argument, 325–326
  importance of competition and,
    319, 320–322
  level of discount rate and, 280
  myth of "low-capital" economy
    and, 313–315
  myth of "no-capital" economy
    and, 315–320
  "national accounting measures
    less reliable than company
    figures" argument, 324–325
  q and, 313–326
  real rates of interest and, 281
  rose-colored glasses and, 234–
    235
  "wall of money" argument,
    322–323
  "world is a safer place" argu-
    ment, 323–324
  yield ratios and, 243–251
Stocks for the Long Run (Siegel),
    24, 42, 99, 118
Stoker, H. M., *41n*
Summers, Lawrence, *289n*
Systemic risk, 193

Taxes:
  on capital gains, 170–171
  cost of capital and, 331
Thaler, Richard, *304n*
Through the Looking Glass
    (Carroll), 310–311
Tobin, James, 4, 34, 109–110,
    147–148, 270, 271, *281n*, 289
Total return:
  on bonds, 176
  capital appreciation in, 83–85
  defined, 84
  dividends in, 59, 60–63, 83–85
  on stocks, 276
Tracker funds, 92–93

Trade deficit, 148, 255
Trademarks, 317, 319–320
Trading rules (*see q*-based trad-
    ing rules)

Uncertainty:
  of market timing, 129, 211
  about mean reversion, 269–
    271
United Kingdom:
  asset bubble, 14
  Bank of England, *41n*
  q in, *261n*
United States:
  asset bubble, 4–5, 7–8, 329–
    330, 332–337
  central bank (*see* Federal
    Reserve)
  economic management of, 8
  q and economy of, 327–343
  stock market bubbles, 4–5, 7–8
U.S. Treasury issues, 51–52

Valuation (*see* Stock market
  value)
Vickers, John, *342n*
Volatility risk, 176–177, 230,
  238–239, 323–324

Wadhwani, Sushil, 234, *288n,*
  304n, 305n, 308n
Warren, G. F., *41n*
Wealth effect, 332–333
Wealth overstatement, 43
Wealth preservation:
  bear markets and, 167
  inflation and, 180
  risk and, 19, 73
Welling, Kathryn M., *191n*
Wiles, Andrew, 303
Wright, Stephen, *34n, 135n,*
  136n, 260, *270n, 307n*

Yield:
  bank deposit, 175, 176
  bond, 175, 176, 177, 280–282
  dividend (*see* Dividend yield)
  earnings, 224, 226, 240–241,
    248, 279
Yield ratios, 243–251
  defined, 244
  as economic indicators of
    value, 249–250

Yield ratios *(Cont.)*:
  equity risk premium and, 307–
    308
  future stock returns and, 250
  long-term history of, 247–248
  mean reversion and, 247–249
  as measurable indicators of
    value, 247
  popularity with stockbrokers,
    243–251